Ancient Egyptian Civilization

Other Books in the Turning Points Series:

Turning|Points
IN WORLD HISTORY

Ancient Egyptian Civilization

Brenda Stalcup, *Book Editor*

Bonnie Szumski, *Editorial Director*
Stuart B. Miller, *Managing Editor*

Greenhaven Press, Inc., San Diego, California

Every effort has been made to trace the owners of copyrighted material. The articles in this volume may have been edited for content, length, and/or reading level. The titles have been changed to enhance the editorial purpose.

No part of this book may be reproduced or used in any form or by any means, electrical, mechanical, or otherwise, including, but not limited to, photocopy, recording, or any information storage and retrieval system, without prior written permission from the publisher.

Library of Congress Cataloging-in-Publication Data

Ancient Egyptian civilization / Brenda Stalcup, book editor.
    p.   cm. — (Turning points in world history)
Includes bibliographical references and index.
ISBN 0-7377-0479-9 (pbk. : alk. paper) —
ISBN 0-7377-0480-2 (lib. : alk. paper)
    1. Egypt—Civilization—To 332 B.C. I. Stalcup, Brenda.
II. Turning points in world history (Greenhaven Press)

DT61 .A62 2001
932'.01—dc21   00-039321
                                                CIP

Cover photo: © Burstein Collection/Corbis
Library of Congress, 117
NorthWind Picture Archives, 31, 134, 165

© 2001 by Greenhaven Press, Inc.
P.O. Box 289009, San Diego, CA 92198-9009

Printed in the U.S.A.

Contents

Chapter 1: The Rise of Egyptian Civilization

Chapter 2: Royalty and Religion in Ancient Egypt

Chapter 4: The Decline of the Egyptian Empire

Chapter 5: The Heritage of Ancient Egyptian Civilization

Egyptian religious and moralistic writings in their own
sacred texts.

Foreword

Certain past events stand out as pivotal, as having effects and outcomes that change the course of history. These events are often referred to as turning points. Historian Louis L. Snyder provides this useful definition:

> A turning point in history is an event, happening, or stage which thrusts the course of historical development into a different direction. By definition a turning point is a great event, but it is even more—a great event with the explosive impact of altering the trend of man's life on the planet.

History's turning points have taken many forms. Some were single, brief, and shattering events with immediate and obvious impact. The invasion of Britain by William the Conqueror in 1066, for example, swiftly transformed that land's political and social institutions and paved the way for the rise of the modern English nation. By contrast, other single events were deemed of minor significance when they occurred, only later recognized as turning points. The assassination of a little-known European nobleman, Archduke Franz Ferdinand, on June 28, 1914, in the Bosnian town of Sarajevo was such an event; only after it touched off a chain reaction of political-military crises that escalated into the global conflict known as World War I did the murder's true significance become evident.

Other crucial turning points occurred not in terms of a few hours, days, months, or even years, but instead as evolutionary developments spanning decades or even centuries. One of the most pivotal turning points in human history, for instance—the development of agriculture, which replaced nomadic hunter-gatherer societies with more permanent settlements—occurred over the course of many generations. Still other great turning points were neither events nor developments, but rather revolutionary new inventions and innovations that significantly altered social customs and ideas, military tactics, home life, the spread of knowledge, and the human condition in general. The developments of writing, gunpowder, the printing press, antibiotics, the electric light, atomic energy, television, and the computer, the last two of which have recently ushered in the world-altering information age, represent only some of these innovative turning points.

Each anthology in the Greenhaven Turning Points in World History series presents a group of essays chosen for their accessibility. The anthology's structure also enhances this accessibility. First, an introductory essay provides a general overview of the principal events and figures involved, placing the topic in its historical context. The essays that follow explore various aspects in more detail, some targeting political trends and consequences, others social, literary, cultural, and/or technological ramifications, and still others pivotal leaders and other influential figures. To aid the reader in choosing the material of immediate interest or need, each essay is introduced by a concise summary of the contributing writer's main themes and insights.

In addition, each volume contains extensive research tools, including a collection of excerpts from primary source documents pertaining to the historical events and figures under discussion. In the anthology on the French Revolution, for example, readers can examine the works of Rousseau, Voltaire, and other writers and thinkers whose championing of human rights helped fuel the French people's growing desire for liberty; the French *Declaration of the Rights of Man and Citizen*, presented to King Louis XVI by the French National Assembly on October 2, 1789; and eyewitness accounts of the attack on the royal palace and the horrors of the Reign of Terror. To guide students interested in pursuing further research on the subject, each volume features an extensive bibliography, which for easy access has been divided into separate sections by topic. Finally, a comprehensive index allows readers to scan and locate content efficiently. Each of the anthologies in the Greenhaven Turning Points in World History series provides students with a complete, detailed, and enlightening examination of a crucial historical watershed.

Introduction

To modern-day people, the world of the ancient Egyptians often seems remote and strange. It can be difficult for us to see any way in which their culture has affected ours. This feeling is quite understandable: After all, more than five thousand years have passed since the civilization of ancient Egypt first arose, over four thousand since the construction of the Great Pyramid, and two thousand since Egypt fell to the Roman Empire. Moreover, there has been no continuity of culture from ancient Egypt to the present day. The religion of the ancient Egyptians vanished, replaced first by Christianity and then by Islam. Their language ceased to be spoken. The hieroglyphs fell into disuse; for two thousand years, no one could unlock their secrets to read the literature and history of ancient Egypt.

It was not until the beginning of the nineteenth century that the hieroglyphs began to be deciphered. At the same time, archeologists adopted a more scientific approach to the excavation of ancient sites and the study of Egyptian artifacts. These two developments have significantly increased our understanding of ancient Egyptian civilization. As Egyptologist Joseph Kaster explains, researchers now have enough information "to make an intelligent comparative evaluation of the civilization of ancient Egypt, and to determine its place in the political and cultural development of mankind. We find, as a result, that the debt of Western civilization to ancient Egypt is far greater than one might be inclined to imagine."

In fact, the legacy of ancient Egypt has turned out to be immense. The Egyptians were pioneers in mathematics, technology, engineering, architecture, astronomy, medicine, political organization, law, art, literature, ethics, and philosophy. Partly through trade and partly through imperial expansion, the Egyptians transmitted much of their knowledge to the surrounding peoples, including the Hebrews, the Syrians, the Phoenicians, the Nubians, and the Greeks.

Whether directly or indirectly, much of that knowledge still impacts the modern Western world. For example, the Egyptians invented the twelve-month solar calendar on which our present calendar is based. Egyptian hieroglyphs served as the basis of the Phoenician alphabet, from which our own alphabet derives. The Greeks adopted and built upon Egyptian scientific knowledge in areas such as medicine, pharmacology, mathematics, and architecture. The translation of Egyptian texts has proven that Egypt's literature and traditions profoundly impacted the Hebrews. Scholars have found many correlations between ancient Egyptian writings and passages in the Old Testament. Furthermore, some researchers believe that Egypt's short-lived monotheistic religion of the Aten directly inspired the Hebrews' development of a faith firmly centered on the belief in one sole god.

The enduring heritage of Egypt is just one of the many topics examined in *Turning Points in World History: Ancient Egyptian Civilization*. Chosen for content and readability, the essays included in this volume discuss the rise, height, and fall of this early civilization. A detailed chronology and historical essay outline the most significant events in the long history of ancient Egypt, while the glossary serves as a further aid to understanding. In addition, the primary source documents featured in the appendix open a window into the life of the ancient Egyptians, told in their own words.

As author Roger Lancelyn Green writes, "It would take a lifetime of thought and study to get to know the ancient Egyptians and feel that one had even begun to understand their thoughts and beliefs, or look for a moment through their eyes." Yet such is the fascinating nature of ancient Egyptian civilization that we cannot help but be captivated. Taken together, the readings presented here provide an introduction to one of the world's most mysterious and most important cultures.

A Brief History of Ancient Egypt

The ancient Egyptians did not refer to their land as Egypt, which actually derives from the Greek word *Aigyptos*. Instead, they called their country Kemet, or the "Black Land." This name described the geographical phenomenon that was essential to the birth of Egyptian civilization—the ribbon of rich black mud and silt left behind by the annual flooding of the Nile River. Lying on both sides of the Nile, this strip of dark soil presented a strong contrast to the pale ground of the desert and barren cliffs beyond the river, which the Egyptians called Deshret, the "Red Land."

Egypt receives such little rainfall that if it were not for the yearly flooding of the Nile, the Egyptians would have never been able to grow enough food to support the rise of a great civilization. The desert was so infertile that the Egyptians used it only as a site for the pyramids and tombs in which they buried their dead. But each summer in the mountains of central Africa and in the Ethiopian highlands, the Nile was swollen by melting snow and heavy rains. The turbulent river then rushed down into the Egyptian lowlands and poured over its banks, bringing life-giving water and depositing fertile soil ideal for the cultivation of crops. "The difference between the fertile Black Land and the infertile Red Land has always been both clear and extreme," explains Egyptologist Joyce Tyldesley, "and many visitors to Egypt have noted how it is literally possible to stand with one foot in the desert sand and one foot on the green cultivation. This perpetual reminder of the stark contrast between the living and the dead, the fertile and the infertile, left an indelible mark on secular and religious thought, and the constant cycle of birth, death and rebirth became an endlessly repeated theme of Egyptian life."

The fertility of the Nile River valley allowed the people who settled there in prehistoric times to flourish. However, it was impossible to predict the amount of flooding that would occur each year. If the floodwaters were too low, drought and famine would be the result; if too high, the raging waters could destroy crops and houses. The prehistoric settlers learned to carefully monitor the Nile, and they built a series of canals and dikes for protection during the flood season. To guard against famine during years of low flood, they constructed reservoir basins and stored surplus grain for times of need. They also began to use the canals to bring water to fields outside of the floodplain, thus increasing the amount of arable land through irrigation.

The complicated system of irrigation and agriculture spurred the growth of government: To be successful, these large-scale projects required meticulous organization and the cooperation of villages all along the length of the Nile. In the early days of Egyptian civilization, small districts called nomes were governed by chieftains, or nomarchs. Eventually, the various nomes of the south and those of the north banded together into two separate kingdoms. The southern region is usually referred to as Upper Egypt; the northern area, including the Nile Delta, is called Lower Egypt. (These designations often look confusing on a map since Upper Egypt is placed lower than Lower Egypt. The names actually refer to the direction of the Nile: Since the river runs northward, Upper Egypt is upstream from Lower Egypt.)

The Two Lands Unified

The kingdoms of Upper and Lower Egypt remained separate political entities for a long time. The two kingdoms of the Nile did not coexist peacefully; when they were not at war, they made raids into each other's territory. They also developed different traditions and cultures. For example, the king of Upper Egypt wore a tall white crown, while the king of Lower Egypt wore a shorter red one.

Owing to a lack of archeological evidence and historical information, the events surrounding the unification of Upper and Lower Egypt are not altogether clear. But sometime between 3200 and 3100 B.C., during another of their many wars, Upper Egypt succeeded in conquering Lower Egypt. According to Egyptian legend, Menes was the king who unified the Two Lands; he appears to have been the same ruler who is identified in inscriptions as Narmer. In order to better unite the two kingdoms, Menes attempted to combine aspects of both cultures. He is portrayed in some pictures as wearing the white crown of Upper Egypt, while in others he

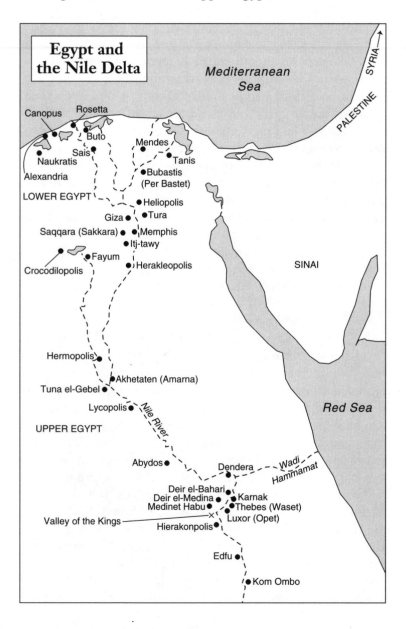

Egypt and the Nile Delta

Mediterranean Sea

SYRIA →

PALESTINE

Canopus
Rosetta
Buto
Mendes
Sais
Naukratis
Tanis
Alexandria
Bubastis (Per Bastet)
LOWER EGYPT
Heliopolis
Giza
Tura
Saqqara (Sakkara)
Memphis
Itj-tawy
Fayum
Crocodilopolis
Herakleopolis

SINAI

Hermopolis
Akhetaten (Amarna)
Tuna el-Gebel
Lycopolis
Nile River
UPPER EGYPT

Red Sea

Abydos
Dendera
Wadi Hammamat
Deir el-Bahari
Deir el-Medina
Karnak
Medinet Habu
Thebes (Waset)
Valley of the Kings
Luxor (Opet)
Hierakonpolis

Edfu

Kom Ombo

wears the red crown of Lower Egypt. (Later these two crowns would be combined into one, known as the double crown.) He also founded a new capital, Memphis, near the meeting point of Upper and Lower Egypt.

The unification of Egypt signals the beginning of the Early Dynastic Period. Not much is known about the First and Second Dynasties, but it seems clear that Menes and the kings who followed him spent much of their time consolidating their power. Lower Egypt did not submit easily, and there are signs of occasional revolts and rebellions. At the same time, however, the unified lands made great strides in cultural advancements. The kings established a complex administrative system to better govern the nomes of Egypt. Paper was invented, made from flattened and dried papyrus reed. Symbols for writing, called hieroglyphs, were also developed during this period. The Egyptians began to study the movements of the stars in order to calculate the date that the Nile flood would occur. By the end of the Second Dynasty, they had invented the 365-day calendar. In many respects, as historian William A. Ward writes, the Early Dynastic Period "must have been . . . vibrant with life and hope for the future."

The Age of the Pyramids

The Third Dynasty of Egypt ushered in the era known as the Old Kingdom, characterized by "the sudden flowering of culture for which the advances of the early dynastic times had prepared the way," in the words of author Jacquetta Hawkes. Blessed with peace and prosperity, the Egyptians of the Old Kingdom produced astounding achievements in art, architecture, engineering, medicine, and literature. The most renowned accomplishment of the Old Kingdom was the pyramid, the world's earliest monumental structure in stone.

The first pyramid was built for Djoser, the founder of the Third Dynasty, by his chief architect Imhotep. Rather simple in design, Djoser's pyramid consists of six rectangular and progressively smaller layers that resemble stairs. As a feat of engineering, though, the Step Pyramid was unprecedented for its time: Never before had anyone attempted to use stone in a building of such enormity. Imhotep designed an ingenious system of internal buttressing to keep the heavy pyramid from collapsing under its own weight—and to this day, the Step Pyramid still stands.

The pharaohs of the Fourth Dynasty improved upon the basic design, constructing pyramids that had smooth, unbroken sides meeting at the top in a point. Far and away the most impressive of these is the Great Pyramid made for Khufu, the second pharaoh of the Fourth Dynasty. The largest of the pyramids, this massive structure covers thirteen acres and rises to a height of nearly five hundred feet. It is composed of an estimated 2.3 million blocks of stone, with an average weight of 2.5 tons each. More than four thousand years later, the Great Pyramid continues to stun and amaze onlookers. According to author Roger Lancelyn Green, "No description can prepare one for the overwhelming experience of size and grandeur, the almost oppressive sense of age and dignity one feels when standing at the foot . . . , scrambling to the summit . . . , or penetrating through its long passages and galleries to the tomb chamber of Khufu in its very heart."

The effort required to build the pyramids was immense; for example, the Great Pyramid is believed to have been constructed over a twenty-year period by approximately one hundred thousand men. Although popular films and novels have often portrayed these workers as slaves forced to toil under the lash of the pharaoh's overseer, research has shown that the labor force was largely made up of peasants who willingly worked on the pyramids during the flood season, when agricultural activity was at a standstill. Many Egyptologists believe that the construction of the pyramids functioned as a giant public works project, providing needed jobs during the three months of the year that the fields lay underwater.

Furthermore, the pharaoh was able to motivate this workforce because by the beginning of the Old Kingdom, he had come to be seen as an all-powerful god. Specifically, he was considered to be the son of Ra, the sun god and the head of the Egyptian pantheon of deities. As the son of Ra, the pharaoh served as the sole intercessor between ordinary humans and their gods. He alone could speak to the other deities on an equal footing, asking them to bless the land and its people. When the pharaoh died, the Egyptians believed, he was reincarnated as Osiris, the lord of the Underworld; through his intercession, other Egyptians could also gain eternal life. The construction of the pharaohs' tombs—the pyramids—was therefore of crucial importance to the ancient Egyptians. "In this period," Egyptologist Rosalie David explains, "the Egyptians perhaps held the clearest idea of their collective destiny and focussed upon one main objective—the building and completion of a monumental burial place for their king, which would withstand the ravages of time and robbery, which would facilitate the god-king's safe passage into eternity, and thus, vicariously, would ensure survival beyond death for all his subjects."

Despite the doctrine of the pharaoh's godhood, toward the end of the Fourth Dynasty the priests and the nobility started to chip away at the centralized authority of the pharaoh. Gradually the balance of power shifted, as can be seen by the fact that the pharaohs of the next two dynasties built much smaller pyramids, reflecting their diminishing status. Then one of the last sovereigns of the Sixth Dynasty succeeded to the throne as a very young child. Pepy II ruled for approximately ninety years, the longest reign on record in the history of humankind. He was a weak pharaoh, apparently hemmed in by the considerable power of the nobility, and after his death the Old Kingdom fell apart.

No one knows exactly why the Old Kingdom collapsed. Certainly the weakened status of the pharaoh played an essential role in the breakdown of civil authority. In addition, the climate seems to have become dryer; for several years, the Nile floods brought less water than normal, which resulted in crop failures throughout the land. External pressures also played a role in Egypt's decline: Tribes of desert nomads infiltrated the Delta, causing continual unrest. The events of the next hundred years are obscure. Pharaohs continued to reign as figureheads, but in reality Egypt split apart into many small warring states, each with its own ruler. Without centralized control, the irrigation system was impossible to maintain, and famines became frequent. It was a chaotic time of civil wars, border raids, economic depressions, lawlessness, and random violence.

Egypt's Resurgence

During the First Intermediate Period, as this period of near-anarchy is called by historians, two powerful families arose at the town of Herakleopolis, approximately fifty miles south of Memphis. These two families comprise the Ninth and Tenth Dynasties, whose pharaohs extended their power over much of Lower Egypt and the northern territory of Upper Egypt. Far in the south, meanwhile, another family of nobles based in Thebes emerged as the dominant rulers of the region. The pharaohs of the Theban family are classified as the Eleventh Dynasty.

For some time, the pharaohs in Herakleopolis and those in Thebes ruled their own territories simultaneously. (This is the reason that the Eleventh Dynasty partially overlaps the Ninth and Tenth Dynasties in chronologies of ancient Egypt.) Around 2060 B.C., the Theban pharaoh Mentuhotep II conquered Lower Egypt and spent the next few years reuniting the Two Lands under his command. Mentuhotep poured considerable effort into pacifying internal rebellions, consolidating and protecting Egypt's borders, rebuilding the nation's army, imposing law and order, and renewing trade and other commercial endeavors.

The latter half of Mentuhotep's reign marks the end of the turbulent First Intermediate Period and the beginning of the Middle Kingdom. His successors continued to work toward restoring Egypt's former grandeur, preparing the way for the country's incredible resurgence under the pharaohs of the Twelfth Dynasty.

The family of the Twelfth Dynasty was also from Thebes, but the first pharaoh relocated the capital to the more central city of Itj-tawy, near the old capital of Memphis. By reorganizing the provincial governments, the Twelfth Dynasty pharaohs placed checks on the power of local rulers and further strengthened the authority of Egypt's central government. They concentrated on repairing and improving the irrigation system, erecting defensive fortifications, and refurbishing the temples. As peace and prosperity spread across the nation, Egypt experienced a new outburst of artistic creativity, most notably in literature.

At the same time that the pharaohs of the Middle Kingdom were renewing Egypt's domestic health, they also embarked on an ambitious campaign of expansion into foreign territory. They conquered northern Nubia, thereby pushing Egypt's frontier about two hundred miles south, past the

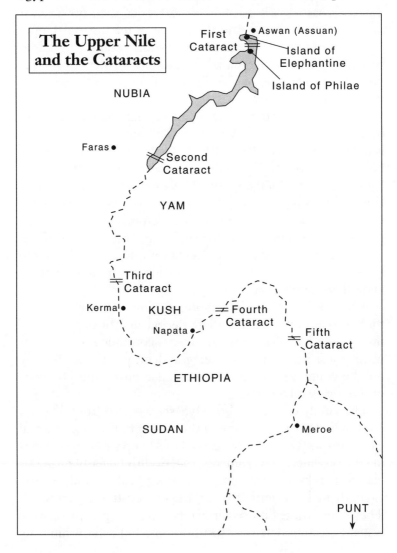

The Upper Nile and the Cataracts

First Cataract
Aswan (Assuan)
Island of Elephantine
Island of Philae

NUBIA

Faras

Second Cataract

YAM

Third Cataract

Kerma　KUSH　Fourth Cataract

Napata

Fifth Cataract

ETHIOPIA

SUDAN

Meroe

PUNT

Second Cataract of the Nile. In the east, the Egyptians carved out spheres of influence containing many Syrian and Palestinian city-states. In addition, foreign trade increased markedly during the Middle Kingdom, reaching as far away as the island of Crete. Compared to the Old Kingdom, the Egypt of the Middle Kingdom was much more interested in developing international ties and expansion via imperial conquest. "Both culturally and politically," author Joyce Milton writes, "the Middle Kingdom laid the basis for the rise of the Egyptian Empire."

Before the empire began to rise, however, Egypt endured another outbreak of turmoil and division, known as the Second Intermediate Period. The disintegration of the Middle Kingdom occurred during the Thirteenth Dynasty, when ineffectual leaders once again allowed the authority of the central government to weaken, leaving the destabilized country vulnerable to infiltration by foreigners. The Egyptians called these people Hyksos, which means "rulers of foreign lands." Their ethnic origins are a matter of dispute, but most likely the Hyksos were a mix of various Semitic tribes from Syria and Palestine. It is also unclear exactly how the Hyksos came to Egypt. The ancient Egyptian texts tell of hordes of warriors pouring over the borders, but the archeological evidence suggests that the Hyksos had been gradually filtering into the Nile Delta for several decades prior to the collapse of the Middle Kingdom. Whichever may be the case, the Hyksos invaders seized control of the Nile Delta and most of Lower Egypt.

Egyptian political history is murky during this time, with the Fourteenth, Fifteenth, Sixteenth, and Seventeenth Dynasties overlapping considerably. The pharaohs of the Fifteenth and Sixteenth Dynasties were the Hyksos rulers of Lower Egypt, who adopted many Egyptian customs. In Upper Egypt, the native pharaohs of the Seventeenth Dynasty maintained a small independent Egyptian kingdom in Thebes. The Hyksos pharaohs did not attempt to conquer Thebes, but they did consider it a vassal state and required the payment of tribute.

The Hyksos's toleration of the Theban dynasty proved to

be their undoing. After approximately one hundred years of Hyksos domination, the pharaohs of the Seventeenth Dynasty took up arms against the invaders and slowly began to regain territory. The last pharaoh of the Seventeenth Dynasty was killed in the fighting. His brother Ahmose, a brilliant military leader and the founder of the Eighteenth Dynasty, drove the Hyksos out of Egypt and pursued them as they fled into Syria and Palestine.

The Egyptian Empire

Having dealt decisively with the Hyksos, Ahmose reunified the Two Lands under his aegis, inaugurating the New Kingdom. His reign also marks the beginning of Egypt's imperial age. The Hyksos interlude had drastically changed the Egyptian perspective on the world. "No more could the Egyptian feel secure in his green 'island,' isolated by sea and sand," explains Egyptologist Barbara Mertz. "The walls had been breached, and never again would Egypt feel the complete superiority she had enjoyed under the Old and Middle Kingdoms." Instead, the Egyptians sought to protect themselves by creating buffer zones of tributary states about their country.

Ahmose set the example that would be followed by the future pharaohs of the New Kingdom. As Ahmose chased the Hyksos from Egypt, writes Egyptologist Joseph Kaster, "he seiz[ed] the territories which they overran in the process and [made] them tributary to Egypt. This was the beginning of the Egyptian empire in Syria." Then he turned his army south and marched into Nubia to reestablish Egyptian control there. His descendants continued his policies of expansion east and south; by the reign of Thutmose III, less than one hundred years after Ahmose's death, the Egyptian Empire stretched beyond the Fourth Cataract of the Nile in the south and as far east as the Euphrates River.

Egypt had never before kept a permanent standing army, but Ahmose and his successors emphasized the importance of maintaining a constant military presence and developing a professional soldier class. They fine-tuned the troops into a well-organized and sophisticated fighting force. According to Egyptologist Barbara Watterson, the New Kingdom was "the first time [that] the army included infantry and chariotry." Ships were used to transport men, horses, and chariots on the Nile—the beginnings of the Egyptian navy. Furthermore, the Eighteenth Dynasty produced an unusually large number of extraordinary pharaohs, intelligent and capable leaders who vigorously defended Egypt's borders and broadly advertised the nation's military might. "For much of the next five hundred years," states author Michael Rice, "Egypt was unequivocally the greatest power in the ancient world."

Among the consequences of Egypt's empire-building was an unprecedented increase in the wealth of the country. The spoils of war and tributes from subject states flowed into Egypt's coffers. Egypt acquired valuable natural resources such as gold and timber from the farthest reaches of the empire. Furthermore, the consolidation of Egyptian control over large amounts of territory enabled Egypt to maintain trade routes to far-distant countries, spurring the growth of international commerce. With their new riches, the Egyptians built colossal statues and magnificent temples. Egyptians from all classes developed a taste for luxuries, including opulent jewelry of ivory and gold.

Cultural and societal attitudes were also affected by Egypt's prosperity and imperial outlook. "The growth of international commerce," as Kaster points out, "is always accompanied by interchange of ideas, the spread of cosmopolitanism, and the broadening of cultural contacts." The highly refined literature and art of the New Kingdom reflected these influences. According to Hawkes, in its cultivation of architecture and the arts, the Egyptian Empire "achieved a brilliance surpassing even that of the Old Kingdom."

However, one innovation that arose during the New Kingdom almost spelled its ruin. Around the year 1350 B.C., the pharaoh Akhenaton attempted to replace the ancient polytheistic religion of Egypt with a new faith centered around one god, the sun-disk Aten. He angered the priesthood by proscribing the old gods, commanding that their temples be closed, and confiscating their lands and goods. "Religious persecution was new to the Egyptians," writes Watterson; moreover, the closing of the temples constituted "a very serious matter, for these institutions played an important part in the economic and social life of the country."

Akhenaton further disrupted the nation by relocating the capital from Thebes to a distant city, where he isolated himself to concentrate on his revolutionary religious ideas. He took little to no action to maintain Egypt's imperial borders. Sensing weakness, enemy forces soon invaded Egypt's territories in Syria. The provincial rulers of these client states pleaded for assistance, but Akhenaton ignored their letters and let large chunks of the empire slip away, seemingly unconcerned. By the time he died, Egypt had lost most of its lands in the Near East, and the once-impressive family of the Eighteenth Dynasty was nearing its end. However, the Egyptian Empire rebounded from this near-disaster. The energetic pharaohs of the Nineteenth Dynasty revitalized Egypt's military might and recaptured the territory that Akhenaton had lost.

The Slow Decline

The Egyptian Empire prospered once more under the rule of the pharaohs of the Nineteenth Dynasty, but its strength was no longer as secure as in the early days of the New Kingdom. During the time span covered by the Nineteenth and Twentieth Dynasties, Egypt periodically faced the threat of invasion from various Near Eastern tribes and the barbarian hordes from southern Europe that they called the Sea Peoples. Although the Egyptians fought off these invaders, the effort gradually weakened the stability of the country. As author Lionel Casson remarks, "The period spanned by these two dynasties presents a curious contradiction. On the one hand, it was perhaps Egypt's showiest age. The pharaohs won victories over foreign enemies, erected monumental buildings, and presided over a luxurious court. Yet it was also the age that portended Egypt's political disintegration and end as a major political power."

Toward the end of the Twentieth Dynasty, a series of weak pharaohs fell under the control of the high priests of Amon at Thebes. The eastern empire was lost, and the country broke apart as the glory of the New Kingdom deteriorated into the confusion of the Third Intermediate Period. The high priests of Amon ruled Upper Egypt from Thebes, while a noble family formed the Twenty-First Dynasty and set up a capital in Tanis from which they governed Lower Egypt. Nubia, the last imperial subject, gained its independence and established its own royal line.

Around 950 B.C., the unthinkable happened: For the first time since the Hyksos invasion, Egypt fell to foreign conquerors. The Libyans who overran Egypt briefly reunited the Two Lands, but the country was soon torn asunder by civil wars between rival dynasties. For the remainder of the Third Intermediate Period, Egypt endured the rule of foreigners: first the Libyans, then the Nubians and the Assyrians.

After the Saïte pharaohs of the Twenty-Sixth Dynasty expelled the Assyrians, the Egyptians enjoyed a short respite from the turmoil of the previous period. For almost a century and a half, the Saïte Dynasty protected the nation from invasion while promoting a revival of the artistic style of the Old Kingdom. "This strong emphasis on all things Egyptian," Tyldesley suggests, was in some respects "a calculated political move designed to emphasize the individual national character of a once-powerful country which was rapidly becoming a bit-part player on the stage of international affairs." Indeed, the Saïte pharaohs attempted to regain the prestige of the former Egyptian Empire, but their military expeditions were largely unsuccessful. Then in 525 B.C., they faced a foe too great to resist: the powerful Persian Empire.

After Egypt fell to the Persians, it never truly existed again as an independent state, despite a few short-lived rebellions during which native Egyptian pharaohs regained the throne. The Persians clamped down on the rebels in 343 B.C., and the last Egyptian pharaoh fled the country. Only a few years later, the Macedonian commander Alexander the Great subjugated the Persian Empire, including Egypt. One of his generals founded a new dynasty, the Ptolemies, who ruled as pharaohs until 30 B.C., when the Roman Empire conquered Egypt. Cleopatra VII, the last queen of Egypt, committed suicide rather than to be taken to Rome in chains.

With Cleopatra died the long history of the pharaohs of

Egypt. Unlike former conquerors, the Romans had no interest in establishing an independent dynasty of pharaohs and instead incorporated Egypt into their empire as a province overseen by governors. Under the influence of the Romans, the remaining remnants of the civilization of the ancient Egyptians quickly faded away—but their timeless monuments, art, and literature survived, waiting to be discovered and treasured by the people of a later age.

Chapter 1

The Rise of Egyptian Civilization

Turning Points

IN WORLD HISTORY

The Unique Geographic Conditions in Egypt

John A. Wilson

Egypt was the birthplace of one of the earliest civilizations. According to John A. Wilson, the Nile River valley possesses a number of unique features that shaped the emergence of early Egyptian civilization. For example, Wilson writes, the annual summer flooding of the Nile allowed the Egyptians to cultivate land that would have otherwise remained arid desert. However, in order to best utilize the floodwaters, the Egyptians needed to devise an intricate system of large-scale irrigation that required constant vigilance. The immense amount of shared effort necessary to keep the irrigation system working encouraged the growth of government and other elements of civilization, the author explains.

Wilson taught for many years at the University of Chicago, where he was the director of the Oriental Institute. His books include *Signs and Wonders upon Pharaoh: A History of American Egyptology* and *The Burden of Egypt: An Interpretation of Ancient Egyptian Culture*, from which the following selection is excerpted.

Most visitors to Egypt are distinctly aware of the exceptional nature of climate and topography along the Nile. They have come from lands of normal rainfall, where meadows run from valley to hill without break and where the clouds may conceal the sun, moon, and stars for days on end. They have come from lands where the roads may run in any direction. Their expectations in terms of terrain or weather have allowed for a wide variety of chance: they have looked to all four directions of the compass; they may have experienced rain in March or August; they are uncertain about the weather for their week-end outing; they may have planted their crops in a riverside meadow or in a highland meadow. Now they find Egypt a land essentially rainless, confined closely to the banks of the Nile River, and thus restricted to a single north-and-south axis. They find the sharpest possible contrast between riverside meadow and highland desert. That contrast between the fertile black land and the red desert sands is marked by a definite margin, which is the extreme limit to which the waters of the Nile may reach. It is possible to stand with one foot on the fruitful alluvial soil and one foot on the lifeless desert sands. As one looks inward toward the river valley, one is conscious of bustling and teeming life. As one looks outward toward the sandstone hills, one is aware of vast desolate stretches where no life is possible. Inevitably, the polarity of attention is the great muddy river which brings the life-giving water and soil. If the Nile were by some chance cut off, that soil would dry to dust and blow away. The land of Egypt would become a vast dry wadi of the great North African desert.

Gifts and Obligations

Because of this dramatic contrast between the desert and the sown, we all repeat [Greek historian] Herodotus' observation that Egypt is the gift of the Nile. One is scarcely aware of the few little oases spotting the Libyan Desert. The Nile has come with pulsing prodigality out of equatorial Africa and the highlands of Abyssinia and has flung fabled riches across one of the world's poorest areas. Only that surging summer inundation of the River makes a land possible here, and the annual gifts of refreshing water and refertilizing soil in a semitropical climate give an agricultural richness which has been proverbial in all times. With the proper use of the soil, two or three crops a year are a happy expectation.

However, as one lives in Egypt, one is conscious that the Nile's gift lays heavy obligations upon the Egyptian peasant. The inundation rushes through the valley on its way to the sea. Unless its waters are captured and retained, the fertility of the soil will last for a few months only. In the spring one hears the ceaseless musical groaning of the water wheel bringing moisture up from deep wells; one sees the back of a peasant, bending and lifting all day long at the well sweep; one sees the heavy work of mending little water channels, which carry moisture off to the outlying fields. Incessant toil is the responsibility laid on the Egyptian peasant by the Nile's great gift. Without that labor to make the most lasting and economical use of the waters, Egypt would be a much narrower country, snatching at a single crop immediately after the inundation.

That observation leads us back into distant prehistoric times, in an attempt to imagine the valley of the Nile before man had developed any system of irrigation. Life then must have been concentrated even more closely at the margins of the River. Each summer the inundation must have rushed through without restraint, spreading thinly beyond the riverside marshes and draining off quickly. The red desert must have come down much closer toward the River, close to a thick, junglelike tangle of marsh at the edge of the stream. The two banks must have been a thicket of reeds and brush, and the profusion of waterfowl and jungle fowl must have provided a happy hunting ground for the smaller animals. That this riverine jungle did exist before man drained the marshes and carried the water up toward the foot of the hills is evidenced by pictures of historic times. There, in scenes of hunting in the swamps, we see the vestiges of earlier conditions, with the tangle of reeds and brush and the swarming of game and fowl. The flora and fauna of Egypt down into historic times were much like the life now present in the southern Sudan. For example, the ibis and the papyrus, so symbolic of ancient Egypt, are now found in the jungle-like Nile reaches fifteen hundred miles to the south.

Thus earliest man in Egypt was trapped between the encroaching desert sands and the riotous riverine jungle. To gain any permanent foothold, he had to drain and root out the jungle, and he had annually to thrust and hold the water out against the greedy desert sands. This was hard work, and it probably was a slow, dogged effort covering thousands of years of prehistory. Indeed, we have no clear evidence of any really important irrigation, involving community effort on canals and catch basins, before historic times. Before then, one infers a clearing-out of swamps by an inching process. It is an inference that late prehistoric times saw major developments in irrigation—but only an inference. The supporting argument would run as follows: large-scale irrigation extended the arable land and produced the necessary food for a larger population and for that element of surplus which goes with civilized living; but large-scale irrigation requires a common effort, binding together different communities, and is a factor promoting the growth of a state; the visible elements of historic times argue that, for several centuries back, there must have been a widespread economy in the utilization of water, to make those historic factors possible.

The Need for Vigilance

The Nile lays another obligation upon the Egyptian. The River is not precise in the timing of its inundation or in the volume of its waters. Man must be on the alert against its antic behavior. In particular, its volume is a matter of serious concern. Only a few inches of maximum height separate the normal Nile from famine or riotous destruction. In modern times, before the Assuan Dam was built, a high Nile at the First Cataract, rising 25 or 26 feet above a zero datum, meant a good, normal inundation, easily controlled and covering enough ground for bountiful crops. A high Nile which fell 30 inches below this normal meant insufficient crops and a pinched year. A drop of 60 inches—80 per cent of normal—meant a fatal famine, with starvation stalking the Egyptians for a year. Too high an inundation was also a peril. The levels of canals and protective dikes were fixed on the expectation of a good, normal flood; only a foot above normal would mean damage to the earth embankments; a 30-foot Nile—20 per cent above normal—would sweep away dikes and canal banks and bring the mud-brick villages tumbling down. The legend of the seven years of plenty and the seven lean years was no fantasy for Egypt; it was always a threatening possibility. The margin between abundant life and hollow death was a very narrow one. Constant vigilance

An artist's drawing depicts the city of Thebes during an inundation of the Nile River.

against the antic behavior of the life-giving River was necessary, and only an orderly government could provide that vigilance for the entire land. Again the gift of the River imposed its hard obligations.

This was the setting in which the ancient Egyptian civilization flourished, and these were the incentives which led the Egyptians to struggle upward toward a fuller life based on the fertile potentiality of their soil. It was no warm and drowsy land of lotus-eaters. In [historian Arnold] Toynbee's terms of an environmental challenge and a human response, there were problems to be met progressively. The full potentiality of climate, water, and soil was a challenge which demanded long centuries of back-bending toil to drain the jungle marshes and reclaim the land nearest the River, then centuries of weary labor to carry the River water against the greedy desert by canals and catch basins. Thereby the ancient won great richness of crops. . . .

The Benefits of Isolation

Another environmental factor which needs attention is the physical isolation of the land of Egypt. The Nile Valley was a tube, loosely sealed against important outside contact. To the west and east of the valley lay forbidding deserts, passable for small caravans of traders but insuperable barriers for any people coming in force. Along the northern frontiers the Sinai desert thinned out and weakened contact with Asia, while the Libyan coast provided a slightly greater potential of traffic for pastoral and nonaggressive peoples. Land communication east or west meant five to eight days of desert caravaning— across Sinai to Palestine, through the Wadi Hammamat to the Red Sea, or out to the nearest of the western oases.

There were also barriers to contact by water. Prehistoric man, with his flexible little boats and his lack of experience in navigation, would not venture across the Mediterranean in force. The Egyptians themselves built boats for the Nile River and adapted them inadequately for the sea. The earliest boats may well have hugged the coast for protection and direction. If that be true, the overseas communication between the Egyptian Delta and the Phoenician coast, instead of being four days' direct sailing, may have been twice as long. . . .

To the south of Egypt proper there were also barriers. The First Cataract was not a serious obstacle, as it could easily be navigated or by-passed. However, the land south of the First Cataract is relatively inhospitable, with the desert cliffs cutting in close to the Nile and limiting the arable land to meager strips. No large and powerful culture was possible between the First and Third Cataracts. South of the Third Cataract the land opens out and provides wider fields and greater pasture land, but the Third Cataract itself, the Second Cataract, and the Nubian deserts were all serious obstacles to movement north and south. There was always the possibility of infiltration from the south, just as there was the possibility of infiltration from Libya or through Sinai. However, the elements which strained out these threats were strong, and a normal Egyptian government was able to handle the threats as a police problem. In earliest times Egypt was well sealed against invasion.

A Relative Sense of Security

The many generalizations made in this essay are subject to modification, exception, or different interpretation. The generalization that Egypt was secure against attack from outside is relative to time and place. There were periods in ancient history when the movements of peoples exerted such pressure that forces broke through the barriers of desert or sea. However, such great folk wanderings as the Hyksos movement or the Sea Peoples' attack come much later in Egyptian history; in earlier times the complacent sense of security was a dominant psychology. Further, there were parts of Egypt where infiltration might be a constant problem: at the First Cataract, at the northwestern frontier against the Libyans, or on the Suez frontier against the Asiatics. In those areas frontier police were necessary, and constant vigilance was an element of the psychology of the region.

Security from foreign threat is also relative in the comparison of different cultures. In contrast to their contemporary neighbors—the Mesopotamians, the Syro-Palestinians, or the Anatolians—the Egyptians were in a happy position of geographic isolation. It was not necessary for them to maintain major and constant force against attack. Any potential threat could be seen at a considerable distance, and it was unlikely that that threat would penetrate Egypt with damaging force. This relative sense of security bred in the ancient Egyptian an essential optimism about his career in this world and the next, and it permitted a marked element of individual freedom for the ordinary Egyptian. In contrast to his neighbors—the Babylonians and the Hebrews—the ancient Egyptian was not constrained to slavish obedience to authority, in the interests of the complete conformance of the community. His rules were general and well understood, but within those rules he enjoyed a relatively high degree of liberty to exercise his own personality. This freedom arose out of his basic confidence in himself and in his world, and this optimism, in turn, was possible because of his relatively high degree of geographic security. . . .

The River and the Sun

One must make a distinction between the sense of insecurity which arises out of the threat of invasion from abroad and the sense of insecurity which arises out of the possibility of a low Nile and famine conditions. The Egyptian did not have the first threat; the second threat was always a lurking possibility. However, that second threat was constantly countered by the hope and expectation that a year of low Nile might be followed by a year of good Nile. It was possible to face the low Nile by a cautious husbanding of Egyptian resources, in order to tide over the famine months of the year until another Nile came. Another Nile always came in its season. That element of periodicity of the life-bringing inundation strongly promoted the Egyptian sense of confidence. Every spring the River would shrink down into its bed and leave the fields to the fury of the hot desert winds—the invader from without—but every summer the Nile would surge again with floodwaters, lift high above its bed, and revive the fields with moisture and new soil. The Nile never refused its great task of revivification. In its periodicity it promoted the Egyptian's sense of confidence; in its rebirth it gave him a faith that he, too, would be victorious over death and go on into eternal life. True, the Nile might fall short of its full bounty for years of famine, but it never ceased altogether, and ultimately it always came back with full prodigality.

The reassuring periodicity of the River was supported by

The Importance of the Nile River

In the following excerpt from his book Egypt: The Black Land, *Paul Jordan maintains that ancient Egypt would have scarcely been habitable if not for the water of the Nile River, which turned the desert into fertile soil.*

Since the alteration of climatic conditions that followed upon the end of the last ice age some ten thousand years ago, Egypt has enjoyed an unusual physical situation. As an habitable country, it has existed since then only because of the presence of the river Nile. The Nile in Egypt is an 'exotic' stream, in the sense that the source of its waters lies right outside the boundaries of the country it flows through and serves. Egypt as a whole experiences a very low rainfall. Without the Nile, Egypt would now be, not the 'Black Land' that the ancient Egyptians called it—'Kemet'—by virtue of its rich and productive mud, but simply a desert.

Paul Jordan, *Egypt: The Black Land*, 1976.

the periodicity of the sun. In a sky carrying few or no clouds, the sun sank into darkness every evening but surged back in power every morning. The Egyptian might be respectful of the sun's heat; he might be grateful for the cooling north wind or for cooling water; but he was happy in the warmth of the sun after the cool darkness of night. He stretched himself thankfully in the morning rays and observed that his animals did likewise. The grateful sense that daylight was the time of life and that night was a time of arrested life was marked in a land where the distinction between night and day came suddenly and clearly. The sun was the great governing factor of his day-by-day life. Its conquest of death every night and its brilliant rebirth every morning were factors of importance; they renewed the Egyptian's confidence that he, too, would conquer death, as did the sun and the Nile.

Density of Population

Let us look at the land of Egypt from a different viewpoint. Only one-thirtieth of the modern state of Egypt is black land, where man may live and plant crops; more than 95 per cent is barren desert. It is as if our entire Atlantic coast were a country, of which only the state of Maryland was habitable territory. At the present day, 99 per cent of Egypt's population lives on this one-thirtieth of the whole land. The density of habitation is more than twelve hundred to the square mile. This is nearly seven times the density of Maryland's population. Egypt is still agricultural, but it has an extraordinary concentration of population, so that the little agricultural towns lie close together and are packed with people. Except in the back districts, there is a kind of semi-urbanism, through the intensity of contacts.

The population of modern Egypt has grown extraordinarily in the past century, and it is certain that ancient Egypt had nothing like the same density of habitation. The point, however, is that its density was relative to its ancient scene. There was still a sharp and dramatic contrast between the teeming life of the sown and the uninhabited stretches of the desert. Modern Egypt has a population of sixteen million. If ancient Egypt had had only one-tenth that population, its density of habitation on the habitable land would have been about twice the density of modern Virginia or nearly three times the density of Mississippi. Such a concentration, sharply separated from the barren desert, promoted internal contacts and led to a kind of urbanity of thought through the constant iteration of such contacts.

The Two Lands

One of the ancient Egyptian terms for their country was "the Two Lands," and this expresses a real geographic truth. Egypt was a single land in its uniform dependence upon the Nile and in its isolation from other cultures. Internally, however, it divided into two contrasting regions, the long, narrow trough of Upper Egypt to the south and the broad, spreading delta of Lower Egypt to the north. Throughout history these two areas have been distinct and have been conscious of their distinction. Upper Egypt may be only four to twenty miles wide; it is always within immediate reach of the Nile and always within immediate contact with the desert cliffs which inclose it; it has only a north-and-south axis. Lower Egypt loses this axis in its broad stretches running out flat in every direction as far as the eye can reach. Still moldering stretches of marshland in the Delta today remind us of a prehistoric situation in which Lower Egypt must have been an almost uninterrupted flat jungle. In the north the great River breaks down into a number of smaller branches or canals, and there is no one artery of movement. Lower Egypt faces out toward the Mediterranean Sea, toward Asia and Europe; its agricultural richness has an overlay of brisk commercial interest. Its contacts are more cosmopolitan. Upper Egypt, held viselike between two deserts, is restrained to Africa; its commerce moves toward the south or toward Lower Egypt; its agricultural richness retains vestiges of a past in which there was a greater interest in cattle-herding. Anciently and modernly, the two regions spoke markedly different dialects and had different outlooks on life. In a true sense, they were "the Two Lands" which were made into one land.

The Influence of Mesopotamian Civilization

Barbara Mertz

Although the civilization that arose in the Nile valley of Egypt was one of the earliest, it was predated by the Mesopotamian civilization in Sumer, located in the Near East between the Tigris and Euphrates Rivers. In the following excerpt from her book *Temples, Tombs, and Hieroglyphs: A Popular History of Ancient Egypt*, Barbara Mertz argues that Mesopotamia had a significant impact on the birth of Egyptian civilization. She explains that at the very end of Egypt's prehistoric period, the Egyptians made a sudden leap in culture and knowledge. According to Mertz, archeological evidence reveals that during this time period the Egyptians came into contact with the more advanced civilization of Mesopotamia and borrowed many ideas from them. Mertz is an Egyptologist and a writer; her books include *Red Land, Black Land: Daily Life in Ancient Egypt*.

When I was a graduate student—back in antediluvian times—we were given neat lists of prehistoric Egyptian cultures, one succeeding the other like steps on a ladder: Tasian, Badarian, Amratian, Gerzean, Semainean in the south; Fayuum A, Merimde and Maadi in the north. Each culture had a few more amenities than the one that preceded it, and the latest, Gerzean-Semainean, had achieved a fairly high standard of living for a prehistoric culture, with painted pottery, beautifully worked flint tools, stone vessels, metal, and neat houses. . . .

Perhaps the most useful remark we can make about the predynastic cultures is that they are related to one another, not only chronologically, but causally; each has certain things in common with the one which followed it. In general, the nearer in time to the First Dynasty, the more complex is the society—the more "civilized," in our terms. Yet conventionally the beginning of civilization in Egypt does not occur until historic times, with the beginning of the First Dynasty. We are cautiously tiptoeing around the edges of a problem which is, in part, one of terminology; scholars are not as precise as they might be in defining words like "culture" and "civilization." The two words are sometimes used interchangeably, but not all cultures are civilizations. Civilization itself may be used specifically, as in the phrases "Egyptian civilization" and "Chinese civilization," or it may be used as an abstraction, to describe a state of affairs which is contrasted with barbarism. The lack of precision is regrettable; however, we may avoid a certain amount of confusion by restricting ourselves, at this point, to the second of the two meanings. We have been talking about prehistoric, or predynastic, cultures. Gerzean, Amratian, and the rest are not civilizations, nor are they "civilization." At what point, then, does a culture acquire the traits which enable it to be considered a civilization? More significantly, perhaps—*from* what point does it acquire such traits?

The Wagon or the Mountain

After the phenomenal leap from nomadism to settled village life, prehistoric culture shuffled along rather placidly for a few thousand years. Then something peculiar happened.

Scholars who concern themselves with the broader problems of history often anthropomorphize the cultures they are comparing. The man-shaped figures that represent civilizations may be pictured as climbing a ladder or a mountain slope, progressing ever higher on their way to—what? The ultimate goal is admittedly hard to define. But if we are determined to have an analogy, we might say that the process of civilization more closely resembles the acceleration of a wheeled vehicle on a downward slope; slow at first, then ponderously gaining speed until it rushes headlong across the level plain beneath. Momentum carries it on for some distance, initially at a speed so great that it may seem as if acceleration were still taking place. But eventually the heavy vehicle slows . . . and slows . . . and stops. And there it remains, in a state of rest, until some unknown force returns to push it toward another slope.

We cannot really compare a culture to a wagon any more than to a human being climbing a mountain. But analogies are a lot of fun, and this one gives a mental picture which may be useful to us. For something did give the Egyptian prehistoric culture a shove, during the late period we call Gerzean. The picture of society we see then is noticeably different from that of the earlier cultures. People lived in houses with windows and doors, and wore clothing woven out of flax. The flint tools are elegant, and copper is increasingly used for artifacts which had been made of stone. Graves are deeper and more carefully built, sometimes lined with wooden planks. The struggle for existence was less agonizing, and men had time for nonproductive activities; they played games and they painted pictures on their pots. The old brown and red pottery continues, but a new type enters, made of a new kind of clay and decorated with quaint little stick figures of men and animals and boats. The boats carry insignias, which may be the standards or devices of small political units; we assume that in this period the land of Egypt consisted of many communities, each governed by a local chief. These changes are striking; but they are not so striking as the further changes which are about to occur. We are very close to the First Dynasty now—to the beginning of history and of civilization, properly speaking. We are curious, not only about what happened, but about why it happened.

The Catalyst of Civilization

Let us go back to the wagon on the slope. We might carry the analogy one step further and ask: Does the wagon creep along (we will grandly ignore the fact that neither a culture nor a wagon can be said to "creep") until it reaches the point at which the ground drops away from beneath its wheels; or does someone come up behind it and give it a shove? More pedantically: Does civilization arise naturally out of a primitive culture because that culture has, by slow accretion, reached a critical stage of development; or does an external stimulus serve as the catalytic agent?

Egypt's Debt to Mesopotamia

Mesopotamia made several important contributions to Egyptian culture, not the least of which was the idea of writing. The Egyptians appear to have borrowed the concept of writing from Sumerian cuneiform, as described below.

There is reason to believe that ideas reached Egypt in very early times through occasional contacts with the inhabitants of other countries, even as far away as Mesopotamia, though by what channel is unknown. A number of inventions including the cylinder seal, stone mace-head of pear-shape and some distinctive artistic motifs, and architectural designs in brick, all of which were employed by Sumerians in Mesopotamia, were suddenly adopted in Egypt at the end of the period which preceded the foundation of the First Dynasty under Menes. Since no corresponding trace of Egyptian influence can be observed in the Sumerian products of the time (the so-called Jemdet Nasr and First Early Dynastic Period) it may be inferred that the movement was not in both directions. Egypt's debt to Sumer, however, does not seem to have been confined to the knowledge of a few artifacts and artistic conventions; certain words in the Egyptian language, particularly agricultural terms and the names of certain cereals, resemble very closely the corresponding terms in Sumerian and are almost certainly derived from the latter. Unquestionably the most important of Sumer's contributions must be counted the imparting of the principles of writing. It is true that the Sumerian syllabic signs expressed both consonants and vowels, whereas only the consonants were indicated in Egyptian hieroglyphs, but the basic method of using a sign to express not only the actual object which it represented but also other words or even parts of words having a like sound (the rebus principle) is common to both scripts.

The British Museum, *An Introduction to Ancient Egypt*, 1979.

We may argue about exactly what distinguishes a civilization from a primitive culture, or even about whether such a clear-cut distinction can be made. Let's not argue about it. Let us merely suggest that certain new elements are found in most of the groups we call civilizations: monumental architecture, writing, centralized government, and a division of labor resulting in social classes. If we think about these elements, we see that each of them implies more than it says about the society in question. Monumental architecture, for instance, requires advanced techniques in the preparation of materials, and some understanding of basic architectural and mechanical principles; it also suggests that the state can spare some of its members from the basic labor of food production to work on labor gangs; further, it implies that there is an elite group within the state which has the power to order and supervise such labor.

Unless we believe in visitors from Mars or supermen from lost Atlantis, we must conclude that some society, somewhere, was the first to discover the various components of civilization. Did the idea spread outward from the original center to other societies, or did it occur independently in all civilizations? If it did occur only once, where was the cradle of civilization?

The problem of Diffusion versus Independent Creation is still being debated by scholars, but for a long time Egypt looked like the best answer to the second question. Recently, Egyptologists have had to relinquish their proud position, for it appears that the ancient Sumerians beat the Egyptians to it. Not only is Sumerian civilization older, but the Egyptians may have stolen the whole idea from their neighbors.

Similarities Between Egypt and Mesopotamia

At first glance this may seem unreasonable. The two cultures appear so dissimilar—the mud-brick ziggurats of Mesopotamia and the stone pyramids, the pretty picture writing of Egypt and the bird-track cuneiform. Yet the signs of Mesopotamian influence in Egypt at the very end of the predynastic period are indisputable. They appear in the Nile valley suddenly and fully formed, whereas in Mesopotamia we can trace their development through various stages. This is always a sure sign of cultural borrowing, and the borrowed elements themselves are definitely non-Egyptian. Cylinder seals are typical of Mesopotamia and atypical of Egypt, but there are cylinder seals in late predynastic graves. Building stone is scarce in the flat plains of the Land of the Two Rivers [Mesopotamia], so the natives of that region built in brick; the earliest large-scale architecture of Egypt is in the same brick, and it imitates a well-known Mesopotamian style, recessed brick niching. Even when the Egyptians began to quarry their numerous fine sources of stone, they cut it up into brick-sized pieces.

Why do we fail to think of these things as "Egyptian"? Because all of them (there were others besides the ones we have mentioned) died out early in Egypt and were replaced by "Egyptian" ways of doing things. Stone architecture began to employ the monolithic blocks we can see in the Giza pyramids; seal impressions were made with stamp seals—scarabs—instead of with the cylinder type. And the writing, of course, is completely dissimilar. The pictures of objects which became the hieroglyphic symbols of Egyptian writing were all Egyptian objects.

Obviously what we have in Egypt is not simple copying; but it is not independent creation, either. The American anthropologist A.L. Kroeber has suggested the term "stimulus diffusion" to cover this type of borrowing. A people may borrow the idea of doing something from another culture, but the way in which it is done may be their own way. The Egyptians did not copy Sumerian writing; all they needed was the great idea that the spoken word could be recorded. Obviously the borrowing culture—the Egyptians here—must have reached a stage of development in which the new concept is understood and desired. In terms of our analogy, both a change in terrain and a push are needed to get the wagon going; the stimulus would not be felt if the circumstances were adverse.

The Unification of Upper and Lower Egypt

Jill Kamil

The history of Egyptian civilization begins with the unification of Upper and Lower Egypt by the first pharaoh of the First Dynasty. However, Jill Kamil maintains, since the unification was achieved by warfare, the succeeding pharaohs had to struggle to consolidate their power. The conquered region of Lower Egypt resisted domination for approximately two hundred years, she states, and it was only through cultural changes emphasizing the unity and equality of Upper and Lower Egypt that the country's political climate finally stabilized. Kamil is the author of several books, including *The Ancient Egyptians: How They Lived and Worked*, from which the following essay is taken.

Menes (the Horus Narmer) is the legendary first pharaoh of the 1st dynasty. According to tradition he managed to gather together the resources of his Upper Egyptian Kingdom and successfully invade the Delta. In subjugating the provinces of Lower Egypt he brought the whole of the Nile Valley under his domination from the First Cataract to the sea. Narmer set up a fortification south of the apex of the Delta near the borderline between the Two Lands. It was known as the 'White Wall', probably in reference to the Upper Egyptian Kingdom it represented, though later known as Memphis.

The legends which have come down to us of Egypt's first pharaoh have undergone thousands of years of embellishment. Traditionally recognised as the founder of Memphis and the Temple to Ptah, its chief deity, Narmer was said also to have surrounded his chosen headquarters with dykes and diverted the river Nile—which hitherto flowed through the sandhills of the Libyan range—through an artificial channel dug between two mountain ranges. It was said, furthermore, that he constructed a lake around the White Wall which was fed by the river. A famous slate known as the Palette of Narmer records his military triumph. Narmer is sculpted in low relief on both faces: on one side he wears the White Crown of Upper Egypt and on the other the Red Crown of Lower Egypt, thus portraying him as monarch of both kingdoms. The reliefs, executed with flair and confidence, show the victorious monarch striking a kneeling enemy with a raised club, inspecting the bodies of decapitated enemies and, accompanied by fan-bearers, symbolically represented as the 'Strong Bull' breaking fortifications of a township as he tramples the enemy. The Horus hawk [the chief deity of Upper Egypt] is symbolically depicted triumphant over the land of the papyrus: the Delta. . . .

Consolidation of Unity

There appears to have been an effort to create a common culture by uniting opposing factions and combining the traditions of Upper and Lower Egypt. Unfortunately the efforts were to no avail. There is evidence of national discord for some 200 years after the so-called unification.

Resistance against Upper Egyptian domination was undoubtedly aggravated by a natural antipathy between the settlers of Upper and Lower Egypt arising out of their cultural differences. In fact earlier traditions had repeatedly to be recognised in order to emphasise a single rule over the Two Lands. For example the pharaohs (who traditionally bore a 'Horus name') adopted, during successive reigns, a *nebty* or 'Two Ladies' title (which was a combination of the cobra-goddess of Buto in Lower Egypt and the vulture-goddess of Nekheb in Upper Egypt), the Double Crown (a combination of the White and Red Crowns) and a *ni-sw-bity* title which also combined two traditions, being a combination of the predynastic symbols of Upper and Lower Egypt, the sedge and the bee. . . .

The geographical and climatic differences in Upper and

Lower Egypt which had resulted in the development of two different cultures were reflected also in the entire political structure of the country; for despite the effort to weld them together, the 'Two Lands of Upper and Lower Egypt' were to remain two united political entities rather than a single political unit. Dualism was finally seen as unavoidable and was used to emphasise unity. There never was a King of Egypt, nor cabinet, nor treasury. There was a King of Upper and Lower Egypt, a Double Cabinet, a Double Granary and a Double Treasury. Even the 'Great House', the palace, which was the seat of the government, had a double entrance representing the two ancient kingdoms, and the hieroglyph for 'Great House' was frequently followed by the determinative signs of two houses. . . .

Though little is known of the activities of the pharaohs of the 2nd dynasty it seems that there was even more active resistance against unity. One pharaoh (Per Ibsen) may have formed a breakaway government in Upper Egypt, for he significantly abandoned his traditional 'Horus' title and adopted a 'Set' title: in other words he exceptionally surmounted his royal emblem with the ancient desert god of Upper Egypt. This move of revolutionary proportions was quashed by his successor, who managed to re-establish the Horus tradition in Upper Egypt, and a Horus and Set title was temporarily adopted. Like the *nebty* and *ni-sw-bity* titles, and also the Double Crown, this combined two ancient traditions: Horus and Set as gods of Upper and Lower Egypt.

The fabric of ancient Egyptian mythological tradition, which survived in embellished or mutilated form for thousands of years, was woven and rewoven, time and again, to justify new conditions, or explain political trends; it was sometimes even entangled to promote a cause. As the country underwent changes in social and political structure there were accompanying changes in the myths which, though radical, did not render earlier traditions obsolete. The battles between Horus and Set, the tribal ensigns, for example, not only reflected opposites—fertile Delta against barren Upper Egypt, and good and evil in the context of the nature cult—but equally portrayed the political friction in the early dynastic period, also expressed in mythological terms as battles between Horus and Set. . . .

The First God-King

Throughout the early dynastic period, as we have seen, concord was short-lived. Periods when the 'Two lands were united' and the 'Two gods were at peace' implied recovery from anarchy rather than peace. Although the pharaoh called himself 'King of Upper and Lower Egypt', combined ancient traditions in his titles, and celebrated the 'Feast of the Union of the Two Lands'; although, moreover, the last pharaoh of the 2nd dynasty probably married a northern princess in order to consolidate the union, this unity seemed no more likely to last than earlier efforts. A strong element was needed to maintain it. This was finally achieved by the creation of the dogma of divine kingship which simultaneously resolved both the problem of unity and the question of political priority.

The ancient Egyptians had learned to predict nature's patterns and control the crops, nature's gifts. The earliest record of pharaonic achievement shows the 'Scorpion King' digging a canal before his rejoicing subjects, and Narmer, the first pharaoh, reputedly diverted the waters of the river Nile. The superimposition of man-worship on nature worship was, therefore, not unfitting. A divine monarch who was neither an Upper Egyptian nor a Lower Egyptian but who ruled as a God-king might finally consolidate the country. Certainly, as a god he would be above challenge and his power would be absolute.

The pharaoh Zoser, whose name is indelibly linked with that of Imhotep, his adviser, administrator and the gifted architect who built his funerary complex at Sakkara, is believed to have been the first God-king. His accession to the throne marks the beginning of the first of Egypt's three 'great periods', the Old Kingdom.

Chapter 2

Royalty and Religion in Ancient Egypt

Divine Rule: The Pharaoh as God

Jon Manchip White

Jon Manchip White is retired from the University of Tennessee in Knoxville, where he was the Lindsay Young Professor of English. His books include *Ancient Egypt* and *Everyday Life in Ancient Egypt*, from which the following essay is excerpted. White examines the pharaoh's special status as both an earthly ruler and a divine god. This combination of spiritual and temporal authority gave the pharaoh unlimited powers while adding to his burdens, White explains. For instance, the author notes, the pharaoh was expected to perform daily religious rituals as well as conducting the business of the state. White also describes other typical aspects of a pharaoh's life, from childhood through marriage and kingship to death.

The government of Egypt was feudal and theocratic. Every thread and filament of social and spiritual authority ran back directly to the hand of the king. The slightest twitch which he gave to the reins of authority was felt from end to end of his kingdom. He was the cone that topped the structure of the Egyptian pyramid. In lands like Babylonia the king was a mere mortal who was chosen by the gods to act as their representative on earth. The king of Egypt was a god in his own right. To be more accurate, he was many gods. He was not only the incarnation of his father, the protean sun-god Ra; he was also identified with Ra's son, the falcon-god Horus. And Horus in turn had a curious dual personality. As the local deity of Hierakonpolis, he was the totem of an Upper Egyptian nome which at the opening of the dynastic

From Jon Manchip White, *Everyday Life in Ancient Egypt* (New York: Putnam, 1963).

epoch is believed by some historians to have conquered Lower Egypt and brought about the union of Egypt. Later the priests of Heliopolis merged the worship of this historical Horus with a legendary Horus who was the son of Osiris, Lord of the Dead. So when pharaoh died he was held to be resurrected as Osiris (or, rather, as *an* Osiris). Thus he was not only Ra and Ra's son Horus, but also Osiris and Osiris's son Horus, all at one and the same time. A confusing situation, admittedly: but one which indicates the rich aura of sanctity with which successive generations of theologians had invested the the ruler of Egypt. No person was ever so hedged about as pharaoh with the divinity that doth hedge a king.

The Pharaoh's Duties

Every morning at dawn pharaoh would go into the House of the Morning, one of his private chapels. There he would perform a ritual laving of his limbs. In the way that the sun-god Ra bathed each morning in the primordial ocean of heaven, so pharaoh bathed his body in order to restore the vital force that flowed therefrom upon the Two Lands. Then he was anointed, robed, and invested with the royal insignia by priests wearing the masks of Horus and the ibis-headed god of wisdom, Thoth. Next he proceeded to the temple, where he officiated at a further ceremony. Its aims were to implant spirituality into the ceremonies that would soon be celebrated in all the other temples throughout the land—a kind of act of transubstantiation. Pharaoh was Egypt's divine catalyst. He was a celestial sparking-plug. The Egyptians did not believe that the whole machine of living could start again at sunrise unless their god-king recited the magic words.

The court of pharaoh was solemn and hierarchical. . . . The king's every move and gesture was endowed with drama. It was a fearful misfortune to find that his shadow had fallen upon one; and to be touched accidentally by his staff might bring very bad luck indeed, unless he was gracious enough to apologise. To be allowed to kiss his actual foot, instead of the dust in front of it, was an extraordinary mark of favour. His personal name was so sacred and fraught with magic that it was dangerous to utter it, and that was why he was called by the impersonal title of 'Pharaoh'. The word comes from the two words *per aa*, 'Great House': that is, 'The Palace'. In a lesser way we still use 'Buckingham Palace' as a circumlocution for the Queen of England, and 'the White House' for the President of the U.S.A.

Childhood and Marriage

As a boy, his daily life was comparatively carefree. He could not foresee the cruel prison of protocol in which he would one day be shut up. He played with his companions, and was taught to swim, to ride, and to shoot with his miniature bow and arrow. As soon as he was old enough, he entered the army to serve a military apprenticeship, in company with the sons of noblemen and foreign princes who had been sent to Egypt to be educated. When the time eventually came for him to mount the throne, he would be changed from a pampered and lively princeling into a withdrawn and frightening god. Here is a description of the solemn moment when King Seti I decided to adopt the Crown Prince, who was about 15-years-old at the time, as his co-ruler.

> The Universal Lord himself [i.e. King Seti] magnified me whilst I was a child until I became ruler. He gave me the land while I was in the egg, the great ones smelling the earth before my face. Then I was inducted as eldest son to be Hereditary Prince upon the throne of Geb [the earth-god] and I reported the state of the Two Lands as captain of the infantry and the chariotry. Then when my father appeared in glory before the people, I being a babe in his lap, he said concerning me: 'Crown him as king that I may see his beauty whilst I am alive.' And he called to the chamberlains to fasten the crowns upon my forehead. 'Give him the Great One [the uraeus-serpent emblem] upon his head', said he concerning me.

The Crown Prince ultimately succeeded his father as the pharaoh Ramses II, and reigned with awe-inspiring pomp and power for 67 years.

A prince or king married young, usually in childhood. He carried in his veins the actual blood of the sun-god Ra, and it was important that this divine liquid should not be diluted;

so he preserved its purity and potency by marrying a member of his own family—sister, half-sister or cousin. In this he was following the example of Osiris, who had married his sister Isis. Pharaohs even occasionally married their own daughters and had children by them. On the other hand, it must not be thought that incest was a widespread practice; as in the parallel case of the royal family of the Incas, it was strictly confined to the royal circle and carried out with religious sanction. It should also be remembered that by the operation of the ancient clan system of pre-dynastic times property and possessions were transferred in Egypt through the female line, that is by matrilineal rather than patrilineal descent. Thus it was nominally the Queen or Crown Princess rather than the Crown Prince who would inherit the throne, and to secure his title to it beyond the faintest shadow of a doubt the pharaoh lost no time in marrying every woman who could possibly lay claim to the throne. He was therefore usually polygamous as well as incestuous; and in addition to his principal and much-venerated spouse, who went by the name of Great Chief Wife, he possessed a number of daughter-wives and sister-wives. He might also possess a further bevy of what might be called political wives: foreign princesses who had been sent by their fathers to marry the king of Egypt in order to cement a diplomatic alliance. A third group of wives would consist of the dancing girls or other ladies who had caught his fancy and had been bought and introduced into the royal *harîm* [harem]. These he might or might not choose to marry, and might or might not recognize their offspring as princes or princesses.

Sometimes a pharaoh might happen to be eccentric, or weak minded, or half-mad, or a child in his early teens. Sometimes the clique who actually ran the country privately despised or hated him. Yet outwardly they always took care to pay him the most scrupulous respect. They knew that the institutions of Egypt would immediately disintegrate if the character of the monarchy were damaged. For the Egyptian state to function the authority of its king must remain unimpaired. Pharaoh was the keystone of the entire edifice. As such he was endowed with exceptional power. His word was literally law. . . . Justice was considered quite simply to be 'what Pharaoh loves', and wrongdoing 'what Pharaoh hates'. His statements were divine statutes. He was Archbishop and Lord Chief Justice combined in a single person.

Strong Rulers

Egypt was commonly fortunate in her pharaohs. She produced some remarkably able, patient and far-sighted rulers. If the kings of Egypt were gods, they were hard-working gods. The sheer weight of the burden that rested on their shoulders, the sheer scale of the challenge, evoked a corresponding response. They usually chose to take up their abode for half the year in Lower Egypt and half the year in Upper Egypt, and from their palaces at Memphis and Thebes expeditions and tours of inspection were made constantly. Their writ ran throughout the whole land by means of a separate royal bureaucracy, operating in the provincial centres side by side with the local civil servants. The conduct of diplomacy became increasingly demanding as the other nations of Hither Asia grew mightier and more threatening as the centuries rolled on. Daily, almost hourly, pharaoh would be closeted with his own senior advisers or with foreign ambassadors. Human nature being what it is, a number of pharaohs were by nature frivolous and self-indulgent, as their images and inscriptions testify; but the scribes and artists of Egypt also reveal, in spite of the habits of conventionalising and idealising, that many of the king-gods were sagacious and energetic men. Some of them seem almost bowed down to the ground by the well-nigh intolerable weight of the sacred trust which had been placed upon them. It was no sinecure to be born to rule the kingdom which had once been ruled by the gods themselves. There exist many portrait-heads of the pharaoh Sesostris III of the exceptionally gifted Twelfth Dynasty, and many of his equally illustrious successor, Amenemhat III. Together these two kings ruled Egypt for nearly 80 years, between 1878 and 1797 B.C. They were called upon to reign after an epoch of appalling chaos. They righted the weaknesses of the state and guided it far along the path to prosperity. The cost of that extreme personal effort has been graven by the sculptors into their stony features for us to see. The force and feeling for truth of these portrait heads place them among the *chefs d'œuvre* [masterpieces] of the sculptor's art. When we contemplate those proud and toil-worn faces, we sense the full authority of the pharaohs of Egypt. We understand why one of Amenemhat's officers of state should have described him to his family in these terms:

> He is the god Ra whose beams enable us to see. He gives more light to the Two Lands than the sun's disc. He makes the earth more green than the Nile in flood. He has filled the Two Lands with strength and life. He is the Ka [i.e. his kingdom's guardian spirit]. He is the god Khnum who fashions all flesh. He is the goddess Bast who defends Egypt. Whoever worships him is under his protection; but he is Sekhmet, the terrible lion-goddess, to those who disobey him. Take care not to defy him. A friend of Pharaoh attains the rank of Honoured One, but there is no tomb for the rebel. His body is thrown into the river. Therefore listen to what I tell you and you will enjoy health and prosperity.

The death of a king of Egypt was always regarded as a shattering and indeed earth-shaking event. Here is the announcement of the death of Amenemhat I, the founder of the Twelfth Dynasty and inspired leader of his country for three decades, until he fell victim to a cowardly assassin.

> Year 30, third month of the Inundation season, day 7. The god mounted to his horizon. The King of Upper and Lower Egypt went aloft to heaven and became united with the sun's disc. The limb of the god was merged in him who made him. The Residence was hushed; hearts were in mourning; the Great Gates were closed; the courtiers crouched with their heads on their knees; and the nobles grieved.

Eloquent and sorrowful words.

The Royal Family

Cyril Aldred

In the following excerpt from his book *The Egyptians*, Cyril Aldred describes the members of the pharaoh's family. Aldred points out that, like the pharaoh, the queen was considered to be the divine incarnation of important Egyptian deities. According to Aldred, the queen was expected not only to produce an heir but also to perform many religious and political functions. In a few cases, he reveals, the queen ascended the throne after the pharaoh's death and ruled the nation, usually as a regent but sometimes as a pharaoh in her own right. Aldred also examines the roles of the pharaoh's secondary wives and the royal children.

For many years, Aldred served as the Keeper of the Department of Art and Archaeology at the Royal Scottish Museum in Edinburgh. His books include *Egypt to the End of the Old Kingdom*, *Egyptian Art in the Days of the Pharaohs*, and *Akhenaten: King of Egypt*.

If the king was the incarnation of the supreme god, the queen was also regarded as embodying the goddess Hathor, 'the Mansion of Horus', i.e. the mother of the sky-god Horus. She was early assimilated to Isis, another goddess of kingship, and also to a very ancient goddess of the sky in the form of a cow, her body speckled with stars. The attributes of Hathor, her headdress with cow-horns, sun-disk and tall plumes, were worn by queens upon their crowns. Her symbols, the sistrum rattle, and the necklace with its *menyet* counterpoise, were carried by her priestesses, of whom the queen was the leader. Both had the power of bestowing a propitiatory blessing upon all to whom they were held.

The Pharaoh's Wives

The chief queen was a lady of great sanctity, and in a number of cases left a greater impression on posterity than her husband. Besides her biological role, her office carried politico-religious functions, which in some cases led to the title being bestowed upon certain kings' daughters, after their mother or stepmother's death. Whether this always implied a sexual relationship between the pharaoh and his daughter remains the subject of debate.

Alongside the chief queen, however, a king maintained a 'harem' of other women, some of whom held the title that we conventionally translate as 'queen'. Ideally, the heir to the throne was the eldest son by the chief queen, but where such a child was lacking, or had died prematurely, the offspring of one of the 'junior' wives would be elevated to the status of Crown Prince. The queen who had conceived the pharaoh of the divine seed was exceptionally privileged among the royal women as the king's mother, even if she had not previously been the late ruler's chief wife.

It appears that the designation of the heir to the throne was the subject of a public declaration by the king. Where there was an eldest son by the chief queen, this must have been a formality, but where a child of a lesser lady was involved, there may have been some jockeying for position to define who was actually the senior prince. Even more significant would have been the declaration when no son of the reigning king's body survived. It is unclear how the succession was formally determined in such cases, but indications are that senior political or military figures were the most likely nominees. Where someone had royal blood, or had married into the royal family, their qualification for the purple was clearly increased.

The Status of the Queen

A number of pharaohs married their full- or half-sisters, which once led to a theory that the royal inheritance passed down the female line, princes having to marry the 'heiress' to qualify for the throne of pharaoh. It is now quite clear that this was not the case, far too many chief queens being of demonstrably plebeian birth to permit such a conclusion. A more likely explanation for consanguineous marriages is the fact that within all systems where a king is divine, a supernatural potential exists in all his progeny. From this would derive a desirability that this be kept within the royal house, and not spread too far outside. However, a number of nobles certainly married royal daughters, and many other cases are doubtless hidden from us: it seems to have been much more acceptable to proclaim one's politico-social relationship with royalty than one's close physical relationship.

The Pharaoh's Daughters

In the following excerpt from her book Red Land, Black Land: Daily Life in Ancient Egypt, *Barbara Mertz explains that some of the pharaoh's daughters served as high priestesses of the god Amon-Ra.*

During the post-Empire period, certain royal women acquired a new position which probably implied genuine political power. This position, held by the virgin daughters of the kings, was signified by the title of "God's Wife," which was originally a religious title belonging to queens of the New Kingdom. Presumably it referred to the intimate relations of the queen with the God Amon, who was, according to one story, the father of her royal son. The later princesses who held the same title may also have been brides of Amon-Re, but their marriages were not blessed with issue. They remained celibate, taking no earthly husband, and they lived in Thebes, where they assumed some of the powers of the High Priests of Amon. Since the capital of Egypt during this period was in the Delta, the king thus secured a valuable viceroy in the south—all the more valuable because she could rule in his name, but never in her own. Since the God's Wife could have no children, she adopted the daughter of the king who succeeded her father, and this girl became God's Wife when her adopted mother died.

Barbara Mertz, *Red Land, Black Land: Daily Life in Ancient Egypt*, 1978.

Naturally, however, where a queen was also a royal daughter, her status was further elevated, something which can be particularly traced in the early Eighteenth Dynasty, though data are unfortunately missing which would enable evaluation of how far the situation is exceptional or conforms to the general rule. The prominence of Ahhotep, one of the first of a line of such queens during the Seventeenth and Eighteenth Dynasties, [received] honours paid to her as the Saviour of Upper Egypt at a time of crisis. Her daughter Ahmose-Nefertiry, married to her son, Amosis, was even more influential, being the first queen to hold the important post of Divine Consort of Amun, before it was limited to virgin incumbents. She was later deified and became one of the great Theban deities for as long as the New Kingdom lasted. Later queens of the dynasty, however, include numerous ladies of non-royal birth—the principal wives of Tuthmosis III, Amenophis II, Amenophis III and Akhenaten were in no case kings' daughters. In spite of this lack of lineage, Tiye, spouse of Amenophis III, and Nefertiti, wife of Akhenaten, attained a prominence almost unparalleled by their earlier sisters, in the case of Nefertiti verging on kingly status. Under the Nineteenth Dynasty, yet another commoner, Nefertari, became a pivotal figure as chief queen of Ramesses II; royal blood was thus not a determining factor in the careers of those holding the highest official female status in the pharaonic state.

The very highest office of all, that of king, was not nominally open to females. However, at least four women obtained pharaonic titles prior to the Ptolemaic Period; on the other hand, in the two best known cases, those of Hatshepsut and Tawosret, the ladies had first come to power as regents for child-kings, and obtained pharaonic status for political reasons that do not seem to have been accepted by posterity.

The Royal Sons

We are ill-informed about the careers of royal sons, and particularly crown princes before the Nineteenth Dynasty. They were usually brought up by high-ranking wet-nurses and formed strong attachments to their milk-brothers who often became companions of their youth and maturity, holding important positions in their households. Royal sons were instructed in the military arts by army veterans appointed for the purpose; military scribes were engaged to teach reading and writing. Princesses also learnt to write and paint in watercolour, judging from the ivory writing-palettes of two daughters of Akhenaten that have survived, showing signs of use. Female nurses and male tutors or major-domos were also appointed to attend upon them. Some of the highest officials in the land filled such posts, presumably after they had retired from a more active role.

It would appear that all the royal sons received the education of a potential pharaoh since no one could know whom fate had in store for the succession. There are many instances of heirs apparent who did not survive infancy. Tuthmosis III while still a child was singled out for kingship by the oracle of Amun. Tuthmosis IV was similarly promised the succession by Re-Herakhty. In the first case it is highly probable that we have a simple declaration of the heir by the king; in the latter, however, there is a suspicion that Tuthmosis' known elder brothers may have been removed from the scene to ease his way to the throne.

There are occasions on which a king associated his eldest son on the throne with him as co-regent and the system is well attested for the Twelfth Dynasty in which every king ruled for his later years with a junior partner. Double datings exist to prove the circumstance, and from these, it is possible to affirm that Sesostris I ruled with his father Ammenemes I for the first ten years of his reign. At other periods a different system of co-regency appears to have prevailed, and double datings were avoided. For this reason there are scholars who in the absence of such proof would deny the existence of co-regency as an institution. As the official statements are very reticent and vague about a practice in which the god incarnate shared in some undefined way his sovereignty with another, the problem is a very thorny one, the little evidence that exists being largely circumstantial. The difficulties are likely to remain unresolved until definite proof is unearthed, assuming that it has in fact survived.

Religious Beliefs and Practices

Lionel Casson

According to many scholars, religion was the most important aspect of life in ancient Egypt. The Egyptians believed
in a large pantheon of gods and goddesses, each with their
own special functions and attributes, who governed every
facet of human existence. Lionel Casson, a retired professor of classics at New York University, presents an
overview of the primary components of ancient Egyptian
religion from its earliest days to the height of the empire.
Casson is the author of numerous books, including *Ancient
Egypt* and *The Horizon Book of Daily Life in Ancient Egypt*,
from which the following article is taken.

Religion permeated an Egyptian's total existence. In his eyes,
every detail of his own life and of the life about him, whether
the annual inundation of the Nile that spelled hunger or
plenty for the whole nation or the chance death of his cat,
was a specific, calculated act of god. We of the West can
place religion in a compartment all its own, we can say,
"Render unto Caesar the things that are Caesar's and to God
the things that are God's," but not an Egyptian. His Caesar
was the pharaoh, and the pharaoh was a god. Egypt's glorious artistic creations were inspired by religion and religion
alone. The Egyptian artist's forte was sculpture, because in
Egyptian thinking a statue erected in tomb or temple was a
way of ensuring an individual's existence for eternity after
death, and all who could afford it provided themselves with
at least one. Egyptians never ordered their sculptors to carve
portrait statues or busts to display in a public square or in a
niche at home; that was a concept for other civilizations to
develop. Similarly, the monuments of Egyptian architecture

From Lionel Casson, *The Horizon Book of Daily Life in Ancient Egypt* (New York:
American Heritage, 1975). Reprinted by permission of the author.

are all religious—pyramids and other types of tombs, temple chapels and halls and sanctums. These were the only structures made of stone, since they were to last for eternity. The dwellings the Egyptians put up for their life on earth, not excepting the palaces of their kings, were of mud brick and have all but disappeared.

Even in politics the ubiquitous presence of religion is clear. The great administrative officials at the pharaoh's court were at the same time prelates of the church: Hatshepsut's factotum [assistant] Senmut, for example, included among his multitudinous titles Sole Companion and Steward of Amon, Prophet of Amon, and others like it. When a pharaoh put men to work for thirty years on a pyramid or called up a veritable army to hack out a three-hundred-ton chunk of granite for an obelisk and transport it from the quarries at Aswan hundreds of miles to a temple precinct and erect it there, he was not whipping an oppressed people into doing repugnant tasks, but simply canalizing a willing service on behalf of the gods.

Early Egyptian Beliefs

Prehistoric Egyptians, like most primitive peoples, were sensitive to natural phenomena, above all the behavior of the animals they came in contact with. They early observed the tender care of a cow for her young, the strength of a crocodile, the ferocity of a lion; in their inexperience they were so impressed that they came to worship the beasts for their special powers, with each village or community or tribe having its particular favorite. Thus, very early in Egyptian history, long before the country became a political whole, its various towns each acquired an animal deity. Bubastis and Buto in the delta became, respectively, the home of the cult of the cat goddess Bast and the cobra goddess Edjo, Hermopolis and Lycopolis in middle Egypt of the ibis god Thoth and the jackal god Wepwawet, Elephantine in Upper Egypt of the ram god Khnum, and so on. With their ingrained habit of never abandoning the old, the Egyptians continued to worship these queer divinities long after they had adopted anthropomorphic gods and had developed a fairly sophisticated theology. . . . For many centuries, a crocodile incarnating the spirit of the crocodile god Sobek lolled at Crocodilopolis, the cat of Bast at Bubastis, and so on.

Worship of animals and nature commonly occurs in very early societies, which are dominated by the world roundabout and exist at its mercy. In most a moment arrives when they learn to come to grips with nature, to master it; this awakens a sense of man's importance, and deities begin to assume the form of man as well as the forms of animals or plants. So it was with the Egyptians: sometime before the rise of the First Dynasty, anthropomorphism makes its appearance. In their traditional way, they introduced it gradually and blended it with what they already had.

One of the first deities to show the effects of the new fusion was Hathor, goddess of love and childbirth: she was given a human body and head but retained an element from her ancient animal manifestation, a pair of cow's horns. Others kept their animal heads and acquired human bodies. Thus Thoth, the scribes' patron deity, became an ibis-headed man. Anubis, who was guardian of tombs and in time was promoted to a role as judge in the underworld as well, became a jackal-headed man. Khnum, originally a ram, and since the Egyptians considered the animal particularly prolific, associated with creation, turned into a ram-headed man often portrayed as a divine potter modeling men on a potter's wheel. Gods that arose later were anthropomorphic from the very beginning. Ptah, the god of craftsmen, who first appears in history when Memphis was founded as capital of the Old Kingdom, was always portrayed as human, and Amon, the obscure Theban god who, emerging during the Twelfth Dynasty, rose to become supreme head of the Egyptian pantheon, was usually so.

The early anthropomorphic deities such as Ptah figure in the creation story, of which the Egyptians had several versions. Most of these rather literally pictured life as coming into being much the way Egypt's land re-emerged after the annual inundation of the Nile. In the beginning there was a dark, watery void. There came a time when this void subsided to permit the emergence of the first primordial hillock of earth—just as the subsiding of the Nile flood permits hillocks of mud to appear with their promise of the life-giving harvest that will follow. On the hillock was the creator-god Atum, who, in some way, brought living things into the world. In the version of the story that arose at Memphis, Ptah, the god of the place, was held to have brought creation about by his "heart and tongue"—that is to say, by mind and speech, by conceiving of the idea of a universe and executing his conception with a verbal command; the physical happenings may have taken place as described in the myth of the void, the hillock, and Atum, but those physical happenings were the result of Ptah's thought and order. Ptah, despite the significant role he is here given and his undoubted importance otherwise, tended to remain the local deity of Memphis and never forged ahead to become of national importance.

The Chief Gods

One god who most certainly did was Re, god of the sun, an inevitable choice for a deity in a land that basked in its benign rays. Re's ascent dates from the Fifth Dynasty, whose pharaohs did not try to outdo their predecessors' pyramid tombs, those structures that dramatically proclaimed the deceased's mighty place in the scheme of things, but, calling themselves sons of Re, built ever more magnificent temples for their father's worship. These were erected at Heliopolis, now a suburb of Cairo, the traditional site of the cult. The version of the creation story current here held that the primordial hillock was located at Heliopolis. A hill in the area was identified with the momentous spot, and on it stood a primitive stone, looking rather like a squat obelisk; it was the inspiration for the slender soaring shafts set up by later dynasties. Re's temples all had open courts where the service could appropriately be carried out in the full rays of the sun, and where there stood a replica of the holy stone of the primordial hillock.

The chief anthropomorphic god was Amon, who, under the title of Amon Re, associated the power of the great sun deity with his own. Amon was the unseen god—the name means "hidden"—who is immanent in all things. He first appears as a local Theban deity during the Twelfth Dynasty, whose kings came from Thebes and elevated the place into the nation's capital. His rise to prominence began in the Eighteenth Dynasty, when he was worshiped as the god who had given victory over the Hyksos to its pharaohs, enabling them finally to rid the homeland of the hated foreign invader. As Egypt acquired an empire, his power grew to embrace the widespread territories over which she held sway. A shrine was established for him at Karnak, not far from the royal palace, and it became fabulously rich on the god's share of the profits of empire. As time passed, it turned into one of the most massive temple precincts of all time, spreading over acres and acquiring new buildings for more than a thousand years. By the time the empire came to a close, Amon's priests owned the lion's share of Egypt's wealth and rivaled the pharaoh in power.

The pharaoh too was a god, not merely anthropomorphic but a veritable man. He represented the Egyptians in the councils of the gods. He ruled—he could not help but rule—in accordance with *maat*, the eternal and unchanging order, the true and proper and just order, that is built into the universe. His death was but his way of leaving to join his fellow gods. His son who replaced him was the same god, and so it had been from the beginning of time and would be to its end. The Egyptians with all their conservative and static ways were not immune to what was happening about them, and in the course of time the pharaoh's status inevitably was modified. His high point was the Fourth Dynasty, when he was able to command the materials and manpower to build a great pyramid as his tomb. By the very next dynasty, he had yielded place to the sun god and by the Eighteenth Dynasty to Amon.

The Osiris Myth

When a pharaoh died he both joined up with the sun god in his circuit of the heavens and at the same time became Osiris, king of the dead in the underworld. The son who took over the throne became Horus, the dutiful child of Osiris who had avenged his father's death (how a god could die, or a post-mortem pharaoh be both in heaven and below the earth, is troubling only to our way of thinking, not an Egyptian's). This brings us to the only members of the pantheon who came to exercise an influence outside of Egypt, the trinity of Osiris, Isis, and Horus.

According to the story, Osiris was murdered by his jealous brother Seth, who savagely cut the corpse up into pieces and scattered them. Isis, Osiris' wife, with admirable conjugal devotion, patiently collected the pieces and by her magic put them together and resuscitated her husband. Horus, their son, with equally admirable filial devotion, hounded Seth, forced him into a fight, and defeated him, thereby avenging his father. The resurrected Osiris (the resurrection element in the story may point to his having been at some time a god of vegetation, one of those primitive deities who consistently figure in resurrection myths) became god of the underworld, identified with the dead pharaoh. Horus, the son, became identified with the living pharaoh, a process helped along by the fact that ever since the First Dynasty, the pharaoh had been identified with a falcon god also called Horus.

In the days of the New Kingdom the trinity gained increasingly in importance. The dead came before Osiris in the underworld for their last judgment. In the upper world Isis, thanks to the magic that had enabled her to bring her husband back to life, became a healing goddess, and, thanks to her devotion to husband and son, the mother goddess par excellence. From the seventh century B.C. on she was Egypt's most widely worshiped deity, and when Rome had converted Egypt into a province of its vast empire, her cult spread from the Valley of the Nile to the farthest reaches of the Roman world. There it left its imprint upon Christianity; representations of Isis and Horus are but pagan versions of the Madonna and child.

Local and Foreign Gods

Despite the many all-powerful national deities, Egypt's local gods never lost their importance. They were usually conceived of as being immanent in their place of origin; so in each locale temples arose to house the resident divinity. In the desert near Memphis was the home of Sekhmet, a fierce goddess with lion's head atop a woman's body who caused and cured plague. At Hermopolis, midway between Memphis and Thebes, was the center of worship for Thoth. At Dendera, near Thebes, was Hathor's temple. Some minor deities, favorites among workmen and peasants, were ubiquitous, like Bes the lion-headed dwarf who scared off evil spirits, or Thoueris, the hippopotamus god, who ensured fertility and safe childbirth.

With their catholic taste for deities, the Egyptians cheerfully accepted foreign immigrants. Government and military personnel stationed abroad easily fell into the habit of worshiping the gods of the locale, often equating them with their nearest Egyptian equivalent. In New Kingdom times, when thousands of prisoners of war, mercenaries, traders, and other non-Egyptians came to settle in the Valley of the Nile bringing their gods with them, these triumphantly survived trans-

The Nature of Egyptian Religion

Joyce Tyldesley is an honorary research fellow at the School of Archaeology, Classics, and Oriental Studies at the University of Liverpool in Great Britain. She is the author of Hatchepsut: The Female Pharaoh *and* Nefertiti: Egypt's Sun Queen. *In the following excerpt from* Daughters of Isis: Women of Ancient Egypt, *Tyldesley compares the ancient Egyptian religion to the primary modern faiths.*
This Egyptian state religion was clearly very different to the major faiths of the present day. Not only was it polytheistic, it was also a theology without a creed, with no real moral undertones and no tradition of pastoral care. Indeed, it was generally more important as a source of continuing unity and stability throughout the country than as a means of spiritual enlightenment. Although it was generally accepted that men and women should choose to lead a good life rather than a bad one, this moral code evolved more for the convenience of society than the gratification of the gods. Virtue did not necessarily reap any heavenly reward, and only the king was required to act in a fitting and proper manner to ensure the preservation of *maat*

planting, particularly the Semitic deities. Shamash, the sun god, was identified with Re, the goddess Baalath with Hathor, the god Baal with Seth. From the late Eighteenth Dynasty on we find priests of Baal and Astarte, the notorious Semitic goddess of love, in Egypt, and Egyptian children begin to bear names like Astartemhab, "Astarte is in Festival."

Religious Concepts

Within this welter of major and minor deities there yet can be distinguished some main lines of Egyptian religious thought. The most obvious is the belief in a life after death, a key tenet. Another is a vague, ill-defined belief in one single supreme god; this found its most distinct expression during the reign of the heretical Pharaoh Akhenaten. Yet another is that, at the creation of the world, a divine order was established, one that embodied *maat*, a key word which, as

throughout the land. The gods themselves showed remarkably little concern over the behaviour of the ordinary Egyptians. . . .

Priests were appointed simply to serve the god on behalf of their king, and consequently had absolutely no interest in the spiritual or other welfare of the people. The temples of Egypt should not be regarded as the ancient equivalent of cathedrals or mosques; they were built simply to be the homes of the gods, housing the cult statues within which the deities were thought to dwell. As such they had no congregation and, indeed, were usually out of bounds to the ordinary people. Access to the back part of the temple, which can be equated with the family rooms at the rear of the private houses, was restricted to the priesthood and the king who serviced the cult by providing food, drink and clothing and burning incense; the front part, which was decorated with scenes of royal propaganda, was thrown open to the general public only on special festival days, therefore there was no Egyptian equivalent of the Friday mosque, Saturday synagogue or Sunday church service.

Joyce Tyldesley, *Daughters of Isis: Women of Ancient Egypt*, 1994.

John Wilson, one of our most thoughtful Egyptologists, explains, had some of the same flexibility as our English terms *right, just, true,* and *in order.* It was

> the cosmic form of harmony, order, stability, and security, coming down from the first creation as the organizing quality of created phenomena and reaffirmed at the accession of each god-king of Egypt. . . . So the relationship of beings was not something which had to be worked out painfully in an evolution toward ever better conditions but was magnificently free from change, experiment, or evolution, since it had been fully good from the Beginning and needed only to be reaffirmed in its unchanging rightness.

Aspects of *maat*, even of the divine kingship, could be subject to misfortune or challenge, but these were only temporary; the nature of the world was that it would ever return to its original rightness, as a sponge reassumes its original shape. This was a concept that arose from, and was fostered by, the land's geography and climate, the barriers of desert that gave it security, the sunny days and life-giving river that made existence so much easier than elsewhere. The Egyptians held by this belief for centuries, until the heartache and the thousand natural shocks that flesh is heir to disabused even their ingrained optimism. We know the Egyptians by the physical remains they have left behind, which reflect overwhelmingly their concern with death, and by the writings of Greeks and Romans, who saw them after they had degenerated into a static superstition-ridden society. Thus our first impression is of a timid, fear-haunted people cowering before terrifying powers, an impression that could not be more wrong. In the great days of the pharaohs, the Egyptian, confident that his world was divinely good, that his ruler represented him amid the very councils of the gods, was garrulous, cheerful, optimistic, often so sure of himself and his future that he turned cocky and arrogant.

Egyptian Temples and Priests

An Egyptian temple was not designed, like our places of worship, for accommodating congregations. Though it was usually large and often grandiose, its *raison d'être* [reason for existing] was to house a rather small cult image of a god. This was invariably tucked away in an inner sanctum, hidden from all eyes save those of the very few qualified to look upon it. From the exterior, a temple's most prominent features were an enceinte [encircling] wall and a massive gateway, or pylon as it is called, which, towering over the rest, formed the façade. Thus it was just the opposite of a Greek temple: it turned inward, it was to be seen and enjoyed from the inside. . . .

The temple proper, vast though it might be, formed only a part of a greater complex. This included living quarters for the permanent staff, workshops, schools, a sacred pool, granaries and other kinds of storage—in short, all the facilities needed to support the large and miscellaneous community that served the god. . . .

In an Egyptian temple the service went on ceaselessly from dawn to dusk to ensure that the spirit of the god be content to dwell in the cult image hidden away in the interior and not abandon it. At dawn the officiating priest approached the tabernacle that contained the awesome statue. It had been closed and sealed as part of the evening ceremonies of the day before; he broke the clay seals and, amid incantations and prescribed prayers and clouds of incense, drew forth the sacred image—probably of wood lavishly adorned with gold—and then did for it what the palace valets did for the pharaoh: he bathed and perfumed it, dressed it in clothes and jewelry, garlanded it with fresh flowers, and, replacing it in its shrine, offered it food and drink. All day long the ceremony went on, a continuum of music, dance, and hymns. At dusk the priest shut the door, resealed it, and backed out of the room, simultaneously sweeping away with a broom the traces of his footprints. . . .

In the most ancient times, it must have been the pharaoh himself who carried out the god's toilette, but other demands on his time soon made him turn the task over to high priests acting on his behalf. As they went through the ritual they were aided by lesser clergy known as the pure or the purifiers, who were entrusted with the censing, dressing, carrying of ritual utensils, and other chores, and who helped to hand the image in and out of the tabernacle. The ranks of the lesser clergy included as well guardians and readers of the sacred books, experts in ritual procedure, and horologers, who watched the heavens in order to set the hours of the daily rites and the calendar dates of festivals. Only the few priests authorized to enter the innermost sanctum and officiate at the ceremony were full-time clergymen. The minor orders were made up of civilians who forsook their secular life one month out of every four to live in the temple and serve the god. This was true of the various specialists as well, the scribes, singers, musicians, even overseers of the temple artisans. . . .

Festivals of the Gods

The daily ritual in the temples . . . was punctuated by festivals. Every god, whether local or national, had at least one annually, an occasion when he left the secrecy of his tabernacle and displayed himself to his worshipers. Many fell, as festivals have always fallen in agricultural lands, at the moments in the year that were critical for the farmer, before the sowing or after the harvest. In Egypt, where such moments were controlled by the behavior of the Nile, the festivals tended to fall during the season of the Inundation, June to September, when the fields were under water and the peasants, spared their endless round of sowing, dike making and repairing, irrigating, and the like, had some moments of leisure. New Year's Day, for example, which naturally called for a celebration, came in July, the month in which the inundation was gathering force, and one could thank the gods if it looked abundant or invoke their help if meager. . . .

Of all the festivals none could match for size and grandeur the Beautiful Feast of Opet. This was the occasion when Amon left his temple at Karnak to make an annual trip to his other temple in Thebes at Opet (Luxor), the one and only time during the year when he generously displayed himself to his worshipful public. Moreover, it was the longest of the festivals; during the time of Thutmose III it went on for ten days, by the time of Ramses II it had lengthened to twenty-four, still later to twenty-seven. It fell during the second and third months of the Inundation, precisely the time when most of the populace was free to enjoy it.

The ceremony began with a monumental procession. We have a good idea of what it was like from scenes painted on temple walls at Luxor and elsewhere. A throng of priests left the grounds at Karnak, some of them carrying on their shoulders three portable boats, and the others purifying the way with censers or shading it with giant fans of ostrich feathers. In one boat, marked by a ram's head at bow and stern, was the precious image of Amon; in another, marked by women's heads, his consort Mut; in the third, marked by falcon heads, his son Khonsu. Headed by a musician banging on a tambourine, the procession made its way to the riverside, where three sumptuous barges, each some sixty to seventy yards long and fitted with a canopied dais, were waiting to receive the distinguished passengers. Each shrine with its cult image was placed on a dais, statues and sphinxes brought from the temple were placed all about it, and in front of it, just as in a temple, were set a pair of miniature obelisks sheathed in gold. The barges were made of the finest Lebanon cedar and decorated lavishly with gold and gems. Since they were too heavy to proceed under their own power, an army of men on the riverside hauled them with tow ropes, urged on not only by their commanders but by the mob that had gathered there to catch a glimpse of the god and to partake in the excitement. Once the tugging men got the barges in the clear, these were taken under tow by boats and, with a fleet of miscellaneous smaller craft all about them, were pulled down the river. A mob of spectators lined both banks; here and there were tents and stalls where drinks were served, where carcasses were cut up and cooked and served, where foods of all kinds were available. Military bands pounded the drums, dancing girls whirled and twisted. At Luxor a procession emerged from the temple leading oxen with gilded horns for the god's table. The barges were moored, the shrines removed, and with the pharaoh himself leading the parade, the gods were carried into the temple, where they resumed their accustomed secrecy. In the meantime, however, the drinking and eating and dancing and singing went on ceaselessly and continued to go on for the duration of Amon's stay. On the last day the events of the first were re-enacted, only in reverse, and perhaps more soberly. . . .

Despite the general carnival atmosphere, there were moments during these festivals that could be deadly serious. During his public appearances, the god might be asked vital questions—to decide a bitter law suit, to indicate his choice of candidate for a high office, even to settle quarrels about the succession to the throne. Once during Hatshepsut's reign, those backing her rival, the young Thutmose, took advantage of the god's public appearance at the Feast of Opet to ask for a sign as to who should be pharaoh. The god could make a forward inclination for assent, backward for dissent, point to a candidate, and the like. How it was done is anybody's guess. Presumably the priests in charge not only worked out the mechanics but consulted beforehand with the appropriate authorities as to what the divine decision should be. . . .

All the festivals, whether public or private, whether annual or occasional, whether for king or god, were done in the typical Egyptian spirit. There was no fasting or solemn prayer, no penances—just music, song, dance, feasting, and lots of drinking.

Death and the Afterlife in Ancient Egypt

Rosalie David

Rosalie David is the Keeper of Egyptology for the Manchester Museum at the University of Manchester in England. She is also the director of the Manchester Museum Egyptian Mummy Research Project and a lecturer at the university. Her books include *Kingdoms of Egypt*, *Evidence Embalmed*, and *Mysteries of the Mummies*. In the following excerpt from her book *Cult of the Sun: Myth and Magic in Ancient Egypt*, David describes the religious beliefs that led the ancient Egyptians to develop the process of mummification. According to the author, the Egyptians' concern with the afterlife caused them to devote a great amount of time, energy, and resources to preparing their tombs, where they believed their souls would reside throughout eternity.

An important factor [in Egyptian thought] was the fundamental concept of the human personality. It was complex and consisted of at least five different elements in addition to the body. These included an individual's name (knowledge of which enabled a man's enemies to do him harm) and his shadow which was believed to enable him to procreate. There were also three immortal elements, possessed at first only by the gods, then by the king, and finally inherited by all men. One of these elements—the *ba*—was depicted as a human-headed bird. It was regarded as an animating force which may have corresponded in some respects to the Christian concept of the soul. Unlike the body which was confined to the tomb, the *ba* could fly to places which the deceased had formerly visited in life. The second element *akh* was a supernatural power which is difficult to interpret in modern terms; it seems to have been attained only after death. The third element was the *ka*, often depicted as a pair of upraised arms. No one satisfactory explanation of this power has been given, and the Egyptians seem to have used the word with different meanings in different contexts. Various interpretations have suggested that it was the double of its owner, or the embodiment of the vital force in living things, or the personification of abstract qualities and characteristics which make up the 'self' or personality of an individual. Again, we do not know exactly how the Egyptian was affected by his *ka* during his lifetime, but after death the *ka* can perhaps be regarded as a man's spirit—the part of him which ensured his immortality as an individual.

The Theory Behind Mummification

At death, the Egyptians believed that the insubstantial part of this complex personality separated itself from the body and was free to travel at will, but that it still preserved a link with the body in the tomb. A king's immortality could continue either by accompanying the sun in the heavens or by identification with Osiris, and ordinary people continued into eternity by travelling in the Osirian underworld— but the spirit still depended upon the body and the food offerings left at the tomb for its sustenance in the next life. Therefore, every effort was made to ensure that the body remained intact and that it retained as close a likeness as possible to the deceased. It was hoped that tomb robbers and evil spirits could be deterred by various architectural devices within the tomb and by magical formulae, but the actual preservation of the body was a complicated procedure. The technique is referred to today as 'mummification'. In fact, the words 'mummy' and 'mummification' are not derived from an ancient Egyptian source, but come from a Persian word *mummia*, meaning 'bitumen'. The Persians greatly prized a black bituminous exudation which occurred in certain areas by oozing from the ground. They believed it could cure certain ailments and gave it the name *mummia*. The embalmed bodies of the Egyptians from the Ptolemaic period onwards frequently had a blackened appearance; and so the bodies were wrongly thought to provide an alternative source of the medicinal bituminous material and the name *mummia* was applied to them. Regardless of the mistaken origin of this name, it was henceforth used to describe the embalmed bodies of ancient Egypt, and its usage has persisted over the centuries until the present day.

We know how the bodies of the deceased were at first naturally desiccated in Egypt by the effect of the heat and of the dry sand in which they were buried, and how increasingly sophisticated brick-lined tombs built for royalty and the nobility resulted in the rapid decomposition of the body. In these early dynasties, there were apparently unsuccessful attempts to preserve the body by applying dehydrating salts to the body's surface to remove moisture before decomposition could occur. However, the method generally adopted throughout the earliest dynasties and, for the nobility, throughout most of the Old Kingdom, was the building up in cloth and stucco-plaster of the bodily contours on a skeletal frame. The discovery of a canopic chest at Gizeh in the tomb of Queen Hetepheres, mother of Cheops, which contained the queen's mummified viscera, indicated that complete mummification involving evisceration and dehydration was being carried out, at least for royalty, in the Fourth dynasty. By the end of the Old Kingdom, use of this process was probably extended to the nobility.

Making a Mummy

Information concerning the various stages in this process is limited. Mummified bodies from later periods provide some evidence, but ancient Egyptian texts do not give any complete record of the various techniques involved. The best account of mummification which we possess comes from the Greeks who wrote about Egypt—Herodotus in the Fifth century B.C. and Diodorus Siculus about four hundred years later. Although they recorded this information thousands of years after the end of the Old Kingdom, the basic process remained the same, with the later introduction of certain elaborations. Herodotus describes three methods apparently in use at his time, but the most expensive of these was obviously based on the method devised to preserve the royal bodies of the Old Kingdom. Except for the heart (which was believed to be the seat of the intellect and of the emotions) and the kidneys, the viscera were removed from the body by making an incision in the right side of the abdomen. They were cleaned, treated with natron [sodium carbonate] and placed in a canopic chest or box. At later periods, they were sometimes wrapped in packages and replaced in the bodily cavities, or they were stored in vessels known as 'canopic jars'. There were four of these to a set, usually made of stone, and each was dedicated to one of the 'Four Sons of Horus'. In the New Kingdom, the stoppers of the jars were carved to represent these demi-gods—the ape-headed Hapy, the jackal-headed Duamutef, the hawk-headed Qebhsenuef, and the human-headed Imset.

After evisceration, the body was cleansed and rinsed, and the cavities were filled with various spices. The body was then preserved by rapid dehydration, so that decomposition would be arrested. To replace the desiccating effect of the sand in the original burial-pit, natron was used as a dehydrating agent. The dispute today is whether the body was actually immersed and soaked in a bath of natron or whether it was packed in a bed of dry natron. Recent experiments suggest that the second method was more commonly used. This process took between forty and seventy days. The body was finally washed again, and strips of fine linen bandaging, treated with a gummy adhesive substance, were bound tightly around the body. The body was finally removed from the embalmer's workshop, and was probably taken to the house of the deceased, before being transported to the tomb.

During the New Kingdom, various advances were made in this process, which are well displayed in the two caches of royal mummies found at Thebes between A.D. 1881 and 1898. Various methods of removing the brain were employed, the most common one being to force an instrument up the nostril and through the intervening bone structure. The brain was then removed, perhaps using a kind of ladle, and resin-soaked strips of linen were packed into the skull cavity. Towards the end of the Eighteenth dynasty, an operation was introduced which was to become increasingly evident during the Twenty-first dynasty. Attempts were made to restore the lifelike contours of the body of Amenophis III, an elderly and obese ruler, by subcutaneous packing. By the Twenty-first dynasty, mummification had reached its peak and techniques attempted to reproduce the lifelike contours and facial appearance of the deceased. A series of small incisions was made in the surface of the skin, through which packing was inserted. The neck and cheeks were also packed, with the face stuffing being introduced through the mouth. Artificial eyes were placed in the eye sockets, the face and often the whole body painted with ochre, and the natural tresses were augmented with false plaits and curls.

A decline in standards is evident from the Twenty-second dynasty, and subcutaneous packing ceased to be used. With a continuing decline in religious beliefs, mummification ceased to have a deep religious significance and became an expensive and commercial exercise. This is particularly true of the mummies of the Ptolemaic and Roman periods, when the bodies are usually poorly preserved inside their gilded and painted cartonnage cases. Mummification continued until the Christian era, when elaborate outer wrappings but superficial treatment of the body signified the final stage of this ancient practice. The Moslem invasion of Egypt in A.D. 641 and the subsequent conversion of many of the Egyptians to Islam meant the end of mummification as a method of preserving the bodies of the dead.

The Tombs

However, we now return to the period when this process was an essential feature of Egyptian funerary beliefs and the correct environment was provided for the mummy and the deceased's continued existence after death. Throughout the Old Kingdom, the mastaba type of tomb was used for the burial of the nobility, although rock-cut tombs, introduced at Gizeh during the Fourth dynasty, gained popularity. These maintained the outward appearance of the mastaba tomb but the associated offering chapels were excavated from the solid rock to allow a greater area for wall decoration. Towards the end of the Old Kingdom, it became increasingly common for the provincial nobility to prepare tombs for themselves in the desert cliffs of their own provinces. However, the traditional mastaba tomb continued to have two main functional parts— the underground burial chamber and the stairway or shaft

---

Essential Elements for Immortality

In the following excerpt from her book Mummies, Myth, and Magic in Ancient Egypt, *Christine El Mahdy describes the Egyptians' belief in the significance of a person's shadow and name. In particular, she writes, the preservation of an individual's name was crucial toward ensuring immortality. El Mahdy is a lecturer, broadcaster, and Egyptologist.*

In the Egyptian concept of human existence there were two other elements [besides the *ba*, the *ka*, and the *akh*] whose survival was essential. An individual was inseparable from his or her shadow, which mirrored every movement, although it was obviously incapable of any act of its own. If anyone behaved badly, there was the potential threat of their shadow being devoured by a demon known as the 'shadow gobbler'. To deprive a living human being of a shadow was to deprive them of existence itself.

But perhaps the most significant aspect of any person was their true essence, the spirit of individuality which distinguishes one being from another. This essence was encapsulated in the name given to the child at birth. So long as one's name was being spoken, so the Egyptians believed, immortality was being assured. So protection of the name of the deceased was vital. The tomb, the mummy, the equipment, the paintings and reliefs were all designed to help preserve the name of the individual. The greatest horror was to have your name destroyed, cut out from a wall.

Christine El Mahdy, *Mummies, Myth, and Magic in Ancient Egypt*, 1989.

which provided access, and the superstructure which marked and protected the burial. . . .

The mummified body and the tomb were believed to be essential to the continued existence of their owner after death. However, this was not guaranteed unless the ritual was properly performed and all material provisions were made in the tomb for the hereafter. The provisioning of a man's tomb with food and drink was mainly the duty of his heir and of his descendants. When performed for several generations of ancestors this became an onerous duty and consequently was frequently neglected after a passage of time had elapsed since the tomb-owner's death. The regular supply of fresh provisions placed on a flat altar table in the tomb-chapel was so important for the sustenance and well-being of the *ka* of the deceased that other methods of insurance against spiritual starvation had to be employed. One way was to enter into a contract with a *ka*-priest. This man and his descendants were paid in kind, with the produce from a piece of land set aside by the tomb-owner or by the king, on his behalf, for this purpose. In return, the priest made regular offerings of food at the owner's tomb; the priest's descendants inherited the income and the obligation to the tomb, and theoretically, the *ka*-endowment guaranteed the eternal sustenance of one's *ka*. However, it soon became apparent that such agreements lapsed after a period of time and the Egyptians were obliged to consider other methods which did not rely on human honesty.

The House of the Ka

The tomb was regarded as the 'House of the Ka', where the dead man's spirit could retain a locality on earth to which it could return to receive sustenance. Only the kings and possibly some of the queens were buried in pyramids, and the nobles built and stocked their mastaba tombs, grouped either around the royal pyramids, or in separate 'cities of the dead'. The life after death was expected to reflect a man's existence in this world, except it was hoped that it would be free from worry, danger and illness. . . . The most commonly held belief was that a man would pass his eternity in his tomb, with access to the pastimes and possessions of his successful earthly existence. Although decorative art and crafts played a part in everyday life, the impetus for the progress made in statuary, wall reliefs and paintings came from their use in tomb decoration and funerary equipment, as magical substitutes to assist the dead. In the Old Kingdom, the decoration of the walls and the contents of the tomb were designed to provide the dead man with the idealized afterlife he expected. Many aspects of his life were depicted; his wife and family; servants; home; clothing; hobbies such as hunting, fishing and fowling; and features of his career, showing his power and influence. The accompanying inscriptions conferred material benefits on the tomb-owner, or provided spells to protect him against evil spirits and dangers which might impede his progress into the next world, or against the constant threat of tomb-robbers. The tomb-owner was himself represented in the tomb by various substitutes—the mummified body, . . . or a full-size statue, or the carved and painted likenesses in the wall-reliefs. Domestic articles were also placed in the tomb; the dryness of the climate preserving them to a remarkable degree, so that we have inherited a wealth of information concerning the everyday lives of the well-to-do Egyptians. However, the most important provision was of course food and drink, and these were originally supplied with varying degrees of reliability by the tomb-owner's family heirs or his *ka*-priest. Another solution to this problem was to ensure that, in the tomb, there were scenes of food-production and the presentation of offerings, which could supply the deceased's needs if the other methods failed. So, scenes of harvesting, slaughtering, brewing and baking were placed on the tomb walls in addition to an offering list and magical formulae to grant the tomb-owner an abundance of food.

A biography of the deceased, in which his achievements were listed, was also included on the tomb wall; this established his name, ownership of the tomb, his family, his *ka*-priest and his rank. This, presumably, would grant him equal status in the next life, and would also impress visitors to his tomb with his success and importance.

The Ritual of Opening the Mouth

It was believed that the transformation of the tomb-reliefs and contents from substitutes into real people and objects, was brought about by the potent magic of the mortuary service. Before burial, the ritual of 'Opening the Mouth' was performed on the mummy of the deceased. The priest would touch the mouth of the mummy with an instrument so that it could speak and eat the funerary meal, so that its nose could smell again and its eyes could see. Similarly, the members of his family and servants, represented in the wall scenes or by tomb statuettes, would come to life. The model boat which formed part of the tomb equipment would become a full-size vessel in which he could sail on the Nile. All the other people and activities shown in the wall-scenes would also become real not just momentarily, but for eternity, to provide company or to add to the happiness of the tomb-owner.

The Sacred Animal Cults

A.J. Spencer

In early times, the Egyptians worshiped animal deities. Later, these animals came to be seen as representatives of various gods and were venerated as such. Many temples housed animals that symbolized certain gods; for example, a living bull was kept in captivity at the temple of Osiris in Memphis. In the following excerpt from his book *Death in Ancient Egypt*, A.J. Spencer explores the Egyptian animal cults, paying particular attention to the treatment the sacred temple animals received after death. These animals were accorded the privilege of mummification and were interned in special tombs, he writes. Spencer is an Assistant Keeper in the Department of Egyptian Antiquities at the British Museum in London.

To the general observer, one of the most peculiar features of ancient Egyptian civilization is the regular appearance of deities in animal form, or with animal heads upon human bodies, in reliefs and paintings. To understand the reasons for the presence of animal divinities it is necessary to examine briefly the origins of Egyptian religion. The beliefs of the early Egyptians grew out of superstitions and traditions of the individual communities which settled in the Nile Valley long before the emergence of a unified state. Each village or town possessed its own local gods, and, despite attempts to rationalize the mass of deities into some kind of order, the local nature of Egyptian religion persisted right through to the latest times. On tomb stelae the visitor is frequently asked to recite the formula of offering, 'as surely as you love your local city-gods'. Amalgamating these many deities into a state religion led to a number of difficulties, but some order was produced by associating the various gods and goddesses into family groups, usually triads, with one member being the child of the other two. For example, we have Amun, Mut and Khonsu at Thebes, or Ptah, Sekhmet and Nefertem at Memphis. But the fact that many of the divinities originated in very early forms of worship, while others were of more recent origin, means that the Egyptian gods cover a variety of levels in the development of thought, with early and later concepts existing side by side. The different stages can be detected quite clearly in the types of gods: animal deities belong to one of the most primitive strata; a later development was to anthropomorphize the bodies and leave only the animal head; fully anthropomorphic gods, like Amun or Ptah, represent a still more advanced philosophy. Other gods may be described as cosmic deities: the sun, moon, earth and the Nile fall into this category. Many civilizations have gone through the same process of adapting their idea of a deity to fit the developing intellect of the time; the special feature in Egypt is the fact that the early beliefs were not replaced by the new ones—instead, the two were merely added together. . . .

The Sacred Animals of the Gods

The origins of animal worship must go back to a very early time, when the creatures themselves were the objects of religious devotion, and different animals may have been the local fetish or totem of individual regions. Later on, the animals serve only as representatives of particular gods and they are sacred because of their association with the divinity, not in their own right. Consequently, it is incorrect to say that the Egyptians of the Dynastic Period worshipped animals; in fact, they worshipped specific gods and goddesses who happened to have links with certain animal species. Even those gods who were normally represented in fully human form had their own sacred animals. Amun is a good example, with the ram and the goose as his animal representatives, while his wife the goddess Mut was linked with the vulture. Provision was made at many of the temples for the animals of the god to be kept in captivity within the sacred precincts. In some temples only a single animal would be kept, like the Apis bull in the temple of Memphis, but other cults required the accommodation of large numbers of animals, which might be ibises, baboons, hawks, crocodiles, rams or cats. A bronze ritual vessel in the British Museum is inscribed with the name of a man called Hor, who was Priest of the Living Baboons in the temple of Khonsu at Thebes. Whether a temple kept one animal or a large number depended upon an important distinction between two different kinds of animal cult, for in certain cases a single animal was selected to be the divine representative on the basis of special markings, whereas in other circumstances all members of a species were considered worthy of particular reverence. The difference is clearly demonstrated by a comparison of the cult of the Apis bull, as an example of the former type, with the ibises of the god Thoth, which must have been kept in thousands. Of course, this difference in the numbers of animals involved in a cult had a direct effect upon the form of burial provided for the animals concerned; in one case there was only a single burial to be provided for a creature of great veneration; in the other it was necessary to supply more modest resting-places for large numbers of individuals. Those cults in which a single animal was chosen as the divine representative were of great importance, by virtue of the special nature of the animal, which placed it apart from other members of its species. The burial of such a creature was a lavish affair, provided for by royal direction. The interment of animals in entire-species cults, on the other hand, was far more simple, often carried out at the expense of private individuals.

The Cult of the Apis Bull

Without doubt, the most important of all the cults was that of the Apis bull, and this is reflected in the elaborate nature of the tombs of the bulls at Saqqara. Although the oldest known burials date from the New Kingdom, the cult of the Apis is known to go back to the First Dynasty, and it is possible that earlier tombs may still await discovery. The known tombs of the bulls . . . are of two types, the earlier burials being individual structures and the later ones, after the reign of Ramesses II, being linked by galleries in the rock. At present, only the western section of the galleries is accessible, where the sacred bulls were interred from the Twenty-Sixth Dynasty down to the Ptolemaic Period. This burial-place is generally referred to as the 'Serapeum', a term derived from the name of the Greek god Serapis, who was linked with the Apis bull. However, despite the apparent similarity between the full title of the deceased bull, 'The Osiris-Apis', and 'Serapis', the two names do not seem to be related etymologically. . . .

The main passage of the later gallery runs for nearly two hundred metres beneath the desert surface, with the vaults themselves ranged along the sides at a lower level, so that one looks down on to the lids of the sarcophagi. These vast stone chests have been hollowed out from individual blocks of granite to provide a final resting-place suitable for the god. In the earlier galleries of the Serapeum, containing the burials of the Nineteenth to Twenty-Sixth Dynasties, and in the older individual tombs, the coffins were made less expensively of gilded wood. One of the isolated tombs was found intact; it contained the coffins of two bulls, both dating from the reign of Ramesses II. The south wall of the chamber bore a painted scene showing the king and the prince Khaemwase making offerings to the Apis. From the coffins came a variety of golden jewellery and amulets, some pieces being inscribed with the names of Ramesses or Khaemwase, together with a number of bull-headed statuettes. . . .

Mummification

The rites of burial were the same for the bull as for any human interment. . . . A demotic papyrus in Vienna records the procedures which accompanied the mummification of the Apis bull, and confirms that the operation was highly ritualized. At an early stage in the proceedings, the bull was housed in a special booth, into which the priests entered to perform all the correct ceremonies. From this temporary shelter the body was transferred to the 'Place of Embalming' for the process of mummification. The instructions in the papyrus state that the corpse was to be laid out upon a bed of sand, to the accompaniment of the lamentations of the priests. The wrappings for the mummy were carefully prepared and were applied according to specific directions, which described the correct manner of wrapping the different areas of the body. . . .

On the site of the ancient city of Memphis are the remains of a structure which formed the mummification-place of the Apis bulls in the Twenty-Sixth Dynasty. The most striking features of this building are the massive alabaster tables, in the form of low couches, upon which the bodies of the sacred animals were laid during embalmment. Each of these tables is equipped with a sloping top, to drain the fluids used in the process into an outlet at one end. After completion of embalmment in this building, the wrapped corpse would have been placed upon a bier for transport to the desert plateau at Saqqara, to rest in the tomb which had been prepared for it in the Serapeum. On reaching the lower desert slopes, the burial cortege would have arrived at the religious and administrative centres which lay along the eastern edge of the plateau, from which the route to the Serapeum was marked by an imposing avenue of sphinxes, at least from the Thirtieth Dynasty. . . . Towards the western end of the route there was a temple built by Nectanebo II and dedicated to the Osiris-Apis, although this structure has been entirely destroyed. . . . The building was called, 'The Place of the Living Apis', and must have been richly decorated, its doors being overlaid with gold and silver. Most of the major cemeteries of sacred animals would originally have had temples nearby, in which the cult of the appropriate deity could be perpetuated, but these places of worship have generally not survived the passage of time so well as the burial installations they were intended to serve. . . .

As a natural extension of the provision of burial-places for sacred bulls, cemeteries of similar character were developed in the Late Period for the mothers of these animals, since the cows were also regarded as divine. . . .

The cemetery of the Mothers of Apis at Saqqara [was] cut in a rock-hewn gallery under the western side of the plateau, some distance north of the Serapeum. The layout of the place is similar to the Late Period galleries of the Apis bulls, although on a much smaller scale and far more ruined. . . .

A Variety of Animal Mummies

Outside the gallery of the sacred cows was a temple built by Nectanebo II, the king that was responsible for the construction of the temple at the Serapeum. The main sanctuary of the building seems to have been dedicated to Isis-mother-of-the-Apis, and to Apis himself, providing a centre in which the cult of the divine cows could be perpetuated. But the temple was not simple in plan, since it also contained separate chapels for two other underground cemeteries of sacred animals. This section of the Saqqara necropolis was honeycombed with such burial-places, and from the temple terrace there opened two galleries into the rock, one devoted to the burials of sacred baboons and the other to falcons. These cemeteries are of a somewhat different character to the tombs of the bulls or cows, because the baboons and falcons belonged to the type of animal cult in which all members of a species were regarded as divine representatives. In some cults of this type a particular animal was chosen periodically as the incarnation of the god, as at Edfu, where the sacred falcon had to be selected and displayed from the temple pylon. But the status of the chosen animal was not so high as that of the Apis bull, who reigned alone among bulls for his lifetime. The elevation of one bird to be the reigning sacred falcon did not cancel the sanctity of other falcons, which were kept in some numbers within the temple complex. The necessity of finding burial-places for large numbers of animals enforced a fairly modest style of interment, although the quantity of animals involved required a cemetery of some considerable size. At Saqqara, the baboon galleries contained over four hundred burials, but the falcons ran into hundreds of thousands, and consequently the individual treatment of the birds was less elaborate than that of the apes. The baboon gallery is on two levels, the lower having been cut after the upper level had been entirely filled with mummies. The animals were embalmed and placed in wooden boxes, which were set into recesses cut in the walls of the passages. The mummy was consolidated in its box by filling the interior spaces with gypsum plaster, thereby setting the corpse rigid in a plaster case, enclosed by the wooden boards of the box.

Each container was sealed into its recess by a limestone slab, on which were written brief details of the baboon, including its name and date of burial. Unfortunately, only a single mummy remained in its original location, the remainder having been destroyed during the early Christian period.

The entrance to the falcon galleries lies in the southern part of the temple terrace of Nectanebo II and consists of a narrow, twisting staircase leading to a roughhewn corridor. This passage winds on into the rock with side-galleries at intervals. The passages are about 2.5 m wide by 3 m high, and extend for a total distance of over 600 m, each lateral gallery being completely filled with pottery jars containing the mummies of the sacred falcons. Many of the birds had been carefully wrapped in intricate linen bandaging, and some had painted plaster masks over the faces. After they had been sealed into their pottery containers, the jars were laid in regular layers inside the catacombs, with a thin filling of clean sand between each row. As a gallery became full it was closed off from the axial corridor by a stone or brick wall, or, in some cases, by mud-plaster applied directly over the ends of the stacked pots. Some birds received special treatment: at intervals along the passages there were niches cut in the rock walls, containing the remains of a falcon mummy within a coffin of wood or limestone. Appearances can be deceptive, however, as some of the finest mummies were found inside plain pottery jars, while more elaborate containers were often found to hold only a few bones wrapped in linen and consolidated into a solid mass with resin. Not all the mummies were those of falcons, for amongst the burials were found remains of ibises and a few very large pottery jars containing what were probably mummified vultures. Mixed in with the pots in the galleries were various objects, including bronze or glazed composition figures of divinities and sacred animals, bronze ritual equipment from the temple and relic boxes of metal or wood. Burying such items with the birds was a method of disposing of excess material which could not be re-used owing to its sacred connections. The relic boxes are an interesting feature of all major animal cemeteries. They consist of rectangular containers of bronze or wood, in which a few bones of the sacred animal could be placed, with a figure of the appropriate creature on top of the box. . . .

The cemeteries of the cows, falcons and baboons at Saqqara lie in an area which seems to have been designated a special animal necropolis in the Late and Ptolemaic Periods, for in the vicinity are yet more underground galleries, this time devoted to the burials of ibises. These are situated to the north and south of the temple of Nectanebo II, forming two separate complexes of great extent, similar in style to the falcon galleries, although with slightly larger corridors. It is estimated that something approaching half a million mummified birds lie in these burial-places, each one contained in the usual pottery vessel. . . .

Saqqara is a good example of the way in which cemeteries of particular animals could develop away from the original cult-centre of the god with whom they were associated. The baboons and ibises were the sacred animals of Thoth, god of writing and wisdom, who had his main religious centre at Hermopolis in Middle Egypt; the falcons represent Re, worshipped at Heliopolis, and only the Apis bull, together with his mother, the Isis cow, originate from the Memphite district. These are not the only animals buried at the site: on the eastern side of the plateau lies the subterranean cemetery of the dogs or jackals sacred to the embalmer-god, Anubis, and further to the south are the burials of cats, here considered as the animal representatives of Bastet. Other animal burials are known only from texts and their location on the ground is still to be determined; these include a cemetery of rams and, most surprisingly of all, a possible burial-place for lions, mentioned in a Greek papyrus.

Another Large Site of Animal Burials

Subterranean galleries like those beneath the Saqqara plateau are known at Tuna el-Gebel, the necropolis of Hermopolis Magna. They date from the Late and Graeco-Roman Periods, and are devoted to the burials of ibises and baboons, both representatives of Thoth, chief divinity of the city. The galleries at Tuna are somewhat larger than their Saqqara counterparts, and they possess many more niches in the walls for individual ibis burials. The latter were contained in small coffins of wood or stone, often with a figure of an ibis sculpted upon the cover. In certain of the passages, rows of such coffins in limestone were found beneath the masses of burials in pottery jars; they were set across the corridors with eight coffins in each row. This number is significant; it is a symbolic reference to the Egyptian name of the town of Hermopolis, which was simply the numeral 8. The reason for the city being known as 'Eight-Town' was due to an early belief that it had been the home of a group of eight divinities who were responsible for the creation of the world. By placing the ibis-coffins in rows of eight, the Egyptians were simply re-stating the connection of Thoth with his city. He is normally referred to in ancient inscriptions as 'Thoth, the twice great, the Lord of Hermopolis', the name of the city being written with eight strokes. Hermopolis is the Greek name for the city, given because the Greeks associated Thoth with [the Greek god] Hermes.

Baboons were interred in the same complex as the ibises at Tuna, the wrapped corpses being placed in coffins of stone or wood and set in recesses in the walls. One mummy found intact was equipped with amulets of gold and glazed composition, attached on the outside of the wrappings. On the desert close to the necropolis some evidence was found of the sacred park in which the live ibises were kept. We know from textual sources that both ibises and falcons were kept at Saqqara, and the remains of birds' eggs found in excavations at that site may indicate areas in which the creatures were bred. The administration of any sacred animal cult-centre and necropolis involved considerable organization and certainly provided employment for many individuals. In addition to the priests of the temples and the embalmers, there must also have been people involved in the provision of food for the animals, stonemasons for work in the galleries, scribes, and persons engaged in pottery manufacture. The last-named must indeed have felt secure in their employment, having been authorized to produce the hundreds of thousands of pots required as containers for bird mummies. Much of our information about the administration of the ibis cult at Saqqara comes from demotic ostraca—memoranda written on sherds of pottery—found on the site. One text refers to the bringing of food for the 60,000 ibises, which, if the figure is accurate, gives some idea of the number of birds involved. It has been estimated that the average rate of burial for ibises at Saqqara must have been in the order of 10,000 birds per annum. There was apparently a mass burial of mummified ibises once a year, the whole process being a rather formal occasion, including a funeral procession to the galleries accompanied by members of the priesthood. The affairs of animal burial, however, did not always run smoothly, and the Saqqara texts describe reforms instituted to stamp out corruption in the administration of the cult. One irregularity which seems to have been checked was the burial of empty pots by the embalmers, when they had taken payment for the complete mummification and wrapping of an ibis. . . .

Were the Animals Sacrificed?

The vast numbers of ibises mummified and buried in the later stages of Egyptian civilization present a problem over the circumstances surrounding the death of the birds. It would seem impossible to have reached such a death-rate if each animal had been allowed to live its natural lifespan, and we are faced with the possibility that the birds may have been deliberately killed. This probability is not limited to ibises, but would apply equally to all those cults in which the mass burial of thousands of creatures was involved. Of course, the dispatch of the animals would have been accomplished in some ritual manner, as befitting divine representatives. It is quite probable that the animals were drowned, although we have no direct evidence, but we know that humans who died by drowning were accorded special reverence and elevated to divine status. . . .

It may seem strange that the vast majority of animal burials belong to the later stages of Egyptian civilization, when one might have expected these primitive cults to have been replaced by more intellectual religious concepts. This is not to say that advanced ideas did not exist, for they certainly did, but, owing to Egyptian conservatism, they had not re-placed earlier beliefs. As explained earlier, animal cults per-sisted right through the history of Egypt. However, the most remarkable feature is the excessive zeal displayed over the provision of temples and cemeteries for animals in the Late and Ptolemaic Periods, and it seems that the explanation of this phenomenon lies in political considerations. During this part of their history, the Egyptians were repeatedly domi-nated by foreigners—first the Persians and then the Greeks. The extension of animal worship at this time may well have been part of a nationalistic movement, probably inspired by the priesthood, intentionally exaggerating the most charac-teristic features of Egyptian culture. Another aspect of the same process is seen in the increasing complexity of the hi-eroglyphic script used for temple inscriptions. If this inter-pretation is correct, then the vast animal cemeteries of the Late Period are to be viewed as a final attempt by the Egyp-tians to assert the superiority of their traditional culture.

Unique Cases

Animal burials, in addition to the examples discussed above, are plentiful throughout Egypt, and it would be pointless to describe each cemetery individually, as the general charac-teristics are much the same. However, a few cults deserve special note. The sacred rams of Elephantine belonged to the same type of cult as that of the bulls, with a single ani-mal reigning at any one time. At the death of the ram the corpse was embalmed and wrapped, decorated with its re-galia, including a miniature crown, and interred in a large stone sarcophagus. The ram of Elephantine was sacred to Khnum, god of the First Cataract region. Far to the north, at Mendes in the Nile Delta, another sacred ram was wor-shipped under the name Banebdjed, which means simply 'The Ram, Lord of Mendes'. Crocodiles were buried in the Fayum and at Kom Ombos, the animals at both places being the representatives of Sebek. The mummies were buried in very large numbers and included crocodiles of all sizes, to-gether with a quantity of eggs. . . . Among the crocodile burials of the Fayum were a number of fake mummies, consisting of a bundle of reeds wrapped up with an odd bone or two, which may represent evidence of corrupt practices among the embalmers, such as is known from the sacred ibis necropolis at Saqqara.

Individual animal mummies were sometimes placed inside a hollow compartment within a wooden statue of an appropriate divinity, dog mummies occurring in figures of Anubis and cats in figures of Bastet or Wadjet. Some such figures may well have served as cult-statues in temples, additional sanctity having been gained by the inclusion of the sacred animal within the image. The practice may seem bizarre to us, but it is not far removed from the preservation of sacred 'relics' in churches.

Chapter 3

The Accomplishments of Ancient Egyptian Civilization

Turning | Points

IN WORLD HISTORY

Writing and Literature in Ancient Egypt

Barbara Sewell

Ancient Egypt was one of the earliest civilizations to develop a system of writing and a comprehensive body of literature. In the following piece, Barbara Sewell traces the development of Egyptian hieroglyphs and the two scripts—hieratic and demotic—that eventually evolved from the hieroglyphic symbols. The different characteristics of these three writing systems suited each one for distinctive functions in Egyptian society, she explains. Sewell also examines the various forms of Egyptian literature and the impact these writings had on other regions of the ancient world. Sewell is the coauthor of *The Story of Ancient Egypt* and the author of *Egypt Under the Pharaohs*, from which the following is excerpted.

Hieroglyphic is the name given by the Greeks to the signs which they found carved on the walls of the Egyptian temples and tombs, on statues and on coffins. It means literally "sacred writing" and was so called because by the time the Greeks came to Egypt this script was used exclusively for religious and ceremonial texts, although originally it was in common use for everyday purposes as well. The hieroglyphic writing was fully developed at a very early date, and had its origins in "picture-writing", the earliest stage of many primitive scripts, where a picture is drawn of an object which is instantly recognizable. These ideograms came to represent abstract ideas and other subjects which had the same sound but which could not be pictorially represented, thus acquiring a phonetic value. For example, a word like "belief" which has no visible quality can be written with pictures of a bee and a leaf, in which case these objects are regarded as phonograms, on the principle of the rebus or charade. Another example is the city of Oxford as the Egyptians might have written it: the coat of arms of the city is an ox upon a representation of water, and this picture on road signs, etc. immediately conveys the idea of the city, and not of an ox or a ford. A further development took place when the hieroglyphic signs came to stand for individual consonants, and it was when this fact was realised by the early decipherers that the key to the reading of the script was found.

Further Developments in Writing

The hieroglyphs were carefully and often beautifully carved and painted, and were used as much for their decorative effect as for conveying information, but as writing became used more and more for administrative and practical purposes a cursive form of hieroglyphs came into use as a result of writing with a rush pen on papyrus. From this developed the hieratic script, the signs at first being not much different from the hieroglyphic forms except that they were often abbreviated. In course of time the hieratic characters acquired distinctive outlines of their own, and bear a somewhat similar relationship to hieroglyphs as that of handwriting to printing.

The hieratic script developed in its turn over a period of time into the latest form of Egyptian writing, demotic, a rapid and degenerate form of hieratic in which it is very difficult to recognize the original hieroglyphic forms, and which is also very difficult to read. Demotic was in common use from about the eighth century B.C. until late Roman times. This "popular" script was used for business and legal documents and for the literary writings of the period. Hieroglyphic and hieratic were used contemporaneously, but hieroglyphic became more and more reserved for religious and ceremonial texts so that eventually it was understood only by the priests and temple scribes.

The Egyptian language survived in Coptic and was written with the Greek alphabet to which were added seven characters taken from the demotic script, and this was the language spoken by the Christian descendants of the ancient Egyptians. It still survives in the liturgy of the Coptic Church, just as Latin has been used in the Roman Catholic Church. The importance of Coptic in deciphering the hieroglyphs is obvious, and it was through the study of this old half-forgotten tongue that the efforts of the early scholars who tackled the problem of decipherment met with success. . . .

It will always remain a mystery, however, how the language was pronounced, since no vowels were written and only the consonantal skeletons of words can be read. The vowels, however, survived in Coptic, which has made it possible to reconstruct some words and names with some approximation to the original pronunciation. The Egyptians themselves must have experienced the same difficulty in recognizing the meaning of different words having the same consonants, and they added determinative signs as a clue to the word's meaning. There are over a hundred of these determinatives, some of the more obvious being the figure of a man, woman or child for words with male and female meanings and those connected with youth; or of a man holding a stick for words conveying any energetic or violent action. A sun is added to words denoting light, or time of day; a sparrow, one of the pests of the fields, denoting anything mean or bad. A picture of the scribe's outfit was used as a determinative for words connected with writing or learning of any kind.

The Surviving Literature

Armed with this knowledge, it has been possible for Egyptologists to probe into the literature of the Egyptians, which by its quantity and quality is unique in pre-classical times, and from which many traditional forms have derived. It is mainly written in hieratic on papyrus rolls, wooden tablets, and ostraca, and, fragmentary though many of these survivals are, their variety and content demonstrate the richness and extent of the literature. The most popular, and therefore the most frequently copied throughout Egyptian history, were the narratives of adventures and stories which constituted a veritable folklore in which the doings of historical kings and famous men are recounted, well laced with magical imagery based on ancient myths and events in the lives of the archaic gods and goddesses.

Probably the most highly esteemed of all were the Wisdom Texts, many of which date from the days of the Old Kingdom; they were attributed to wise men of old like Imhotep, Djoser's architect, and were written in the form of an instruction by a father to his son. In fact, they took the place of religious teaching in moral education from generation to generation. They contain a fund of sound precepts based on tradition and worldly experience, and display a remarkable degree of humanity, circumspection and excellent advice for restraint in speech and action, and decent conduct towards one's fellow men, and are amplified by much sagacious advice on worldly advancement. The importance of good manners and observance of the correct etiquette in all situations of daily life are also stressed.

The teachings of one New Kingdom sage contain several maxims which are recognizable in the Book of Proverbs, which they obviously inspired. Egypt's early and continuous contact with the Near East must have disseminated many Egyptian tales through the oriental love of listening to the story-teller in the market-place; so much so that common elements in Egyptian stories—of travellers' tales, of shipwrecked sailors on magic islands peopled with friendly monsters who talk in human language and who turn out to be benignant deities, of magical transformation of humans into flowers or animals, of prophecies and erring wives—can be traced in the Greek romances and have faint echoes in popular tales the world over.

Medical Knowledge and Practices

Eugen Strouhal

Trained as both a physician and an archeologist, Eugen Strouhal is the director of the Institute of the History of Medicine at Charles University in Prague, Czech Republic, where he specializes in ancient Egypt. Strouhal examines Egypt's medical accomplishments in the following excerpt from his book *Life of the Ancient Egyptians*. According to Strouhal, ancient Egyptian medicine was very limited compared to modern-day practices: Doctors did not fully understand how the body works, and they often relied on useless "cures" or magical spells. On the other hand, he writes, Egyptian doctors could identify and treat many diseases and could even perform successful surgeries. Strouhal concludes that despite their limitations, the ancient Egyptians possessed a degree of medical knowledge and skill that was unique in the ancient world.

Of all the branches of science pursued in ancient Egypt, none achieved such popularity as medicine. The Greek poet Homer put it aptly in the *Odyssey:*

That fecund land brings forth abundant herbs,
Some baneful, and some curative when duly mixed.
There, every man's a doctor; every man
Knows better than all others how to treat
All manner of disease. . . .

There was even a degree of specialisation quite remarkable for the time, if we are rightly informed. The Greek historian Herodotus asserts that 'The practice of medicine is so divided among them that each physician treats one disease, and no more. There are plenty of physicians everywhere. Some are eye-doctors, some deal with the head, others with the teeth or the belly, and some with hidden maladies. . . .'

Ancient Egyptian Doctors

The usual term for a doctor was *sunu*, written with an arrow-shaped symbol that, it had been suggested, was an allusion to the use of arrowheads to lance abscesses.

Some doctors belonged to the priesthood, including priests of the goddess Sakhmet, patroness of diseases, remedies and physicians, and of the lector-priests (*khery-heb*). Some again were counted among the scribes, as shown in such titles as 'chief doctor and scribe of the word of god'. Many enjoyed ecclesiastical as well as lay titles.

Like other professions doctors had their hierarchy. Besides ordinary doctors there were senior doctors, inspectors, overseers and masters of physicians and the 'Chief of Physicians of the South and the North', a kind of minister of health. Royal and palace doctors had their special hierarchy and titles.

The Belgian scholar Frans Jonckheere counted 82 doctors known by name, many with titles suggesting specialisation in some defined area. However, Hermann Grapow, a specialist in Egyptian medicine, is probably right in thinking of them as simply exemplifying the various skills which the doctor might possess. Thus the 6th-dynasty court physician and high priest Pepyankh, known as Iry, was not only 'doctor to the king's belly' and 'shepherd of the king's anus', but also 'the king's eye-doctor'. There has been much dispute recently as to whether dentistry ranked as a separate calling; there are only five references to it in the Old Kingdom and another isolated one in the 26th dynasty. Nor has it yet been settled whether any of the doctors known to us conducted research.

There were no female nurses to help the doctors, but we do know of male nurses, dressers, masseurs and lay therapists.

It would be wrong to see connections between the medical profession and that of the embalmers, priests of the god Anubis. Contrary to older ideas that Egyptian doctors took part in the preparation of mummies to improve their knowledge of anatomy, it must be re-emphasised that most of their information came from ancient texts in which descriptions of the internal organs were based on analogy with animal bodies. The embalming procedure had nothing in common with medical autopsies.

The physician learnt his trade in the Houses of Life, notably at Per Bastet in the New Kingdom and at Abydos and Sais in the Late Period. He was no doubt given some practical experience, but chiefly he had to study what was already written. As the Ebers Papyrus says: 'His guide is Thoth, who lets the scrolls speak for themselves, compiles treatises and expounds knowledge to the savants and doctors who follow in his path.'

The Greek historian Diodorus too confirms this: '[They] administer their treatments in accordance with a written law which was composed in ancient times by many famous physicians.' From his further statement that 'on their military campaigns and on their journeys in the country they all receive treatment free of charge', it appears that for some people, at least, there was a system of free medical aid. But on other occasions doctors expected to be handsomely reimbursed, as we can tell from a scene in the 18th-dynasty tomb of the doctor Nebamun at Dra Abu el-Naga. There we see a patient, supported by his wife (both dressed in Syrian style), being handed some medicine by Nebamun's orderly. Behind this group and on another register is a file of servants bringing the doctor his fee—a copper ingot, a set of vessels (full, no doubt) and several little slave-girls.

The medical texts were not only the fount of professional knowledge but an insurance against possible failure. Diodorus saw this clearly: 'If they follow the rules of this law as they read them in the sacred book and yet are unable to save their patient, they are absolved from any charge; but if they go contrary to the law's prescriptions they must submit to a trial with death as the penalty.'

Of the eight extant medical compendia the most impor-

tant is the Ebers Papyrus, a collection of about 700 prescriptions for treating internal diseases arranged according
to the organ concerned. This was built up between the 4th
millennium B.C. and the New Kingdom through the continual addition of fresh material. The Hearst Papyrus, by contrast, probably represents the memoranda of a practising
doctor of the 18th dynasty in which he had written out
remedies from other works, the Ebers Papyrus among them.
The Edwin Smith Surgical Papyrus shows a profound em-
pirical knowledge of the different types of injuries and how
to treat them: this is a copy from the Second Intermediate
Period of a work at least 1000 years older. Other medical
documents include the Great Berlin Papyrus, the London
Papyrus, Chester Beatty Papyrus No. VI, Papyrus Ny Carls-
berg No. VIII and the Kahun Papyrus, the last dealing with
gynaecology. These are largely copies of Old Kingdom treatises made during the Middle and New Kingdoms.

Medical Knowledge and Beliefs

Examination of both medical and non-medical documents
has convinced many investigators that the ancient Egyptians
knew their anatomy in fair detail. In addition to externally
visible features there are many names of internal organs well
known from butchery and cooking.

Notions of physiology and disease were all anchored in
the concept of the heart as the centre of the organism. It was
the site of the soul, the reasoning faculty, qualities of character, and emotions. It was through the heart that god spoke,
and the Egyptian received knowledge of god and god's will.
The heart was one's partner; it spoke to a person in his or her
solitude. It was at the same time the engine of all the bodily
functions, not only of one cardinal function, the circulation,
as modern science revealed. From the heart proceeded
channels (*metu*) linking all parts of the body together. These
channels, the Egyptians believed, conveyed not only the
blood, but also air (reaching the heart from the nose, they
thought), tears, saliva, mucus, sperm, urine, nutriment and
faeces, as well as harmful substances (*wehedu*) conceived to
be the agents of pain and illness. Not only blood vessels were

considered as *metu*, but also the respiratory tract, tear duct, ducts of various glands, spermatic duct, the muscles, tendons and ligaments. The female organs were likewise seen as tubes open into the internal cavity; the eye was supposed to communicate with the ear and the only purpose of the brain was to pass mucus to the nose, with which it was also thought to be connected. The Egyptian idea of the human body, then, was as a network of interconnecting channels and analogous to the branches of the Nile and the artificial canals of their own country.

The Medical Pioneers of Egypt

In the following excerpt from his book Ancient Egypt: Its Culture and History, *Jon Manchip White lists some of the medical discoveries made by the Egyptians and notes their far-reaching influence on later civilizations.*

The powders and concoctions of the physician were composed of a variety of plants, seeds, piths and such fruits as dates and figs. Many of the plants were grown in the herb gardens of temples. Tuthmosis III, whose army included a corps of surgeons, sent back to the temple of Karnak botanical specimens culled during the course of his Asian campaigns. Plant juices and the fat or blood of a large number of animals were incorporated in suitable liquid vehicles. Among the drugs whose properties were recognized for the first time by the ancient Egyptians a medical authority lists hartshorn, castor oil, mandragora, cumin, dill and coriander. Medicaments plainly borrowed from Egyptian sources are said to occur in the works of the Roman scholar Pliny, the Greek scholar Dioscorides, the Greek physician Galen, and in the Hippocratic Collection. The Greeks frankly acknowledged, in this as in other fields, the debt their own men of science owed to Egypt. The Romans, Arabs and Persians also availed themselves freely of Egyptian medical lore. The Egyptian doctor was undoubtedly the first great pioneer of serious medical investigation.

Jon Manchip White, *Ancient Egypt: Its Culture and History,* 1970.

It was soon realised that in some of the *metu* the heart 'spoke' and a doctor could 'measure the heart' from this beat. But he could only tell if the heart was going faster or slower by comparing the patient's pulse with his own. The concept of circulation was still beyond the Egyptians' knowledge, since they did not distinguish between arteries and veins, nor appreciate that the blood returned to the heart.

The precondition of good health, they thought, was free flow through the *metu*; ailments arose when they became blocked, just as with irrigation canals. Thus if a woman was infertile this was because the sexual channel was closed, and constipation or accumulation of the blood were likewise causes of disease.

Harmful substances might find their way into the *metu* through the natural orifices, mainly by the ingestion of bad food. But they could also originate inside the gut, and doctors were therefore much exercised to ensure its regular evacuation. Sometimes seeing worms in the stool, they deduced that these too might have come into the body through the mouth and cause a disease. They gave them various names, such as the '*hefet* worm in the stomach', and the '*pened* worm', and attributed toothache to the *fenet* worm gnawing at the tooth.

With externally visible damage like wounds and fractures the causes were often obvious. But with many internal ailments doctors were at a loss, so they imputed them to irrational influences, usually gods—either hostile and malignant deities, or well-intentioned ones who sent down plagues as a punishment for wrongdoing. Sickness might also be the work of evil demons, or of an envious neighbour's evil eye.

Diseases and Injuries

It would far exceed the scope of this essay even to enumerate the diseases of ancient Egyptians that our researches have so far revealed. The evidence comes from several sources; from identification of their names and from their description in the texts, from their characteristic appearance in portrayals of the human body, from the study of pathological tissues in mummies and, in the case of diseases of bones and teeth, from the examination of human skeletal remains from burial sites. The study of all these sources constitutes the recently defined discipline of paleopathology.

According to medical texts the ancient Egyptians recognised some 200 types of sickness, though there is no mention of diseases of the lungs, liver, gall-bladder, spleen, pancreas or kidneys—the symptoms evidently eluded them. We can of course never be sure what any named disease refers to unless its symptoms or recommended treatment are mentioned in the same context.

The descriptions of external lesions and in particular of wounds are fairly clear. A wound is said to have a 'mouth' and 'lips' and may 'go as far as the bone'. It is usually accompanied by bleeding, which in the case of severe injuries to the skull, may come from the nose and ears too. The Ebers Papyrus mentions that a skull fracture haemorrhaging into the brain can cause paralysis, on the same side of the body it says, not the opposite side—perhaps this was a copyist's error. The Smith Papyrus quotes a man with a gaping head-wound as showing the symptoms of tetanus: 'His mouth is locked tight . . . his brow is convulsively contorted and he has the expression of a man crying.'

The Egyptians distinguished simple fracture, *sedj*, where the bone is broken in two, and complicated fractures, *peshen*, resulting in numerous fragments.

Conditions characterised by a bulging of the affected part were classified either as *shefut*, commonly translated as 'swellings' but in view of some scholars' references to a liquid content possibly including abscesses too, or as *henhenet* and *aat*, thought to denote tumours. The former were treated with dressings, the latter by excision. . . .

Types of Remedies

Over 200 remedies are mentioned in the texts, but not all of them would have been pharmacologically effective. They were derived from about 70 species of animals, 25 plants, 20 minerals and a number of common foodstuffs, drinks and secretions. Among them were the flesh, fat, blood, milk, gall, faeces and urine of animals and humans, and the leaves, fruit and powdered roots of such plants as henbane, thornapple and mandrake, to mention only the three most likely to have produced results. Some of the less convincing remedies were fresh dew, lumps of Nile mud, dirt from a patient's finger-nails and mouse excrement. The active ingredients were mixed by the doctor himself with bases such as milk, honey, sweetened beer or oil, and for ointments oil or fat. There is no evidence of specific pharmaceutical equipment, so pre-sumably household vessels, mortars, rods, spoons and so on were used.

Enemas and vaginal douches may well have been admin-istered through an animal horn with the tip cut off. Believ-ing that noxious substances enter the body in food, or arise in the digestive tract itself, the Egyptians 'look after the health of their bodies by means of enemas, fasting and emet-ics, sometimes every day and sometimes at intervals of three or four days. For they say that the larger part of the food taken into the body is superfluous and that it is from this su-perfluous part that diseases are engendered,' to quote Diodorus. Modern dieticians will no doubt applaud.

Eye-drops were administered with a vulture's quill. In-halations were prepared by heating a given substance on a hot stone, the vapour being breathed in through a reed com-ing out of an inverted pot placed on top. For genital fumi-gation women sat on a pot in which the recommended sub-stances were similarly heated.

Surgical Operations and Other Treatments

Surgery was performed with knives, forceps, and wooden or metal probes. A relief in the Ptolemaic temple of Kom Ombo shows a case of instruments which might have been used for surgical, dental or cosmetic purposes, though some commentators suggest that they were objects ritually de-posited at the foot of the foundation wall when the temple was being built.

For dressing wounds ordinary linen bandages, sutures, nets, pads and swabs were used. In setting fractures recourse was made to palm ribs, strips of bark, reeds or wooden splints bound with canvas or plant fibre.

Treatment of wounds was something Egyptian doctors

were quite skilled in. References to 'threads' in this context suggest that they may have sewn them sometimes, but normally they drew the edges together with bandages. For the first day they would cover a wound with fresh meat, then on each of the following days apply a dressing soaked in oil or honey. Severe or inflamed wounds were left uncovered, drenched in oil, kept cool and allowed to dry.

The Edwin Smith Papyrus shows how competently they dealt with dislocations.

> If you have to treat a man whose lower jaw is dislocated, so that his mouth stays open and he cannot shut it, you must place both forefingers on the ends of the arms of the jawbone inside his mouth and both thumbs under his chin. Then you must draw [the heads of the dislocated bone] downward until they are resting in their right place. At the same time you must say: 'A man with a dislocated jaw—that is the sickness I shall treat.' Then you will put on a poultice with *imeru* and honey each day until it is better.

When knives were used for opening 'tumours'—the same word applied to abscesses—they were first heated over a fire so that they would staunch the bleeding: unwittingly, of course, the physician had thereby sterilised them too. Blisters and warts were pierced with glowing splints or red-hot metal probes. The medical texts make no mention of any more sophisticated surgery, and yet 10 cases have been described of skulls that had been trepanned, in four cases demonstrably for medical reasons, and probably in the others too. The operations had in all cases been carried out on living patients who survived them for long periods, as the extensive subsequent healing shows.

No dental fillings have been found; there was a recommended mixture, of resin and malachite, but this was probably short-lived. Of 16 dental prescriptions mentioned in the papyri, seven are for treating loose teeth by enclosing both tooth and adjacent gum area in a casing made from wheatgrains, with ochre or honey (the same as was applied to splints for supporting broken bones). Some of the remedies mentioned in the Ebers Papyrus for dental treatment contained copper sulphate, an astringent still used for chronic gum inflammation.

If a tooth fell out, Egyptian dentists were able to fasten it to its sound neighbours with gold or silver wire; five examples of such 'bridges' have been recorded so far.

The Use of Magic

Where rational medicine failed, magic stepped in. Indeed, some of the medicines could only work by magic, as when baldness was treated with a mixture made from a rook's vertebra, a burnt ass's hoof and the lard of a black snake. The repellent nature of some prescriptions, such as faeces, urine or blood, was supposed to exorcise the demons that had caused the disease. Consumption of medicine, application of dressings and the preparation of drugs were all accompanied by the recital of magic spells.

At other times people turned to those gods credited with healing power, either by praying to them or writing them letters. The gods in question included Amun, Thoth, Min, Horus, Isis and Serapis. Three mortals were also promoted into their company, namely Imhotep, vizier and architect to King Djoser and identified by the Greeks with Aesculapius; Amenhotep, son of Hapu, who was an architect and senior officer in the reign of Amenophis III, and finally Antinous, the Emperor Hadrian's lover.

Magical cures also took place in some of the temples. The oldest evidence is from the Ramessid period at Deir el-Medina, other sites being the upper terrace of Hatshepsut's temple at Deir el-Bahari, the Serapeum and Anubieion at Saqqara and the temples at Canopus and Abydos. Remains of a sanatorium have been found on the grounds of the temple of Hathor at Dendera, where patients stayed isolated in small rooms recalling monastic cells, praying, meditating and benefiting from healing sleep, during which truths would be revealed to them in dreams. The use of bathing pools fed from the temple's sacred lake was also part of the cure.

There were always magicians at hand to rid the patient's body by incantation of demons that had caused his disease. People also sought to ward off these demons by wearing amulets, one of the most popular being the Eye of Horus, *wedjat*, the 'moon eye' which Seth had injured in combat with him and Thoth had restored to health. This story was connected with the phases of the moon, which Seth caused to wane and Thoth to wax again. Protection against snake bites, scorpion stings and crocodile attacks was conferred by a stele showing the god Horus doing battle with these dread creatures. It sufficed to pour water over the stele, catch it as it ran off and drink it. . . .

In sum, an Egyptian who fell ill could always rely on some cure being available, whatever the problem. The most rationally based branch of medicine, incomparably more advanced than that of other countries at the time, was certainly surgery. When it came to internal medicine there were some potentially beneficial drugs, but most prescriptions could only have psychotherapeutic effect.

The Solar Calendar

M. Abdel-Kader Hatem

In the following essay from his book *Life in Ancient Egypt*,
M. Abdel-Kader Hatem describes how the ancient Egyptians developed the world's first solar calendar. Because
the Egyptians needed to predict the timing of the annual
flooding of the Nile, Hatem writes, they began to study
astronomy and to divide the year into twelve months. As
Hatem explains, the Egyptians were the first ancient peoples to regulate the year according to the movement of the
sun rather than the moon. Eventually, he states, the Egyptians' solar calendar displaced the lunar calendar of other
civilizations, becoming the basis of the same calendar that
the modern world uses today. The author of several
books, Hatem had a long and active career in Egyptian
politics and government, including a term as acting prime
minister.

Science is a product of the mind and spirit of man. Although
science takes as its object of study the material side of nature,
its origins and functionings mark it as a spiritual and moral enterprise. This is true even when a distinction is made between
pure and applied science. Thus it is right to speak of science as
one of the great spiritual achievements of ancient Egypt.

In all periods of Egyptian history, learning, knowledge,
and science have been revered as sacred. It would not be an
exaggeration to say that Egyptian civilization could never
have reached its peak had not science contributed to the
achievement. . . .

The first and perhaps the greatest achievement of ancient
Egyptian science was the solar calendar, the development of
which was not only an epoch-making event in Egyptian his-

tory but an unparalleled advance for the whole of mankind. In the creation of the solar calendar the Egyptians were without predecessors; it was a product of the Egyptian mind alone.

The creation of the solar calendar came about in the following manner. The annual flooding of the Nile inspired the ancients to divide the year into three seasons, with the "first" day of the flood counted as the first day of the year. The first season of the year was therefore the flood season, lasting four months, the second the seed-sowing season, and the third the harvest season. Using the phases of the moon as the basis of calculation, the year was then divided into twelve months. With this system, however, there were five extra days at the end of the year that had to be set aside in calculating the twelve-month year. Discovering that their calcula-

Insights into Astronomy

Guillemette Andreu is an Egyptologist at the Louvre Museum in Paris, France. In the following passage from her book Egypt in the Age of the Pyramids, *Andreu describes the Egyptians' astronomical knowledge and their division of the day into twenty-four hours.*

The Egyptians distinguished stars grouped in constellations from the planets, which they called "the unwearying stars." Five planets were recognized: Mars, Saturn, Jupiter, Venus, and Mercury. To determine north and the other cardinal points, so important in the orientation of pyramids and sacred buildings, astronomers had to sight the middle of the ellipse formed by the maximum deviation of one of the stars of the Big Dipper. The polestar of the Little Dipper could not be used; for the earth's axis was not aligned on that star in the time of the pyramids.

We owe the division of the day into twenty-four hours to the Egyptians. Their hours, however, varied in length with the season: in summer, the hours of the night were very short because darkness did not last for an actual twelve hours, but the hours of the day were quite long.

Guillemette Andreu, *Egypt in the Age of the Pyramids*, trans. David Lorton, 1997.

tions were imprecise, the ancients, before the first of the historic dynasties, decided to undertake a systematic study at Adan University in Memphis.

This study resulted in one of the major discoveries in the history of mankind. Observing the movement of the planets over a long period of time, astronomers noted that the distribution of the stars formed certain patterns. They then divided the stars into thirty-six areas, each comprised of the brightest stars observable every ten days. From this emerged the idea of dividing the month into three periods, or weeks.

The astronomers noticed that the coming of the flood coincided with the appearance of the star they called Babrot, the first of the group of stars known as the Great Bear. The star appeared once a year, to coincide with the rising of the sun over Heliopolis. The ancients now confronted the problem of how to reconcile the difference between the Nile year of 365 days and the astronomical year as calculated by the Babrot star of 365¼ days.

These ancient astronomers realized that every four years the beginning of the astronomical year was one full day later than the Nile year, and were therefore able to work out a scientific basis for the calendar. They noted that the astronomical year would be coincidental with the Nile year according to their calculations. This was in the year 4241 B.C., but it was not until the years 2781 B.C. and 1321 B.C., as pointed out by later astronomers, that the astronomical year and the Nile year did coincide in actual fact, proving that the ancients could have arrived at such a conclusion only through astronomical observation. Eventually the Egyptian solar calendar was made up of 365 days, divided into twelve months, and four seasons. The months were named after various feasts and special events, and still retain these names today in rural areas.

The solar calendar worked out in ancient Egypt eventually became the calendar of the whole world. Julius Caesar replaced the lunar calendar with it, calling it the Julian calendar. In A.D. 1582 Pope Gregory revised the Julian calendar and called it the Gregorian calendar. In essence, however, it is still the same solar calendar devised by the Egyptians six thousand years ago.

The Pyramids of Egypt

John Romer

Art historian John Romer is the author of numerous books, including *Ancient Lives: The Story of the Pharaohs' Tombmakers* and *The Valley of the Kings*. He is also the president of the Theban Foundation in Berkeley, California, which is devoted to preserving and studying the Royal Tombs of Thebes in Egypt.

In the following selection from his *People of the Nile: Everyday Life in Ancient Egypt*, Romer outlines the development of one of the greatest architectural achievements of all time, the pyramids of Egypt. During the Third Dynasty, he recounts, Egyptian architects devised a pyramid in the form of a stepped structure; this Step Pyramid was the forerunner of the smooth-sided pyramids that arose during the Fourth Dynasty. Romer provides an overview of the methods used to design and build these immense structures, as well as the religious and political significance the pyramids held for the ancient Egyptians.

By the end of the First Dynasty, the desert spur that formed the greater part of the western skyline of Memphis had been quite filled with royal tombs, and the kings of the Second Dynasty started a new royal cemetery half a mile to the south. Here the skyline was less regular and parts of the ridge were buried deep beneath the drifted sand of a great dune. Two kings built their tombs behind this dune and, in turn, they were followed to the area by some of the tombs of the next dynasty. Rather than placing their monuments side by side as their forerunners had done, these kings had their tombs sited behind those of their predecessors, going ever further into the desert in a general retreat from the sharp edge of the Memphis horizon.

An Innovation in Architecture

It was on this desert plateau that the architects of one Third Dynasty king, Djoser, came slowly to the realization of a new form for the royal tomb: the pyramid; and in this they made an image that dominated the life of the nation for a hundred years. In the century that followed Djoser's death, the Egyptians made pyramids so large that to this day they remain the biggest stone structures in the world. The king's tomb had become the site of a national celebration of the potential and power of the nation's culture, a statement in architectural form of the order that had been created in the land.

Small stone structures had been built since the days of the First Dynasty—usually as parts of other buildings made of mud brick—but Djoser's craftsmen transformed this simple technology, which never seems to have consisted of more than a few hundred roughly dressed stones set into a coarse plaster, and, at the site of the royal tomb, made buildings all of stone. These were bounded by a magnificent stone wall, this a great rectangle decorated with the same pattern as the panelled façades of earlier royal tombs. Djoser's walls were, however, nearly six hundred yards along their longer sides and slightly more than half that distance along their shorter. . . . But there the architectural similarities ended, for neither the Egyptians nor anyone else in the world at that time had seen anything quite like those smooth, shining white stone walls.

If these great walls, their design steeped in the traditions of royal tomb architecture, did not sufficiently emphasize the new-found vigour in the land, then the buildings that rose inside them certainly did. Because the tomb was set back from the Sakkara ridge Djoser's architects had to build high to enable it to regain its position of dominance on the Memphis skyline, and that's exactly what they did. They had started by making the tomb a low square structure of well-finished stone with battered walls some 20 cubits (10.6 m) high that was reminiscent of the superstructures of the earlier royal tombs at the Umm el Ga'ab. On top of this sturdy monument Djoser's workmen first built three smaller similarly shaped structures of stone that rose in a series of equal sized steps. Then, in a final dramatic gesture, as if they were intent on taking the royal tomb up into the sky itself, the entire monument was enlarged at its base, enabling two more steps to be added to its top. In this process of transforming the shape of the royal tomb they had built a pyramid—the Step Pyramid—the first in the world.

The Significance of the Step Pyramid

Many different factors influenced the mechanics of this revolutionary process. For example, the traditional material for a royal tomb, mud brick, would never have been able to withstand the stresses of compression in a building nearly two hundred feet high. Pyramids were born of stone, and virtually in the same breath as stone architecture itself. The new material had given immediate expression to a form that the Egyptians could not previously have realized. The whole architectural tradition had been transcended. By piling form on form the Egyptians had created a shape so dramatic that, in unison with its commanding position at the horizon, had joined heaven to earth, earth to heaven. Djoser's pyramid and the buildings that accompanied it were a philosophical statement, part of the language of a nation that thought and responded to their situation in concrete images. And the pyramid's form so charged this nation that for a hundred years the national life revolved around the royal tomb, reducing many of the cities of Egypt to comparative poverty in the process.

For the ancient Egyptians, who viewed their history in terms of monuments and monument making, the almost mythical reign of Djoser was regarded as a time of great wisdom and achievement. The sole architect of these buildings, they believed, was Imhotep, known in Djoser's time as sculptor-builder and chief minister of the land. He was later revered as a god of medicine and wisdom, a deity to whom the scribes would sprinkle a few drops of water from their ink palettes before they started to write. . . .

Djoser brought the royal presence of death to one place. And by bringing together the royal tombs on the Sakkara plateau he literally gathered the nation about him in death. It was the beginning of a massive focusing of royal power in one location that reached an extraordinary climax during the next dynasty. The likes of most of Djoser's buildings, however, innovative in size, material and ritual purpose as they were, were never made again. They remain, therefore, unique; some of the gentlest and most exquisite architecture ever made: the deified Imhotep has made one of the magical places of mankind.

The Era of the Pyramids

From the reign of Djoser until the beginning of the New Kingdom almost every king of substance and authority was buried under a pyramid. At the end of this long tradition the splendid visions of the earlier dynasties had shrunk to monuments of poorly built steep-sided mud brick that were often no larger than about 40 feet square, but a thousand years before, pyramids had been measured in hundreds of feet, their masonry in millions of tons. The largest of all, the Great Pyramid on the Plateau of Giza, near modern Cairo, is still the biggest stone building ever made by man and one of the most accurately constructed. It was built less than one hundred years after Djoser's craftsmen had started their work on the Step Pyramid.

Singularly, the kings of the Third Dynasty who followed Djoser to the throne have not left any finished monuments—though there might still be some surprises lying under the desert sands at Sakkara. It was at the beginning of the Fourth Dynasty, in the desert north of the older monuments, that pyramid building on a quite unprecedented scale was started. These Fourth Dynasty monuments are the finest of the pyramids: seldom do they measure less than 350 feet along their sides and most are double that. After this time there was an immediate reduction in size and quality of construction that continued throughout the rest of the Old Kingdom. During the Middle Kingdom, however, the pyramids once again reached the colossal measurements of their forerunners, but these monuments were of carefully but-tressed mud-brick cased with stone, some of which had been quarried from the monuments of their predecessors to fit over the fresh mud brick like the shells of hermit crabs. Later, this fine stone skin was removed by other parasitical masons and the soft mud-brick cores have now eroded into unrecognizable shapes that require the paper plans of arche-ologists to recover something of their former magnificence in the mind's eye.

Despite this decay, there is little doubt about what the Middle Kingdom rulers thought of their monuments: 'the High and Beautiful', 'the Mighty', 'the Pure', 'the Peaceful' are some of the names of these sad ruins. Several of these ep-ithets recall the days of the Fourth Dynasty: 'Rising in Splendour' for example, is a title similar to that held by two of the largest monuments of that time. The scanty inscrip-tions connected with the Old Kingdom monuments also show, perhaps, a feeling of exultation at the power in the state, and some of the names of the Fourth Dynasty stone-hauling gangs reflect this same feeling; 'Sceptre Gang' (a reference to an emblem of kingship), 'Vigorous Gang' and, appropriately enough, inscribed on a block of the Great Pyramid, 'Craftsmen Gang', after which is added, perhaps in wonder at the monument that they were making, 'How powerful is the White Crown of Cheops!' (i.e. the organiza-tion of the state).

Cheops, or Khufu to give him his Egyptian name, was the king for whom the Great Pyramid was made. He was the second king of the Fourth Dynasty and reigned from about 2589 B.C. for a period of twenty-three years. The construc-tion of his pyramid must have taken up most of those years. What extraordinary confidence possessed the architects of this great pyramid as they strode over the bare desert plateau marking out the size of the projected monument! At that time they were committing the primary resources of their nation for generations. That such extraordinary optimism was sometimes misplaced is seen at less-visited sites where the construction of similarly vast monuments hardly pro-gressed beyond the cutting of a huge trench that was to hold

The great pyramids of Egypt are living proof of the advanced mathematical, astronomical, and architectural skills of the ancient Egyptians.

the royal burial chamber. This stopping of the work, it is assumed, was due to the premature death of the king.

But such cancellations were not the rule. In the reign of Cheop's father, Sneferu, no less than three mighty pyramids were built south of Sakkara, each one of which, in its size, comes close to rivalling the single monument of his son. It is interesting to observe that the buildings that accompanied these three pyramids were extremely simple, that all the architectural ritual of Djoser's great complex was discarded, freeing the workforce and its resources, allowing it to concentrate on the pyramid itself. It was during the reign of Sneferu that the final form of the pyramid, the straight-sided version that covered over the stepped structures of Djoser's monument, was established and this survived right through the monuments of the Old and Middle Kingdoms, built in a seventy-mile band down the western bank of the Nile near Memphis. Moreover, it was during Sneferu's reign that the considerable technical problems involved in building such enormous structures were overcome while at this same time, the nation was welded into a veritable race of tomb builders. It was a potent legacy that was eagerly grasped by Sneferu's son.

The Great Pyramid of Giza

For, despite the three majestic monuments of Sneferu—the combined masonry of which has been estimated at some nine million tons—the pyramid field *par excellence* must surely be the Plateau of Giza. There, during the greater part of the Fourth Dynasty, multitudes of masons' gangs chipped and chiselled at the landscape to re-form it into the pyramids of three kings, and into hundreds of other, smaller monuments. It was a grand gesture that, stretching out over the landscape, printed the hand of man next to the forms of God. These mountainous efforts must have taken virtually the entire energy of the nation which, according to modern estimates, stood at that time at about 1.6 million people. The pyramids, therefore, *are* the history of the Fourth Dynasty. But for historians who like to chew over family relationships, battles, treaties and all the normal burdens of history, the period remains practically an empty book. Yet these people left buildings as finely made as watches and so large that they defy imagination.

Indeed, the accuracy of Cheop's pyramid is no less phenomenal than its bulk. The maximum error in the four sides at their bases, the mean length of which is about 755.8 feet, is just 8 inches. The faces of the pyramid, sited on the points of the compass to provide a fixed point with which to check the progress of the work, show a maximum error at the base of a little over one twelfth of a degree. The right-angles at the corners are equally precise: the largest single error in them amounting to less than one twentieth of a degree. As are all the others, the Great Pyramid is virtually a solid structure composed, in the most part of blocks of limestone numbering, it has been estimated, some 2,300,000 averaging 2½ tons each. It has also been calculated that with eight-man gangs each moving one of these blocks from the quarries to the pyramid that the entire structure could have been assembled by 100,000 men in 'less than twenty years'.

An Expression of Faith and Strength

In some ways, this extraordinarily intense activity, which continued on the Giza Plateau for the better part of a century, can be likened to the cathedral building of medieval Europe—an expression of faith that is reflected in the quality of the architecture, the activity of building as an act of worship. In this sense, the pyramids may be seen as the memorials of a vital process, and it was this *process* that was the real core of the enterprise. We are merely left with the results. But there is one vital difference. The accuracy of the pyramids was not prompted by sentiments of piety but was the result of necessarily strict controls instituted so that the form of the monument would retain its accuracy during the lengthy period of its construction. Such plain geometric shapes as the pyramids will clearly show any deviations from true, and their extraordinary accuracy is an incredible demonstration of the strength of the ancient state.

This building programme, then, was a demonstration of the successful application of the mechanisms of state. And, as the accuracy of the pyramids was maintained during the long periods of construction, so the culture of Egypt was itself maintained throughout thousands of years by the similarly strict application of rules and methods. As they built their pyramids so the Egyptians built their state. It was a dramatic climax to the culture that was made during the first two dynasties and it left Egypt with a cultural self-confidence and self-awareness that survived the tribulations of more than 2,000 years of history.

Building the Pyramids

There is, now, broad agreement among scholars concerning the outline of the techniques that were used to build the pyramids, though many details, especially of the methods used for the initial survey and the subsequent geometric controls, remain obscure. One old theory that has collapsed following fresh research into the ancient flood levels in the Nile Valley was the proposition that stone used in the pyramids was brought to Giza on barges that were able to cross the Nile Valley at the time of the annual inundation. It now appears that the shallow depth of the annual floods during the Old Kingdom would not have allowed the passage of barges of sufficient draught to carry such huge blocks. It is more likely, therefore, that special canals were dug from the Nile bank to the bottom of the desert ridge and the stone barges came up these specially constructed waterways to the foot of the pyramid.

Of course, the Nile was an essential transportation system for the enormous tonnages of hard stone that were brought to the pyramids from the deserts and the cataracts of Upper Egypt. Aswan granite was especially favoured as a finishing stone, often used to line the interior chambers and corridors of the pyramids and also for the massive lintels that spread the huge loads of the masonry above the burial chambers. The fine white limestone used for the outer surfaces of many of the pyramids was brought from the quarries of Tura on the eastern bank of the river opposite Giza. The bulk of the limestone used in the pyramids, however, was quarried from the surrounding plateaux.

The huge stone blocks were handled by gangs using sledges, rollers, ropes and rocking platforms that, with the use of wedges, could be used to raise the blocks small distances. For the final ascent to their position in the pyramid the blocks were dragged by the gangs up ramps of mud brick which, when they were lubricated with water, would have had a surface almost as slippery as ice. Traces of such ramps are still in position by their pyramids, and other more complete examples have been cleared from later temples where they were used in the same way. A New Kingdom papyrus preserves the mathematical formula used for a rough calculation of the volumes of such enormous constructions.

Building the ramps to allow the transportation of large blocks of stone as much as 600 feet up to the top of a pyramid would have been equal to the effort of constructing the pyramid itself, and this fact has sometimes been used as an argument against their use at the larger monuments: that no builder would ever employ such an uneconomic method. But it is false to judge these ancient buildings by the rules of modern economics. There are very many instances where the ancient Egyptians devoted long periods of time and much skill to tasks which by modern standards would not be acceptable. And this is a basic reason why many of the products of the ancient Egyptians are so profoundly different from those of modern cultures. The Egyptians made their monuments for reasons other than those that govern the work of most modern architects and artists: as the economist John Maynard Keynes succinctly observed, 'Two pyramids, two masses for the dead are twice as good as one; not so two railways from London to York'.

Two cultures, ancient and modern, have expended quite different amounts of time and effort on quite different aspects of their architectures, and they have, therefore, developed two quite separate technologies. In the process, the Western world has largely lost the skills of managing large numbers of manual workers which the ancient Egyptians possessed to a remarkable degree. Further, modern notions of what is practical are severely limited by factors of time. Our methods of moving blocks as large as those used at Giza, for example, require engineering skills that, ideally, will resolve the problem at a touch of a button. Yet in Egypt today, the villagers employed for manual labour on archeological excavations still easily shift ancient blocks about with great skill. They have a sensitivity towards the special properties of friction and balance that such loads have, they share a confidence in each other, and work easily in group rhythms. How much more skilful must the ancient gangs of Giza have been, with a hundred years of experience behind them!

Changes in Emphasis

After the Fourth Dynasty the royal pyramids were greatly reduced in size, and paradoxically it is this dynasty, an age virtually devoid of recorded political history, an age of national absorption in building and architecture, that is often regarded as the apex of the ancient Egyptian culture. However, with the reduction in size, the accompanying facilities became greatly elaborated. Texts were inscribed in the chambers inside the pyramids, and the temples that had always accompanied the monuments became increasingly complex and lavishly decorated: theological exposition partly replaced the sheer bulk of the Fourth Dynasty monuments.

The natural conclusion of this tendency was reached during the Twelfth Dynasty. One of the pyramid temples of that era has since entered legend, as the Labyrinth, one of the seven wonders of the world. . . . In their architectural convolutions, especially the complex security systems that surrounded the pyramids' burial chambers, these Middle Kingdom monuments seem more worldly wise than the Old Kingdom models on which they were based. Some of them contained hydraulic mechanisms that worked with sand, blind passages leading prospecting robbers away from the burial chamber—in fact, much of the paraphernalia so beloved of Hollywood epics.

The Middle Kingdom kings were well aware that the massive yet simple security devices of the Old Kingdom pyramids had, without exception, failed their owners during the anarchic time of the First Intermediate Period; the kings who had supervised the building of the Giza pyramids were now 'cast out upon the high ground', as an ancient scribe wrote of their dismal fate. The elaborate security systems of the Middle Kingdom pyramids are an architectural expression of the physical insecurity of the kings themselves; anarchy, after all, had proved that the god-king was not invulnerable. However, these extraordinarily ingenious systems, too, failed their hopeful owners, for with the exception of some pyramids whose burial chambers have been submerged with the rising of the Nile's water table, all were robbed in distant antiquity.

Egyptian Art

Paul Johnson

To the modern eye, Egyptian artwork often seems primitive and unskilled, especially due to its odd rendition of
the human form. For example, Egyptian paintings typically depict the human body in profile except for the eyes
and shoulders, which are shown frontally. However, as
Paul Johnson explains, Egyptian artists purposefully chose
to utilize this mixed perspective in order to represent the
human form as fully as possible. He asserts that the art of
ancient Egypt was regulated by specific codes influenced
by religious and cultural factors; seen within this framework, Johnson argues, Egyptian artists produced exceptional pieces of art. Johnson is a journalist and a staff
member of the *New Statesman*, a British periodical of current affairs. His books include *The Civilization of Ancient
Egypt*, from which the following essay is taken.

The very essence of Egyptian civilization was its art. If we
can understand Egyptian art we can go a long way towards
grasping the very spirit and outlook on life of this gifted
people, so remote in time. The dynamic of their civilization
seems to have been a passionate love of order (*maat* to
them), by which they sought to give to human activities and
creations the same regularity as their landscape, their great
river, their sun-cycle and their immutable seasons. In public
affairs, the quest for order produced the pharaonic political
and religious system which, with all its limitations and weaknesses, endured in some form for 3,000 years. The same
spirit organized the early pictograms and phonograms into a
highly disciplined system of communication, and regulated
the diverse artistic expressions of proto-dynastic and early

dynastic times into the most coherent and orderly code of art in history. Two or three pioneering generations of leaders accomplished these massive and related transformations at the outset of the Old Kingdom, perhaps within a span of a mere fifty years. Already, by the time of Djoser, it was all there: the visible, unmistakable majesty of a great civilization.

Unity in Diversity

The creators of the monolithic Egyptian state were also the patrons and marshals of its art: they drew no distinctions between religion, politics and creativity, and it is important we should draw none either. Unity is the key to understanding. All aspects of Egyptian civilization were informed by the same drive, but they were most successful in art because there the spirit of unity in diversity was most convincingly established and tenaciously retained. In art, the ordering process achieved a wonderful clarity of form, almost from the start, and retained it almost to the end—whether the magisterial simplicity of the monumental sculpture and architecture, or the simple elegance of the merest everyday utensil: the objects produced at every level of expression, cost and material were bound together in aesthetic unity by the same manifest style.

However, when we use the word 'aesthetic' we must beware of giving it a nonfunctional significance. The unity of the civilization forbids this separation. All art in ancient Egypt, even the shaping of an ordinary spoon in the form of a goddess, had religious, social or political meaning and purpose. We can understand it best if we regard art as an enormous system of communication. An artistic object was a message, usually a message to the gods. The artist encoded it; the gods—or we, if we know the rules—decode it. The language of art was not divided into strict compartments. Almost without exception, for instance, sculpture and its architectural setting were designed together; or, to put it another way, architecture was conceived as incomplete without its sculptural adornment, as that was a key part of the message. There is an analogy here with the façade of a Gothic cathedral. Hence we must remember that the figure of a pharaoh or a god seen in a Western museum, even if complete in itself, was a severed fragment in Egyptian eyes. Equally, a great tomb complex, temple or palace, shorn of its statues, is blind and lifeless by the criteria of its creators. The unity would have been blazingly apparent if we could have seen these creative ensembles in their pristine state, not least because all was painted, the colours having meanings and being part of the system of communication.

The Connection Between Words and Art

Above all, we must not distinguish between hieroglyphs and purely plastic art, since that is not a distinction the Egyptians could or would have made. During the formative period of Egyptian art, these two forms of expression or communication advanced with the same deliberate speed in the direction of clarity. The axis on which Egyptian civilization revolved was the mastery of stone-carving: it is significant that the basic hieroglyph for arts of all kinds is the sign for the borer used in hollowing a stone vase—marking the first unequivocal victory in Egypt of skill over matter. Hieroglyphics began as raised carvings on stone—brushmanship and penwork followed much later. During the Second Dynasty, the signs were first arranged in harmonious lines, acquired well-defined relative sizes, and were gradually arranged into elegant square or rectangular groups; at precisely the same time Egyptian sculptors were first mastering the human form and giving it order in stone. The artistic process was the same in each case and possibly the same hands were at work. The great ceremonial palettes of early dynastic times, with their combination of raised low-relief sculpture and raised glyphs, are plainly the work of single artists. . . .

I think if we could get inside the mind of a literate Egyptian at any epoch before the first millennium B.C., we would find that he did not distinguish between words and art. Both were seen as the process of communicating and clarifying. So intense was the clarifying urge that there is hardly a picture, sacred or profane, in the whole corpus of Egyptian art, without an accompanying text—often an integral part of the picture—which tells us what is happening, who the people are, the speeches they address to each other, and much other information, often superfluous when the paintings or sculptures are self-evident. In three-dimensional sculpture, the hieroglyphic lines are ordered with immense and delicate skill so that they gently and unobtrusively emphasize the principal forms of the mass, without losing their own significance. On the great wall-paintings and low-reliefs, the writing often plays a central role in the organizing of space, the balance of masses and the conveyance of meaning. That is why the script, as it were, retained its protean character: travelling in either direction horizontally, and vertically too—though it is notable that the signs always face in the direction in which the person to whom they are attached is speaking, moving, looking or performing. The integration of script with art is of course the reason why the hieroglyphs never lost their pictorial element and became a pure alphabet. By a curious paradox, they could not escape from their primitive origins because they were part of a sophisticated artistic process. And, equally, in their intense search for clarity and their desire to communicate, the Egyptians never allowed their purely pictorial forms to escape from their primary task of communicating information. If, for instance, an Egyptian artist wanted to show the contents of a basket, he drew the objects—bread, vegetables, fishes and so forth—in such a way, and so arranged in relation to each other, as to give the impression almost of an artistic code, having more in common with hieroglyphic signs than, say, a European still-life of the eighteenth century.

Hence we should see the ancient Egyptian artist as a communicator. To understand what he is doing it is necessary to learn the code within his art just as we need to know what the signs of the hieroglyphs stand for, alone or in combination. Egyptian art was dominated by an immensely powerful studio tradition, perpetuating itself from generation to generation. . . .

Egyptian painters, sculptors and architects did not have the self-confidence of the modern individual artist. Their art, at its best, is immensely assured and confident but it is the confidence of the collective. An Egyptian artist saw him-

self as part of an immensely powerful tradition which had always existed and always would exist, and which was followed
by all his colleagues. In individualism lay disaster; in the collective lay strength and security. This professional approach
itself reflected the social and religious beliefs common to all
Egyptians. Man arrived at knowledge and so justified himself, not by exercising his critical faculties and by his own
perception, but by the acceptance of dogmatic truth. The
artist is obedient and submissive before the divine order. He
does not express a personal viewpoint, his own order as it
were, but seeks to integrate himself with the universal order,
or *maat*, laid down by god.

The Artistic Code

All this implies a code, and in fact the Egyptian artist worked
within the restraints of an immensely comprehensive and
authoritative code, taught by example in the studios and so
passed on, and occasionally modified, from generation to
generation. As an individual, he could not change the rules
any more than a scribe could alter the hieroglyphics. First
there were the restrictions imposed by the material. Egyptian sculptors worked in stone as a rule, and by preference in
very hard stone, using tools of comparatively soft metal.
They eventually coped with this difficulty very successfully,
but their initial strivings were inevitably reflected in their
traditions, which sought to reconcile treatment of the
human figure with the rectangular solidity of the block. The
backboard and the seat, originally employed (we presume) to
help overcome the problem of rendering a free-standing figure, remained part of the artistic idiom long after they had
ceased to be necessary. Conforming to and expanding this
tradition, sculptors during the Middle Kingdom introduced
the device of the squatting figure, which aligned itself even
more closely to the block of undressed stone. This marrying
of plastic shapes to the demands of the material was conducted with immense elegance and an authority which
rested on faith. Indeed, it was faith, for Egyptian art was in
no way anthropocentric. The object was more important
than the man looking at it. The object, in fact, had religious

significance even before the sculptor got to work on it. Gold was for the gods, stone for eternity. A particular stone was never selected arbitrarily but according to well known religious criteria—its very availability might well be the result of divine intervention, as the claims of many stone-quarrying expeditions testify. . . .

Then there were social restrictions, inevitable in any court art, but in Egypt of peculiar power and complexity—so complex that we, in our ignorance, cannot know them all. If the artist owed duties to his material, he also owed respect, in varying degree, to his subjects. The Egyptians seem to have regarded themselves, in a state of nature, as highly emotional and volatile people—mercurial, excitable, galvanic. The essence of civilization, as they saw it, was the subordination of these wild instincts to order, conformity, self-discipline; *maat*, in short. They would have agreed with Irish poet William Butler Yeats's definition of civilization as the search for self-control. Hence a human form possessing a plenitude of *maat*—a god or goddess, a pharaoh or, in descending order, a member of the royal family, an aristocrat, a priest or high official—had visibly to exercise restraint by an absence of motion, a fixed, stationary, self-consciously 'noble' posture. From this necessity came the dominant idiom of the standing figure, left foot forward in arrested motion, arms to the sides in alert repose. We imagine that the pharaoh himself in real life—at any rate when he was on public show—was so burdened with his stiffened linen robes and top-heavy ceremonial headgear that he had no alternative but to adopt statuesque postures and slow, magisterial gestures. . . . In art at least, members of the ruling class took on the pharaonic immobility.

However at a certain point down the social scale, movement became permissible, almost mandatory, and artists portrayed it. Stone monumental sculpture did not, of course, deal with the lower classes but the group models, or miniatures, placed in tombs often show them in vigorous motion. In two-dimensional paintings and reliefs, servants, peasants, workmen, artisans, soldiers and sailors, dancers and musicians, could be supple, dynamic, even frenzied, jumping, running, leaping and fighting, hammering and pulling. They were imprisoned in much less rigid conventions of depiction. So, too, were enemies and foreigners, whatever their rank. The artist owed them little or no respect and could show them in unusual or uncanonical postures, old and ugly, obese or starving, ill, wounded, dying or dead. . . .

Measuring the Human Form

Of course the conventions which underpinned the style were supplemented by more mechanical devices. The Egyptian artist was the first to develop a systematized canon for the human form. The human canon was a metrological concept in origin, the Egyptians having noted the reliability of human proportions. But this was an aesthetic and religious observation, as well as a metrological one, the artist perceiving that, in the divine wisdom, the diversity of human forms was contrasted by their proportional unity and that it was the harmony of the latter which made humanist art so satisfying. The artistic canon was very likely worked out at the same time as the system of measurement and was certainly

The Main Themes in Egyptian Art

In the following excerpt from his book Egyptian Art in the Days of the Pharaohs, *Cyril Aldred comments on the unique qualities of ancient Egyptian art, particularly the emphasis on a well-ordered and cultivated society.*

In examining any large collection of ancient Egyptian art, the spectator cannot but be conscious of its unique quality which is usually instantly recognizable, apart from the exotic charm of its ethnic features and fashions. The dominant impression is of its humanity. The main subject of this art is man and his many activities in an Egyptian milieu. Colossal figures may exist (though they are rarer than is commonly supposed and most Egyptian statues, even of gods, are of less than life-size), but they magnify only the heroic and beneficent qualities of divinities and kings, and not the horrific power of tyrants or demons. Sinister and hostile forces are tamed into intellectualized concepts and often reduced to a contemptible size, with little in existence by the beginning of the Old Kingdom. Its accuracy and strict observation had a religious sanction, since the usual purpose of Egyptian art was to guarantee the immortality of the body, whose appearance therefore had to be rendered correctly.

For this purpose, the earliest Egyptian sculptors of the dynastic period used a grid which was a geometrical projection in measured squares of the agreed proportions of the body set out in the metrological canon. The rough-hewn blocks used for sculptures were squared on at least two sides—possibly on all four and on top as well. The axis ran between the eyes, down the nose, across the navel and between the feet. Thus, for sculpture, the body was divided into identical halves. For the two-dimensional low-reliefs and paintings, grids were also used stretched over the surface (sometimes strings dipped in paint), but, except for the shoulders, the figure was turned round on its sculptured axis, so that head, trunk and legs were shown in profile. If these parts in profile are turned back on their axis, the figure then

power to impress by their intrinsic appearance, but able to terrify only by what they symbolize. With few exceptions Egyptian art mirrors an ideal aspect of the natural world in which calm, successful men and women are shown acting in a rational manner. The scenes that are depicted express for the most part piety, family affection and social harmony amid a sympathetic nature. Scenes of violence and disorder are confined to the butchery of the sacrificial ox, the gala fights of the clownish boatmen or the overthrow of the forces of evil, whether in the form of the animals of the wild or the human marauders of the Nile Valley. Egyptian art at its best reflects the restraint and sense of proportion of a sophisticated society that in its formative period was counselled by its philosophers to follow moderation in all things, to beware of the passionate or sensual man, and to cultivate 'silence' or the qualities of temperance, patience and benevolence.

Cyril Aldred, *Egyptian Art in the Days of the Pharaohs*, 1980.

resumes the appearance of a three-dimensional sculpture seen from the front. The same canons of proportion and the same basic outline applied, therefore, to the rendering of the human form in both two and three dimensions. In either case, the canonical height of the male standing figure, from the hairline to foot, was the one-fathom metrological unit, marked into eighteen squares on the grids; each square was a full headsbreadth of four fingers and thumb. The seated figure was measured and set out according to the same ratios, the parts being moved round the axial system as required. In short, the canon and its axis, though notional or merely set out in grid form, acted as a kind of lay-figure, with articulated joints, which the sculptor or artist could arrange for his purpose to discover the exact length and width of each member he wished to paint or sculpt, whatever the position of the figure as a whole. The combination of canonical ratio plus axis therefore gave the artist a precise and dependable code for all his renderings of the human form, down to the smallest gesture. . . .

There is no evidence that artists found the canonical code irksome. . . . To the artist, the canon was simply the recognition of an (to him) obvious fact, that the harmonious proportioning of a well-built man was the supreme standard of beauty—something the Egyptians recognized long before the Greeks. Most artists, as a rule, prefer to work within the restraints of a system, particularly a classical one not subject to fundamental change, where the artist explores and exploits the limitations of the framework by virtuoso techniques. The system led to very exacting standards among artists: considering the enormous quantity of Egyptian art we still possess, the proportion of high quality is impressive by any comparison; poor or even mediocre work is very rare.

Use of the canonical system explains the essential characteristics of Egyptian art in both three and two dimensions—conventionalism, standardization, the geometrical drift, the stress on typology. It also makes it clear beyond any possibility of error that the Egyptian approach to art was severely intellectualized, not emotional. The Egyptians did not have a different way of seeing things. The way in which they portrayed the human form, or space or distance, or any objects whatever, was determined precisely and logically by the application of their code, which itself was a rationalization of the visual world.

Learning to "See" Egyptian Art

It is important to remember this when we look at Egyptian works of art. If our response to them is instinctive, we will undoubtedly misconceive them because we will be distorting the purpose of their forms to make them fit into the assumptions of our own artistic system, which is quite different. We will, as it were, be seeing Egyptian art as an emotional aberration from our own code, instead of as the normative product of theirs. We have to learn how to look at Egyptian art, and this is not easy because it involves deliberately suppressing the powerful dictates of our code. But at least the methods to be employed have been authoritatively set down by Heinrich Schäfer, the great Berlin Egyptologist, in his *Principles of Egyptian Art*, one of the most remarkable books ever written about aesthetic history. He provides a detailed explanation of the Egyptian visual code which, though open to challenge in certain respects, unlocks most of the doors for us.

In the late sixth and early fifth centuries B.C. Greek artists invented a new kind of illusionist art in which artists began to adopt a purely visual response to their subjects, portraying what they saw to be there, rather than what they knew to be there. In fact they began to perform, in many respects, as cameras. This involved the use of aerial perspective and all kinds of distancing techniques, *chiaroscuro* (treatment of light and shade), shadows and distortions, which are visual rather than actual.

Now this perspective revolution of the Greeks was the product of an intellectual decision, the growth of a new adventurism of the mind, which manifested itself in many other ways. The Greeks did not *see* things any differently from their artistic predecessors: they simply decided, in revolt against the limitations of the old codes, to portray what they saw. It is evident from the literary sources that earlier peoples saw with the same perspective vision as we do. A famous and much-quoted Akkadian poem, which may well go back to about 1750 B.C. (though the oldest manuscript which we have dates from the seventh century B.C.), shows a mythical figure called Etana flying up to heaven on the back of an eagle, and looking down: each time he looks the world appears smaller. The poem gives us, as it were, a series of aerial perspective snapshots.

Yet it is one thing to give away a sense of perspective in words, almost accidentally; quite another to employ it deliberately in visual presentation. Among primitive people—and for this purpose we must include the Egyptians among them—there is no, or little, distinction between a created image and the reality. Indeed, it was of the very essence of the Egypt cult that the image was the god. This being so, it was essential that the rendering of the image should approximate as closely as possible to reality—not the illusionary reality seen by the fallible human eye, from one viewpoint only, but the true reality of the actual appearance of the person or object, as known intellectually and by experience. Usually this takes the form of rendering the frontal image, irrespective of the artist's viewpoint, the frontal image being chosen because it is the one which most immediately conjures up to the viewer the reality. Or, to put it another way, it is most characteristic of the object concerned, and conveys to the viewer the most information about it. In yet another sense, it is also the most objective way of portrayal, since the subjective eye of the artist is subordinated to the objective characteristics of what he is portraying.

Providing Information

Hence, when we look at Egyptian art, we must remember that the artist is not striving primarily to present, whether in two or three dimensions, what he sees in his eye, but to give the maximum information, in pictorial or plastic shorthand, about what he knows intellectually to be there. Once again, we have to see the artist as communicator and his work as closer to hieroglyphics than to photography. Hence, when we look at the Egyptian rendering of human figures in two dimensions, we should never judge them as human forms

Egyptian art frequently depicted religious scenes. In this painting, the star-filled sky goddess Nut shelters her tired husband, Geb, the earth god.

comprehended in one glance from a single viewpoint. They are in fact composites, jigsaw puzzles of frontal images and characteristic images, put together with right-angle turns in the axis, to provide the archetypal human form, rather than the one seen in the artist's eye. The Egyptians reduced all this to a code which laid down these multiple viewpoints and the images of reality judged to be most characteristic.

Every part of the body was shown from the side which revealed it most characteristically. Thus the head was shown in profile, because that told us more about the nature of the face than the frontal image; but the eye was shown frontally, because it was the only view giving the complete circle of white, iris and pupil. The neck was also shown in profile as part of the head, but it had to be presented in a twisting motion (which was in fact natural) because the shoulders were most characteristic when shown full frontally. The legs, feet, hips and bottom were in profile, chest and stomach acting as transition between them and the frontal shoulders. Here the code became a little awkward, the chest being, as it were, pivoted at forty-five degrees. In the case of a man, one nipple may be shown frontally, the other in profile. With a woman, both are covered by the straps of her dress, which is shown frontally; but one nipple is also, as a rule, shown exposed and in profile. This is a contradiction and a visual impossibility, but it did not seem wrong or absurd to the Egyptians, since it conformed to the code of giving the maximum information by portraying the characteristic profile shape of the female breast—the fact that it could not be seen under the dress was irrelevant since everyone knew it was there.

This two-dimensional rendering of the human form, with its multiple points of reference, . . . remained absolutely standard for the Egyptians for 3,000 years, and all other renderings of the human form were variations from it. The more important the person in the social or divine hierarchy, the more closely the rendering had to conform to this pattern (workmen, being relatively unimportant, were often shown in strict profile or even with their backs to the viewer). With work in three dimensions, the human form, in addition to conforming to the canonical proportions, could only move on fixed axes. The plane in which it was set was unalterable: it could bend forwards or backwards, but not sideways at the neck or at the hips; and it could not turn within its axis. Sometimes angles of eighty degrees approximately were considered permissible, but any drastic variation from the right-angle approach was ruled out. Hence, Egyptian sculpture is basically composed of four views, each at right angles to the other. Schäfer calls this 'the law of directional straightness'. It enclosed the statue in an invisible rectangular box. Seen from the front, as it was meant to be seen, it does not, to our eyes, give an impression of depth. The Egyptian viewer apprehended the frontal image, then viewed the image at right angles from the side; then, in returning to the front, superimposed the two images in his mind to acquire depth and reality. Modern photographs which show Egyptian sculpture at an oblique angle, so that both front and side images are combined in distorted form, defeat the purpose for which the sculptor was striving and wrench the statue out of the code in which it was composed. . . .

The same principle of providing information, and of presenting objects in their most characteristic shape, rather than rendering the image from the fixed viewpoint of a 'subjective' artist, applied to all forms in Egyptian art. A table was shown with its legs and top, irrespective of what could actually be seen from the angle of vision subjectively chosen; and if there were loaves and fruit on the table, these were simply piled up vertically on top of the table and presented frontally to bring out their characteristics. If the artist is painting a pool surrounded by trees, the shape of the pool seen vertically is chosen, because that is the pool's characteristic shape; but the trees surrounding it are shown from a horizontal angle, because that brings out *their* characteristics. Again, a storehouse is shown by portraying its doors and horizontal profile of roof; but the grain within is also shown in its jars, because the picture would otherwise be meaningless to Egyptians. The fact that objects are opaque is not allowed to hinder the process of information-conveying since the artist is not only allowed to change his viewpoint in composing his picture but may, as it were, walk through doors and wander around inside, sketchbook in hand. There is no distinction in the Egyptian code of art between an outline drawing of a building and a topographical sketch, plan or map, or a series of architect's elevations—all are combined together when and if they exhibit characteristic features and convey the maximum information in the space available. To the Egyptian artist, a picture was closer to an inventory than to a snapshot.

Designed to Be Read

Egyptian low-reliefs and paintings must therefore be 'read', as well as looked at. They were designed to convey information but they also demanded from the viewer a series of intellectual reactions or, rather, a continuous process of analysis as his eyes moved over the surface and translated the pictorial code into the realities as he knew them. In the big compositions combining hieroglyphics with strictly pictorial forms, the mental process involved in apprehending both of them was roughly the same. The art of viewing them intelligibly lies in being able to isolate each point of reference or unit within the picture and move from one to the next changing the viewpoint, while at the same time keeping the mass of the picture, and its overriding unity, in mind. This is not easy: it requires a fierce intellectual self-control.

But, equally, it was not easy to compose and execute the multiple reference pictures. Therein lay the civilized art of the Egyptians. As with their ordinary tools and technology, they were operating what was essentially a very primitive method of creating art, but with such refinements of skill as to give it an appearance of immense sophistication. One could draw a similar analogy with their theology: a primitive structure with a dazzling veneer of subtlety. At no point were the Egyptians prepared to adopt illusionist art: they were absolutely committed to the frontal image-based rendering of characteristics. But within this limitation they employed a number of elegant clarifying devices. One was size: size stood for power, authority and importance, so artists drew attention to the pharaoh by size, and to the actual occupant of the tomb, as opposed to relatives and mourners. A chief wife was not shown smaller than her husband, but in the natural human ratios laid down by the canon: lesser wives could be smaller, and servants smaller still. Relative sizes were also dictated by rank in battle scenes. Gods, however, were no bigger than important human beings, since, in strict theology, the latter could become 'like unto gods'; the key dividing line, as with artists' attitudes to movement, seems to have been drawn on an occupational basis—a man or women was diminished by being condemned to manual labour. These gradations of size were not arbitrary; the dimensions of the subordinate figures in a composition depended on the main figures, being inscribed in grids of simple fractions of the scales used for the master-figures. Hence, even in the great court and battle scenes of the Eighteenth Dynasty and Ramesside periods, covering enormous areas and combining multiple incidents, there was a carefully worked out inner harmony of scale. . . .

There is no doubt that Egyptian artists could have used perspective in portraying landscape. They certainly possessed the technical skill to do so. But it was unacceptable to their search for the timeless archetype of things, their compulsion to break down a picture into its component parts and present each of them as it is in known reality, ideally, always, everywhere and for everybody.

Chapter 4

The Decline of the Egyptian Empire

Turning Points

IN WORLD HISTORY

The Heretic Pharaoh

Elizabeth Riefstahl

Toward the end of the Eighteenth Dynasty, Pharaoh Amenhotep IV converted to a new monotheistic religion, which centered around the god Aten. The pharaoh changed his name to Akhenaton, moved the royal capital from Thebes to the desert city of Akhetaton, and attempted to eradicate the ancient polytheistic religion of Egypt. In the following excerpt from her book *Thebes in the Time of Amunhotep III*, Elizabeth Riefstahl describes Akhenaton's unusual reign and the disastrous effects it had on the Egyptian Empire. According to Riefstahl, Akhenaton destabilized Egyptian society by persecuting the priests of the old gods and isolating himself from the Egyptian people. Moreover, Akhenaton's single-minded focus on instituting his new religion caused him to ignore foreign threats to the empire, she maintains. For many years an associate curator at the Brooklyn Museum, Riefstahl is the author of several books on Egyptian art.

In the thirty-seventh or thirty-eighth year of his reign, Amunhotep III died and was buried with suitable pomp in his unfinished tomb in the Valley of the Kings. Though he was hardly in his mid-fifties, modern historians are unanimous in referring to him as an old man; and there seems little doubt that he was prematurely aged, perhaps even senile, as the result of excess and sickness. He was succeeded by the son of his Great Wife Tiy, who came to the throne as Amunhotep IV but is better known to history as Akhenaten.

The new King was not a prepossessing figure. Sculptured likenesses from a Theban shrine which he erected in the second year of his reign show him with brutal realism as grossly

From *Thebes in the Time of Amunhotep III*, by Elizabeth Riefstahl. Copyright © 1964 by the University of Oklahoma Press. Reprinted by permission of the University of Oklahoma Press.

emasculate, with the swelling hips and belly and breasts of a woman, but with sunken chest, skinny neck, and spindly shanks. In the far from pleasant features of his narrow face— coarse nose and lips, almost mongoloid eyes, and long, stubborn chin—sensuality and fanaticism seem to struggle for dominance. These representations and later portrayals in similar style have been cited as examples of Akhenaten's passion for truth. They seem rather to indicate a total lack of self-irony.

Akhenaten has come down in history as the first monotheist. He is today widely known for his vain attempt to clear Egyptian religion of the debris of ages and to substitute one god, the Aten, the visible disk of the sun, for the vast pantheon. He has become a legendary figure, shrouded in half-truths and myth. In scholarly circles an endless and often bitter controversy is waged over the interpretation of the meager records of his reign. Arguments wax hot about whether or not the young King shared the throne of his father as co-regent during the latter's declining years. Historians indulge in widely divergent speculations concerning the tangled relationships of the royal family. They offer the most disparate estimates of the motives and character of the unfortunate ruler who was mentioned in later Egyptian records (when at all) only as "that enemy from Akhetaten."

Akhenaten's Reign

The main facts concerning the King and his career can be briefly stated. He was crowned Amunhotep IV, but by the sixth year of his reign (or toward the end of his co-regency with his father), he had changed his name from Amunhotep, "Amun Is Pleased," to Akhenaten, "Serviceable-to-the-Aten." In the same year, he journeyed down the Nile and marked out on the site now known as Amarna the city of Akhetaten, "Horizon of the Aten," which he destined for his capital. Since the region was wasteland, he claimed that it had belonged to his god from the beginning of time and set up boundary stelae to mark its limits. On these stelae, he vowed never to exceed the limits thus set: "May he [the King] sojourn here," later prayed one of his followers, "until the swan turns black and the crow white, until the hills arise to depart and the water flows upstream." By his eighth year, the King and his court were settled in the new capital, where he erected new stelae reaffirming his oath.

He was already married to Nefertiti, the beautiful. Her antecedents are unknown. Among the many guesses concerning her origin, one of the most plausible is that she was Akhenaten's cousin, the daughter of Ay, who was possibly a brother of Queen Tiy and certainly a power behind the throne during the reign of Akhenaten and his successors. He himself ruled briefly as the last king of the Eighteenth Dynasty. Nefertiti bore six daughters, one of whom died young and two of whom were married to Akhenaten's immediate successors, Smenkhkare and Tutankhamun, putative sons of Amunhotep III, although if the latter was related to him at all, he was more likely (unless an extraordinarily elastic chronology is employed) to have been his grandson. While the beautiful Nefertiti was accorded more prominence in pictorial and written records than any of her predecessors, including Queen Tiy, she apparently fell from favor in Akhenaten's twelfth year of rule, and was relegated to the palace that had been built for her in the northern suburb of Amarna, which offers some evidence of her sojourn, none of her ultimate fate.

Her place in Akhenaten's affection, together with many of her epithets, seems to have been usurped by her son-in-law Smenkhkare, who disappeared from history in the third year of his reign, during part or all of which he may have acted as co-regent. Akhenaten died after seventeen years on the throne. The manner of his death and his place of burial are unknown, though speculation is rife over remains hastily interred with remnants of royal trappings in Tomb Fifty-five of the Valley of the Kings. . . .

Akhenaten did not succeed in establishing his god without a struggle. While he had erected shrines to the Aten in Thebes during the early years of his rule, the worship of the old gods still continued. But after his removal to the new capital, he sent his cohorts far and wide in an attempt to eradicate all traces of the ancient faith. Although they ranged from Memphis far into Nubia, their venom was vented chiefly on

Thebes and Amun. Temples were closed, their cult images destroyed, their wealth diverted to the new capital and the new god. The King's bullies swarmed through the Theban necropolis, entering rich tombs (and perhaps looting them en route) to hack out all reference to the old deities. Private names—even royal names—compounded with that of Amun were systematically obliterated. The City must have experienced great terror, but there is no evidence that Akhenaten's rabble met with any resistance. The faithful adherents of the old religion must simply have gone underground. That there were such among the priestly and official families seems clear from the alacrity with which the ancient worship was reinstated after Akhenaten had disappeared from the scene. As for the populace, they were apparently little moved by the storm that raged above them. In Amarna itself, the necropolis workers still cherished their amulets of the good Bes and Tauret, of the protecting Eye of Horus.

In view of the piety and stubborn conservatism of the Egyptians, it is to be wondered that Akhenaten's revolution could succeed even temporarily. There is evidence that he may have had the support of certain elements of the army, which seized their chance of gaining control of the government; it may well be that his iconoclasts were recruited from the horde of soldiers and foreign conscripts left idle during long years of peace. Probably an ingrained reverence for the divinely ordained kingship aided in holding revolt in check. It may also be, as has been suggested, that a natural portent—famine, pestilence, or earthquake—frightened Egyptians into a suspicion that the old gods had deserted them and into a desperate acquiescence to the will of the King. Any or all of these factors may have been involved. All that can be said with certainty is that Akhenaten managed to remain on the throne for seventeen years.

Years of Disintegration

They seem to have been years of administrative disintegration and economic distress. One can well imagine that the collapse of the traditional religion left impoverished great numbers of persons who had been dependent on the temples. While the peasants continued to work the fields of the former gods for the profit of the King and the Aten, and large numbers of artists, craftsmen, and laborers found employment at Amarna and in the construction of shrines to the Disk erected by Akhenaten elsewhere in Egypt, the vast personnel formerly employed directly or indirectly in temple service could hardly have been absorbed.

We know of the state of Egypt during the religious revolution only from sparse and hardly disinterested records of the counterrevolution, but contemporary archaeological evidence seems to indicate that all may not have been well with the land. The remains of Akhetaten give the impression that it was an embattled city, a luxurious concentration camp. Along the encircling cliffs that formed its natural fortifications can still be seen the track worn by the weary feet of sentries who guarded the King and his followers. Below, at the edge of the desert plain, a long line of barracks for foot soldiers and chariotry protected the city still further, and one can well believe that boats patrolled the river to defend any approach to the capital from the west. While Akhenaten's vow never to pass the limits set by his boundary stelae may have been simply a legal phrase used to define property rights, there is no hint that he ever left his capital once he had taken up residence there.

He seems to have lived in complete isolation from reality. The encroachments of the Hittites into northern Syria and the frantic pleas of Egypt's Asiatic allies apparently left him unmoved. The eastern empire gradually slipped away; by the time of his death, the hard-won control of the pharaonic armies did not extend beyond southern Palestine. Some scholars have regarded Akhenaten's attitude toward Asia as evidence of a convinced pacifism. It was probably the result of inertia—and of troubles nearer at hand. It was no mean task he had set himself, that of eradicating in a lifetime a tradition reaching back into a past beyond memory.

At this distance, the real character of Akhenaten defies analysis. One school of contemporary thought sees in him the inspired prophet of the One God, a god of all-embracing love and universal peace. In certain liberal churches his story is told with reverence, almost as if he were a forerunner of Christ. Another school regards him with some disgust as a degenerate, at best as an ineffectual weakling. The truth probably lies between the two extremes.

The representations of the King certainly suggest a physical degeneracy of the sort that is frequently accompanied by a brilliant, if unstable, mind. There is small doubt that Akhenaten had vision. The monotheistic religion he sought to impose on Egypt had, in contrast with the involuted traditional faith, the grandeur of simplicity. He had vision and, as Egyptologist Sir Alan Gardiner has said, he had courage. But his vision was limited and his courage was the blind daring of fanaticism. The Aten, with its rays ending in blessing hands, was quasi-anthropomorphic (for it is given to few to conceive deity save in their own likeness), but it was, nevertheless, remote and impersonal, more distant from mankind than the very human old gods had been. There was still no question of popular participation in the cult. The King was sole mediator between God and man. He was the son of the Aten, as his ancestors had been sons of Amun-Re. Even more: while his father had set himself up as a god, Akhenaten went a step farther—he was the One God. He and his family alone were pictured as receiving the gift of life from the Aten, and his followers prayed to him and the Disk in the same breath. The King offered the god the symbolic figure of Maat. That figure was the same old Maat, not factual truth, but divine order; only the order was now of the King's own devising, not that handed down through the long line of royal ancestors. One of Akhenaten's great errors in judgment lay, as Egyptologist T. Eric Peet long ago remarked, in thinking he could balance two decades of monotheism against two thousand years of tradition.

An Unattractive Religion

Some such balance might possibly have been attained had the new religion proffered anything that was really new, but it destroyed without building. As it offered the people no participation in its mysteries, so it offered no spiritual guidance, no rule of conduct. Above all, it offered small comfort.

While tombs were built during the Amarna period, bodies mummified and laid to rest with appropriate and, to some extent, traditional ceremonies, Osiris, both as judge and sav-

The Rising Tide

A former librarian, freelance writer Joyce Milton has written extensively on historical subjects. In the following paragraphs, Milton presents archeological evidence showing that Akhenaton's counselors repeatedly warned him of the threat posed by outside forces.

After effacing the name of Amon from his temples, Akhenaten ordered the abandonment of Thebes and founded an entirely new capital, Akhetaten, or "Horizon-of-Aten." The city, more often known by its modern name of Tell-el-Amarna, was situated on a rather unpropitious strip of land on the east bank of the Nile halfway between Memphis and Thebes. . . .

He insisted upon his own privileged status as a god—the only deity other than the one Aten—and tried to return his kingdom to the days when the pharaoh was the sole link between his people and the spiritual world. But a god must be surrounded by at least an aura of success, and Akhenaten was not. By the end of his brief seventeen-year reign, Egypt was, as contemporary inscriptions were to say, topsy-turvy.

Even while Akhenaten remained in his new capital pursuing his experiment in a new order, the rest of his kingdom was in ferment. Egypt's foreign situation had been deteriorating since the reign of his father. A cache of clay tablets inscribed with diplomatic correspondence, discovered during excavations in a field near Tell-el-Amarna, is full of missives from distraught client priests. They warned Akhenaten of the rising power of the Hittite Empire and of the threat posed in Palestine by marauding tribes known as the Habiru—a name that tantalizes scholars because of its similarity to "Hebrew." Whether Akhenaten could have done anything to stem this rising tide is debatable, but his influential subjects, many of whom had refused to follow him to his new capital, must have longed for some decisive action.

Joyce Milton, *Sunrise of Power: Ancient Egypt, Alexander, and the World of Hellenism*, 1980.

ior, recedes into shadow along with the other gods. Though
he seems not to have met with the vindictive official hatred
accorded to Amun, for the most part he suffered the obloquy
of silence. It is true that the dead were sometimes promised
eternal existence by favor of the King, sleeping the sleep of
death by night in their tombs but awakened each morning to
breathe in the life offered them by the vivifying rays of the
Aten. Those favored men who were granted burial in the
rock-tombs of Amarna might go forth by day to serve the
Disk in his temple, to haunt, unseen, the fair villas and gardens they had made in Akhetaten, until sunset recalled them
to their eternal homes. But there was now only one road to
bliss; it was closed to all save the followers of the Aten, and
the only righteousness and its chief reward seemed to lie in
perpetual adoration of the God-King. . . .

The new religion brought with it no administrative reforms, no alleviation of the condition of the masses. On the
contrary, if one can judge from scant documents of the following periods, it resulted in the breakdown of the machin-
ery of government and general hard times. The King was as
aloof from common life as any of his predecessors had been.
While sculptures and reliefs portrayed his physical idiosyn-
crasies and the domesticity of the royal family with frank-
ness and shockingly bad taste, no one dared to presume on
the intimacy thus invited. Courtiers bowed lower than ever
before, and commoners still kissed the dust before a sovereign who seemed to have small doubt that he and his god
were one. The extravagance of the court was no less than it
had been in the past, and its luxury was still maintained at
the expense of the populace.

It became increasingly a court of dark intrigue, permeated by a miasma of decay. The general malaise is evident
in the art of Amarna. Like the new religion, the art sought
freedom from the binding conventional forms of the past.
It is full of sunshine and flowers, of genre scenes executed
with liveliness and frequently with humor; but for all its
febrile charm, much of it breathes decadence in every line.
One suspects some artists of working tongue in cheek.
From the rubbish of Amarna come little sculptured groups

of affectionate monkey families, unmistakable caricatures of the royal ménage. . . .

Akhenaten's Successors

The disappearance of Akhenaten from the scene did not mean, as has sometimes been stated, the immediate release of the vengeance of the followers of Amun and the summary destruction of the city of the Aten. Akhenaten's successor, Smenkhkare, if he ruled at all in his own right, may have made his peace with Thebes, but apparently the next king, Tutankhamun (born Tutankhaten), abandoned the new capital only in the fifth year of his brief reign. Even then, houses and palaces were left standing: villas were carefully locked as if their owners expected to be absent only briefly. The temple of the Aten was not, as is frequently stated, completely razed under Horemheb, who demolished the great temple which Akhenaten had built to the Disk at Karnak. The city of Akhetaten only gradually became anathema, shunned and feared by all; and Ramesses II did not hesitate to quarry from its sanctuary stones that pictured the heretic and his god, to use them as fill in the foundations and pylons of the temple he built to Amun at Hermopolis, a short distance across the river from the accursed site.

Tutankhamun might well have been forgotten by history, but as a result of the discovery of his Theban tomb, with its dazzling royal equipment all but intact, he is perhaps better known today than any other ancient ruler; his name seems likely, as he would have wished, to "live forever." He was a mere child when he came to the throne, only about eighteen when he died, and his reign was brief, lasting not more than ten years. It seems significant of the very gradual rise of resentment against the Amarna heresy and the family that promulgated it that Tutankhamun was permitted to ascend the throne at all. Even more, he ruled under the tutelage of Ay, the putative uncle of Akhenaten, who had been a pillar of the heretical faith, and it was the aged Ay who (as has previously been noted) briefly succeeded the boy king as ruler of the Two Lands.

Both Ay and his ward had recanted; they emphasized their

orthodoxy in every pictured scene, every text of their reigns. On a stela which Tutankhamun erected at Karnak and which Horemheb later usurped, he records that he expelled deceit from the Two Lands and re-established Maat "as in its first time." He adds that he had found the temples desolate and overgrown with vegetation; "their halls were a footpath." The gods had fled and turned a deaf ear to the entreaties of suppliants. All this the young King changed. He rebuilt and refurbished the temples, replaced the vanished cult images with statues of "fine gold from the highlands," re-established the priesthood, carefully choosing men "from among the notables of their towns" for the divine service. He doubled, tripled, and quadrupled, so he claimed, the treasure of the temples, especially searching his heart for acts of devotion to Amun. In his piety and bounty he "went beyond what had been done since the time of the ancestors."

His apostasy was of no avail. Future generations sent Tutankhamun and his co-regent and successor, Ay, into limbo along with the heretic Akhenaten. The Eighteenth Dynasty ends with the name of Amunhotep III. There, too, ends the history of Thebes as a capital. Though it was nominally the seat of the first rulers of the Nineteenth Dynasty, their activities were centered chiefly in Lower Egypt, and it was in the Delta that Ramesses II, the third king of the dynasty, established his "fair throne, after the pattern of Thebes."

Akhenaten and his sole god were as if they had never been. But though Thebes became richer than ever before, The City and Egypt as a whole never recovered from the shock of the reformation. Thebes was no longer a world center, the capital of an Empire, and Egypt never fully regained her supremacy in the ancient world.

The Last Moment of Greatness

Torgny Säve-Söderbergh

An esteemed Egyptologist, Torgny Säve-Söderbergh was a professor and field archeologist at Uppsala University in Sweden. He was also one of the leading participants in the international campaign to relocate the ancient Nubian monuments that were threatened by the construction of the Aswan High Dam during the 1960s and 1970s. In the following passage from his *Pharaohs and Mortals*, Säve-Söderbergh describes the reign of Ramses III, whom he characterizes as Egypt's last great pharaoh. Ramses saved Egypt from being devastated by warlike barbarian tribes, he writes, and ushered in a new era of peace and prosperity. However, the author notes, Ramses was unable to fully restore the Egyptian Empire to greatness before he was tragically murdered.

In the 1200s before Christ the catastrophe came. For some reason barbarian tribes in the Danube region began to rouse themselves. Some moved down in plundering bands toward Greece, where the Mycenaean culture flourished. City after city, town after town fell to the invaders; but the chief city, the storied Mycenae, managed to hold out. The folk wave moved on over Crete and southwestern Asia Minor and then to the North African coast, where the tribes combined with the Libyans to attack Egypt. The invasion was thrown back, but this was only the first warning.

Another tribe, the Phrygians, rolled in over Asia Minor from the Danube region. The Hittite kingdom, which had not long before been one of the strongest military powers in the Middle East, was shattered and annihilated. After about 1200 B.C. historical sources are silent about this realm.

From *Pharaohs and Mortals*, by Torgny Säve-Söderbergh, translated by Richard E. Oldenburg (Indianapolis: Bobbs-Merrill, 1958). Copyright © P.A. Norstedt & Söners Förlag, 1958). Reprinted by permission of the Estate of Torgny Säve-Söderbergh.

The pressure of the ravaging migrations only increased. Tribes from Greece in the west and Asia Minor in the north gathered in northern Syria for the final assault upon the richest and most tempting region in the eastern Mediterranean world, the fertile Nile Delta of Egypt. . . .

Crushing Egypt's Enemies

There is no doubt that danger was imminent. What had quickly to be done was to collect the land's scattered forces and carry out an effective preparedness program. Hundreds of thousands, both Egyptians and foreign mercenaries, were enrolled in the infantry and the chariot forces, Ramses III tells us.

This was at the last minute. Now the assaults came, one after another, first from Libya to the northwest. To pacify this region, Ramses had tried to put in a Libyan prince raised in Egypt as king of Libya. The attempt failed, and the Libyan tribes, in one combined force, broke into the Delta in northern Egypt. But before they had time to reach the heart of the land, Ramses managed to inflict a stinging defeat, and they were forced to retreat.

In the meantime, up in the northeastern corner of the Mediterranean, where the coasts of Asia Minor and Syria meet, the threat was growing.

"The foreign nations," we are told, "had conspired together on their islands. All lands were annihilated and crushed [by them]. No land could hold out against their weapons, neither the Hittite land, Kode, Carcemish, Cilicia, nor Cyprus. All were annihilated. They made camp in one place in the land of the Amorites and plundered its people, and the land looked as though it had never existed. And now they neared Egypt."

These were the so-called "peoples of the sea"—the Peleset (which is to say the Philistines), the Thekel, the Danai, and others who had formed a terrifying coalition. One group moved by oxcart, like a swarm of lemmings, along the coast through Syria and Palestine. Another group steered their slender sailing ships toward the mouths of the Nile. The time was long past when the Egyptian fleet controlled the ocean, and there was no possibility of countering the enemy sea power along the way. But Ramses III made a virtue of necessity and permitted them to enter the narrow Nile channels unopposed. There the trap was sprung, like a birdcatcher permitting a flock of ducks to settle on his net only to close it about them at the right moment.

The ships of the sea people, under full sail, had barely veered into the Nile when they were showered with well-aimed arrows and spears from the Egyptian infantry drawn up along the shores. Before the enemy had time to recover, Egyptian river boats swarmed around the fleet. The sea peoples' ships had no oars, and they were speedily outmaneuvered by the more easily guided, rowed vessels of the Egyptians. The Egyptians boarded the enemy ships, seized the ropes of their sails, and forced them to capsize. The catastrophe for the enemy was total. . . .

The sea peoples' assault by land also failed, and they were forced to retreat north. The Peleset, the Philistines, settled in Palestine. Their allies, the Danai, we find later in southern Turkey, near the Syrian border; the others met unknown fates.

The triumph was complete. At the last moment Ramses had succeeded in saving Egypt from the terrible fate which had befallen all the other lands, large and small, in the western part of the Near East. There the old states had been splintered as though by an atom bomb, and nameless suffering was the people's lot in this witches' brew of migrating tribes.

Egypt was saved, but still no rest was possible. A new ruler in Libya, named Kaper, had once again united all the Libyan tribes for an attack on Egypt. Under the leadership of Kaper's son Mesher the Libyan forces had soon advanced deep into the land. But once more Ramses succeeded in winning a glowing victory. Among the numerous prisoners was also the Libyan prince and army chief, Mesher. His aged father pleaded for his son's life. But in vain. The son was killed, and the father dragged off into slavery.

The Libyans in general were too valuable as warriors simply to be slaughtered in honor of Amon, the god of their realm. They were put in prison camps, where "they may hear the speech of people in the retinue of the king," as the

Egyptians put it, "and he saw to it that their own language disappeared and that they forgot their own tongue." After this re-education they were enrolled in the Egyptian army.

A Golden Age?

Now began a golden age in Egyptian history. The tax system was reorganized, and riches in never-ending supply flowed into the state treasury. In all directions expeditions were sent out to procure precious raw materials—gold from the south, copper from the Sinai, incense and myrrh from Somaliland. Enormous temples were built to the gods, these gods who had been so badly treated but who had given Ramses glowing victories and rescued the land in its hour of danger. The temples, filled with gold and silver, precious stones, and mounds of grain and other foods, were decorated with brightly painted reliefs, not a few of them pictures of the king's shining exploits in war. . . .

Not only the king and the gods enjoyed the fruits of the victories and the work of reconstruction. At least, not if we may believe Ramses III: "Throughout the whole land, I planted trees and greenery and let the people sit in their shade. I made it so that a woman in Egypt might go wherever she willed without anyone accosting her on the way." Both Egyptian soldiers and foreign mercenaries could stretch out on their backs, since there were no longer any enemies to fight, neither in Nubia nor in Syria. "Their bows and weapons lay in the storehouses, and they were sated and full of happiness with their wives and children, who were with them. I supported all in the land, both foreigners and Egyptians, both men and women.". . .

It sounds almost too good to be true. If we look at the monuments which have been preserved, at the handsome buildings, the riches in the hands of the state and the priesthood, it seems like a Utopia. This state splendor and the flowery phrases of the official texts were meant to bear witness to posterity of Ramses III's fortunate reign. If pure chance had not preserved for us some insignificant papyri and inscribed pottery fragments, we should almost have taken him at his word. But when we read these everyday documents, the picture becomes quite different—a fascinating contrast to the glossy exterior.

In Thebes a rather large group of families specialized in the pious work of digging and painting handsomely the royal tombs in the Valley of the Kings in the desert mountains west of Thebes. Their small city, Deir el Medineh, as it is now called, has been closely studied by archeologists, who have found a large number of texts and other materials which give us an insight into the life and times of these workers. . . .

Among these things we find the earliest testimony regarding strikes by workers.

It begins with an inscription on a little pottery fragment, which tells us that on the twenty-first day in the second month of the twenty-ninth year of Ramses III's reign, the clerk Amennacht said to the workers: "Now twenty days of the month have passed, and we have still not received our rations." So he went to a temple in the vicinity and there managed to obtain a portion of their pay. This first time it seems to have been possible to pacify the workers by borrowing from temple stores in the region. Properly, it was the state treasury and not the temples which should have paid the workers.

But then come more difficulties, so severe that Amennacht thought it best to keep a record of them, which has been preserved. On the twenty-ninth day of the seventh month the workers in the Valley of the Kings stop their work and make their way past the five guard walls at the entrance to the valley. The work on the royal grave was watched over carefully, and guards were necessary to protect the unbelievable riches which had been placed in the graves of earlier kings.

The workers march down to the large temples in the Nile Valley and institute a sit-down strike. One night is passed in great disorder in Ramses II's temple, the Ramesseum, and neither fair means nor foul can get them back to work.

"We are hungry," they shout. "Hunger and thirst have driven us here. We have no clothes, no oil, no fish, no vegetables! Send a message to Pharaoh, our master, or the vizier, our chief, so that we may receive something to survive on!"

Only after several days of disturbances are the rations for the previous month paid out to them, and the workers content themselves with this—for a while. Next month is just as bad, and the month following the vizier himself has to appear before them to calm them. Not even he can pay them in full, but by his authority he manages to make them accept half their pay. The administrative apparatus no longer functions as it should. The vizier tells them frankly, but also indignantly: "Have I not given you as much as all the other viziers? And if it should now happen that nothing is left in the grain supply, I have given you what I could find [from other sources]."

It was apparently common for the workers in the necropolis, who still were among the most privileged workers in the land, to have to wait long, and often in vain, for their pay. Even the vizier himself, like his subordinates, had to go out and borrow in order to make the salary payments. . . .

In such circumstances it is no wonder that Ramses III had to begin looking after his own house. Around his luxurious temple in Thebes and the adjoining palace he built a strong fortified wall, with battlements and towers, to safeguard the temple treasures from disorderly elements. A large fortification in the very heart of the land—a defense against the land's own people—made a striking image of the beginning dissolution.

Intrigue in the Palace

If we look more closely at this structure, we find other features which indicate that Ramses III's life, despite the outward splendor and the handsome phrases, was not a bed of roses. In the largest gate tower in the fortification wall we find pictures of the king surrounded by a crowd of charming harem women. And in his palace within the temple walls lies a series of rooms for the harem women, just in back of the king's grand audience chamber. These harem rooms are all exactly like one another, as though Ramses had wanted not to show his particular favor to any of his consorts, to avoid all nagging and envy among the wives. . . .

More was at stake here than simply keeping peace among the wives. It was a question of who among all the sons of his wives should be the successor to the throne. This would be that prince whose mother had been designated as the favorite, "The great royal consort." This was a vital affair of state, not a question of peace in the family.

For as long as possible Ramses postponed this choice, as though he foresaw its consequences. But not even the divine Pharaoh could hope to live forever here on earth. Finally he had to decide, but when he did, frightful turmoil was the result. In the tangle of intrigues and counterintrigues, Ramses III himself was murdered, and as victor among the candidates stood his successor on the throne, Ramses IV.

We have good reason to believe that he was not the one whom Ramses III had chosen as crown prince; the later kings regarded Ramses IV as a usurper without legitimate right to the throne. Ramses IV did what he could to cleanse himself and to justify his role in the terrible blood bath among his opponents. Among other things, he issued an account of their trial which has been preserved down to our own day. . . .

Among those most seriously charged is Prince Pentawer, probably the one whom Ramses III had chosen as crown prince. He is accused of having placed himself on his mother's side when she, together with other harem women, conspired and tried to stir up the people against their lord. "They found him guilty; they left him where he was; he took his own life," the record tells us.

A number of higher officials, among them an officer and a police captain, are accused of having been in collusion with some women who had sneaked away from the harem, and even of having a beer party with the women, instead of reporting them. Their terrible punishment was to have their noses and ears cut off. One of them committed suicide after undergoing this torture.

Numerous officials and others fell victims to the stern judgments. The normal punishment was death. That this was more than the usual harem intrigue common in the Orient is obvious. Not only harem officials were involved, but also representatives of the police power and of the troops in Egypt and in the rich Nubian province to the south. Civil war threatened until Ramses IV managed to usurp power before the other side had time to strike.

Egypt seems never to have recovered from this internal crisis, of which the worker strikes and the harem conspiracy were symptomatic. After the death of Ramses III the realm begins its decline. The royal power becomes a plaything in the hands of the various political groups—the priesthood, foreign mercenaries, and Nubian provincial officials. The economic situation deteriorates, food prices rise, and the administration of justice declines more and more. The police power can no longer even protect the honored graves of past kings from plunder by conscienceless individuals, in collusion with the authorities in charge. Culturally and politically Egypt has played out its role as the leading great power in the Near East, and soon foreign rulers succeed each other on the Pharaohs' throne—Libyans, Ethiopians, Assyrians, and Persians.

Ramses III, the man who saved the land in its fateful hour, who granted it one final flowering, and who finally fell prey to the intrigues of his own family, proved to be the last great Pharaoh.

Centuries of Decline

Lionel Casson and the Editors of Time-Life Books

Lionel Casson is a professor emeritus of classics at New York University and an authority on life in ancient civilizations. In the following selection, Casson recounts the turmoil that Egypt experienced as its empire disintegrated over a period of several centuries. During this era, he explains, Egypt's political situation changed constantly: Sometimes the nation was ruled by foreign leaders, while at other times it split apart into its ancient divisions of Upper and Lower Egypt. Although the Egyptians of this time did enjoy some brief periods of renewed strength and tranquility, he relates, never again did the nation hold sway as an important world power.

For 2,000 years and more, the Egyptians had met and surmounted the crises of war, drought and famine. The civilization they had built seemed impervious to the assaults of time. But during the 20th Dynasty, a combination of factors—loss of empire, steady shrinkage of the pharaoh's prestige, and the impact of the Iron Age—signaled danger. The impressive achievements of 20 centuries of civilization were too solid to crumble under these blows, but an irrevocable process of decline had begun.

Chaos and Conquest

After 1100 B.C., Egypt's role as a great political power approached its end. Racked by internal dissension, the nation broke apart at its traditional geographic seam, and weak successors of the mighty pharaohs took over a land that henceforth would be frequently divided. At first merchant princes from Tanis ruled Lower Egypt, while high

From *Great Ages of Man: Ancient Egypt*, by Lionel Casson and The Editors of Time-Life Books. Copyright © 1965 Time-Life Books Inc. Reprinted by permission of Time-Life Books Inc.

priests of Amon succeeded the last of the Ramesside kings and held sway over Upper Egypt. The nation now entered upon a chaotic period. Although it would enjoy occasional eras of prosperity and unity, never again would it be a world power.

The bounty of the Nile, which had assured Egypt its wealth, had always aroused the envy of less fortunate neighbors. So long as the nation retained sufficient power to guard its frontiers it had little to fear from these covetous enemies. But in the process of taking these precautions, Egypt laid itself open to internal overthrow. For long years it had assigned much of the task of manning the desert bulwarks to foreign soldiers. Many of these mercenaries were Libyans who were paid in land grants on which they settled with their families. Profiting from a period of divided rule, the Libyans increased their power in Lower Egypt until they rivaled in power the priests in Thebes and the court in Tanis.

Around 950 B.C. one of these Libyans, named Sheshonk, seized control over both Upper and Lower Egypt. The change was made with a minimum of confusion or resistance. Sheshonk could hardly be called a foreigner, for he came of a family of high priests that had lived in Herakleopolis for many generations. At the outset, Sheshonk's regime seemed promising. With considerable energy, the 22nd Dynasty set about restoring Egyptian prestige. Sheshonk embarked on a foreign policy of conquest. He invaded Palestine, which under King David had become a power to be reckoned with. Taking advantage of the civil war that followed the death of David's son Solomon, Sheshonk raided a number of Palestinian cities and about 930 B.C. plundered the Temple of Solomon in Jerusalem. At home the economy prospered.

But under Sheshonk's son, rivalry between the powerful priests at Thebes and the court began to undermine the Libyan Dynasty. By 730 B.C., civil wars were occurring regularly and local princes were asserting their autonomy. Egypt, splintered and helpless, was an inviting target for invasion.

Once again, when interlopers came they were scarcely

strangers to Egypt. Indeed, the Nubians from below the Fourth Cataract who now took over the country were in a sense as Egyptian as the Egyptians themselves.

Upper Nubia had been within the pharaohs' orbit since the time of the New Kingdom, and its culture had become largely Egyptian. Following the last, hapless days of the New Kingdom, Nubia broke away and became independent. A few centuries later it mustered the strength to conquer its former overlord: about 730 B.C., Nubians stormed across the border to dominate most of Egypt. The Nubians, orthodox in their religious observance, brought with them the puritan atmosphere of an older Egypt, the source of their religion, and the strict, theocratic ways of Napata, their small-town capital on the Fourth Cataract. To Nubian eyes, the Egypt they now encountered must have appeared worldly, lax and impious.

Nubian control, concentrated in the area of Thebes, lasted only 70 years. Almost from the time the newcomers took over, they found themselves threatened by bloodthirsty conquerors from the east. Egypt had long been invulnerable to attacks by envious neighbors. For centuries its rich copper mines had guaranteed a supply of the vital war material that gave an era its name: the Bronze Age. When iron weapons came into wide use in the middle of the 12th Century B.C., bronze armaments became obsolete. Lacking iron ore, the Egyptians could now be challenged by other powers which had equal access to this metal, which was unmatched for the fashioning of arms.

Of all Egypt's iron-armed neighbors the Assyrians were perhaps the fiercest warriors. In 663 B.C. they finished off 80 years of intermittent warfare with an overwhelming invasion. There was not much doubt about the issue. As the Assyrians had once warned the Israelites (at a time when the latter were looking to Egypt for military support): "Lo, thou trustest in the staff of this broken reed." The Assyrians, coming down "like the wolf on the fold," stormed all the way to Thebes to end the rule of the Nubians, who withdrew to their own land and in time abandoned Egyptian ways.

A Brief Egyptian Resurgence

The Assyrians enjoyed their triumph only briefly. Within a short time a wily Egyptian prince, brilliant, lucky and shrewd, had tricked the conquerors into departing. His name was Psammetichus, and he managed to convince the Assyrians that they could more profitably rule Egypt through a native nobleman than by instituting military government. The nobleman he had in mind was, of course, himself. Once the Assyrians had withdrawn their troops, they were out of Egypt for good. They became occupied with other matters; meanwhile Psammetichus established a remarkable dynasty, the 26th, with his birthplace as its capital, and Egypt entered a period of relative tranquillity and prosperity.

The secret of Psammetichus' domestic success lay in his talents in the marketplace. In the manner of a modern chamber of commerce, he invited Syrians, Jews, Ionian Greeks and other profit-minded peoples to settle down in Egypt and develop the nation's trade. Egypt became a leading exporter of grain. For centuries thereafter, the crops grown along the Nile were to be a vital element in feeding the Mediterranean area. Political control of this granary became the key to world dominance, and as a consequence a series of powerful nations henceforward would strive to exercise authority over Egypt.

When Psammetichus died after a reign of 54 years, he was succeeded by his son Necho II, who was as shrewd as his father. Hoping to enhance Egypt's role as middleman in the trade between the Mediterranean and the distant east, he began to dig a canal from the Red Sea to the Nile to provide an all-water route for this profitable traffic. Forced to abandon the project because the techniques available to him were not equal to the brilliance of his plan, he cast about for an alternative and conceived the idea of circumnavigating Africa. He equipped an expedition, manned it with Phoenician sailors and sent it off to explore the feasibility of the route. The voyage was successful, but the time it took—three years—could not have been very encouraging; the world had to wait until the 15th Century A.D. for Vasco da Gama to open up an all-sea route to Middle Eastern waters.

The use of Phoenician sailors was typical of the 26th

Dynasty's reliance on foreigners for many important jobs: Phoenicians did Egypt's exploring; Greeks and Syrians conducted overseas business; Israelites built a thriving colony at the frontier on the First Cataract; and Greek mercenaries served Egypt in Nubia (among other things, they carved a record of their exploits on one of Ramses' colossal statues, a custom followed by military expeditions since time immemorial).

The 26th Dynasty gave Egypt an Indian summer of independent rule that lasted almost a century and a half. It was brought to an end by a new invasion. In 525 B.C. the Persians overran Egypt and incorporated it into their growing empire. They maintained their dominance (except for brief periods when the Egyptians gained temporary freedom) for two centuries. And then the Persians were themselves humbled by that most spectacular of conquerors, Alexander the Great.

The Greek Rulers of Egypt

Desmond Stewart

Alexander the Great, a Macedonian Greek, conquered Egypt in 332 B.C. After Alexander's death, one of his soldiers—known as Ptolemaeus or Ptolemy—founded a dynasty in Egypt that endured for three centuries. The Greek Ptolemies ruled as pharaohs, wearing the ancient Egyptian crown and adopting many aspects of royal Egyptian life. However, the Ptolemies also introduced elements of Greek culture and scholarship into Egyptian society, which most Egyptians resented. In the following excerpt from his book *The Pyramids and the Sphinx*, Desmond Stewart traces the reign of the Ptolemies from the beginning of the dynasty to the demise of the last ruler, Cleopatra VII. The author of numerous books and articles, Stewart lived in Egypt for many years, where he was the Middle East correspondent for the *Spectator*, a British magazine of news and current events.

In its long and mortal disease, Egypt learned too late that foreign mercenaries represent a short-term tonic and a long-term poison. Once hirelings find their way into the barracks and then the palace, it is but a step to their taking over. What imperial Rome later experienced from German praetorians [bodyguards], or medieval Islam from its Turkish Mamelukes, Egypt experienced from the Greeks.

The Greek View of Egypt

Since early in their history Greeks had been finding their way to Egypt. The seafarers of Crete and Mycenaean Greece knew that to the south, across dark, glittering waves, lay an immeasurably rich and ancient culture. In the prime work of Greek literature, the epic poems of Homer, names were mentioned that later voyagers equated with what they found in Egypt. "There is an island in the surging sea, which they call Pharos, lying off Egypt," Homer wrote. "It has a harbor with good anchorage, and hence they put out to sea after drawing water." Besides mentioning the nucleus of what would one day be Alexandria, Homer spoke of "hundred-gated Thebes." Such a city could only be the southern Egyptian capital with its many pylons—and so the metropolis known in Egyptian as Waset became Thebes for the Greeks and the West. Greeks also gave names to Egyptian things: *obelisks*, because these sun-symbols resembled little spits; *pyramids*, because they were shaped like wheaten cakes. The Greek visitors took back with them recognizable cultural influences. For example, archaic Greek statues show young men standing with one foot before another in the stiff Egyptian manner.

Only the earliest Greeks knew an Egypt still independent. Around 1100 B.C. an eleventh Ramesses had ended the Twentieth Dynasty and Egypt had fallen under the rule of first Libyan, then Nubian rulers. The latter had proven unable to defend Egypt against the aggressive new empire of Assyria. Instead, a last vigorous dynasty, the Twenty-sixth, managed to reestablish, with the help of Greek mercenaries, a phase of independent power. This Saite dynasty, so named from its delta capital of Saïs, labored to restore the artistic and religious heritage of the Old Kingdom. Looted pyramids and tombs were piously resealed. Sculptors were commanded to labor in the ancient style, and their reproductions were remarkably fine, being sometimes hard to distinguish from the real thing. But although testifying to the reserves of talent still latent in Egyptians, Saite art tells another story—for the wish to revive former artistic modes is rarely a sign of artistic vigor. Although it is true that Victorian railway builders sponsored a neo-Gothic revival, nineteenth-century Europe was pioneering new forms of power. Saite Egypt, on the other hand, was living in a world where the balance of power and technology had moved against it.

Efforts at reviving the Egyptian empire wilted ignominiously each time they were exposed to the sun. And reconstruction of the waterway that purportedly linked Memphis to the Gulf of Suez during the Eighteenth Dynasty—and thus provided communication between the Mediterranean and the Red Sea—only made Egypt a more tempting prize. The revival of ancient power was finally proved a sham when, in 525 B.C., the Persian Great King Cambyses invaded and conquered Egypt. His successor, the talented Darius (521–486 B.C.), was to make some Greeks as well as all Egyptians subjects of a vast empire ruled from the Persian plateau.

Herodotus was one such subject of the Great King. His home town of Halicarnassus in southwest Anatolia (modern Turkey) was as much under Persian rule as was Egypt. Yet there was an important psychological difference between being an Egyptian vassal of Persia and a Greek one, for a Greek living in the eastern Aegean looked across an island-studded sea to independent Athens, not captive Thebes. Herodotus had been a small child when a Greek fleet at Salamis defeated the last serious Persian attempt to subjugate mainland Greece. He was a spiritual citizen of Hellas in its golden age, a contemporary of the Greek tragedians, of Pericles the democrat and of Socrates the questioning philosopher.

Herodotus, the product of this new Greek culture, visited Egypt in the middle of the fifth century. At the time of his visit, which probably lasted no more than three months, the country was temporarily in successful rebellion against Persia. What he saw and heard fills the second book of his *History*, whose main theme is the conflict between Greeks and Persians. His account is sympathetic, for the ancient country appealed to his Greek fondness for the mysterious and the spectacular. . . .

Alexander the Great

The writings of Herodotus helped to familiarize his countrymen with the Nile valley and delta. So did the experiences of a growing number of veterans who settled in Egypt and traders who opened stores there. But the man destined to take over both barracks and palace was Alexander the Great, a Macedonian from the Hellenic fringe. As a Macedonian, he lacked the sceptical, rationalist temper of the Athenians. As a pupil of Aristotle, who had been a disciple of Plato, he must have heard about that conservative philosopher's visit to Egypt and his conversations with the priests of Heliopolis. The autocratic majesty of Egyptian monarchy and the Egyptian reverence for the past had impressed Plato. In one of his dialogues he quotes an Egyptian as saying: "There is nothing beautiful nor great nor remarkable done, be it in your country or here, or in another country known to us, which has not long since been consigned to writing and preserved in our temples." Alexander was thus prepared by temperament and education for an encounter with Egypt.

The most enduring achievement of Alexander the Great's conquest of Egypt was the founding of Alexandria (pictured).

He led his army into the Two Lands in 332 B.C., after defeating the Persians at the battle of Issus. Far from resisting, the Egyptians were prepared to accept him as a liberator. After visiting Memphis, Alexander went as a pilgrim to the oracular shrine of Amen-Re at Siwa, an oasis on the northern edge of the Libyan Desert. There Amen-Re, whom Alexander recognized as Zeus, purportedly recognized Alexander as his son. Alexander took this as seriously as did his new subjects. The superstitious Macedonian found it possible to balance his important earthly paternity, as son of the King of Macedonia, with an immortal paternity as son of Amen-Re. . . . Wearing the ram's horns in his curly hair, Alexander was acclaimed pharaoh by the Egyptians. They needed a strong pharaoh, and the handsome Greek conqueror was preferable to a Persian one.

The most durable achievement of Alexander's year in Egypt was his foundation of a new capital named after himself. Compared with all previous Egyptian capitals—Memphis and Thebes, Akhetaten and Saïs—Alexandria embodied a new orientation, or more correctly, an occidentation. The city's two great harbors were linked to the West by the Mediterranean, and the city was severed from Egypt proper by the fresh-water lake of Maraeotis. It was also a new kind of city whose pattern of colonnaded streets, the chief of them two hundred feet wide, foreshadowed imperial Rome and even Manhattan. Despite religious ceremonies notorious for debauch, the city was primarily dedicated to the commerce, arts, and sciences of man, not to the cult of the gods. It was an Egyptian capital in which foreigners outnumbered Egyptians at least two to one.

Alexander did not live to enjoy the cool breezes and cultivated talk that were features of the new city. A year after the conquest Alexander returned to Syria to confront the Persians—and soon after subduing Darius's empire the thirty-three-year-old conqueror contracted a mysterious fever and died. One of Alexander's seven bodyguards, the Macedonian Ptolemaeus, by securing the hero's corpse and conveying it from Iraq to a central tomb, or *soma*, near the intersection of Alexandria's two main streets, helped to confirm his control over Egypt during the subdividing of Alexander's empire.

In a sense, Ptolemaeus was the founder of a thirty-first dynasty, which lasted through sixteen Ptolemies and seven Cleopatras. The members of this Macedonian family ruled as pharaohs, wearing the ancient crown and uraeus and practicing the custom, abhorrent to real Greeks, of royal incest. To bind their Greek and Egyptian subjects in one happy family they patronized a composite god, Serapis. The god's name and nature combined the two most popular Egyptian deities: Osiris, the immemorial god of the dead, and the Apis bull, to whom Alexander had sacrificed on a visit to Memphis. This Apis cult marks the decadence of Egyptian theology. The days had gone when animals and birds were merely manifestations of the cosmic diamond; now a particular, living bull, chosen by certain signs on the death of his predecessor, was worshiped in his lifetime and after death was entombed in an underground complex of tunnels at Sakkara known as the Serapeum. In appearance Serapis was in the Greek tradition: a sceptered Zeus-like figure whose long, curly locks supported a basket containing god-knew-what mysteries.

But despite the imposing Serapeum in which this synthetic god was worshiped, despite temples in his honor as far afield as Britain and Italy, it is doubtful if Serapis united the Greeks and Egyptians. Although some Egyptians undoubtedly became Hellenized and many Greeks adopted Egyptian mystery cults and funerary habits, Alexandria remained a physically and spiritually divided city. . . .

For a thousand years the Greeks were to dominate Alexandria and Egypt, either directly during the three Ptolemaic centuries or indirectly under the Roman empire and its Byzantine successor. Greek was the language of government, taxation, and commerce. The building that symbolized

The Romans and the Christians

Paul Johnson is the author of several books, including Civilizations of the Holy Land *and* The Suez War. *In the following excerpt from* The Civilization of Ancient Egypt, *Johnson takes a look at Egypt after the fall of the Ptolemies.*

The Romans, who took over in the first century B.C., had no respect for the Egyptians whom they regarded as orientalized Greek troublemakers, like Cleopatra, or faceless, incomprehensible natives, no better than slaves. Egypt was important to them because of its continuing ability to produce corn for export. They treated it accordingly and Egypt was sealed off from the normal processes of Roman politics and reserved for tourists. Like the Ptolemies and the Persians, the Roman Emperors played the role of pharaoh, but with increasingly less conviction. . . .

By the third century A.D., there was very little left of the elements of the ancient Egyptian way of life. Emperors no

Ptolemaic Alexandria took its name from Homer's island: the Pharos, a gigantic lighthouse, rose to a height of four hundred feet and was surmounted by a great polished mirror of steel lit by beacons. In being gigantic, the Pharos was in the Egyptian tradition; in being dedicated to a secular purpose—the guidance of seafarers into the city's two harbors—it was Hellenic. For the Ptolemies, despite their acceptance of pharaonic costumes and customs, promoted an essentially humanist culture. Alexandria could never rival Athens, focus of the Greek golden age, for even at their early best the Ptolemies were despots; they could never offer scholars the groves of Akademe, since these had been defoliated by the very victories that had given these despots their power.

Alexandria was the focus of a silver age, but even so it was an age that witnessed important contributions to the arts and sciences. The nautical lighthouse had its cultural counterpart in the great Library and Mouseion that the Ptolemies built south of their own seaside palace. In reigns spanning a century, the first three Ptolemies attracted leading Greek

longer bothered to pretend they were pharaohs; the temples were often in ruins; the clergy had lost their status and prestige and their learning was held in contempt. Nothing remained of the old Egyptian ruling class. The Nile Valley was swept by the fierce economic storms which ravaged the empire at this period. Christianity, originally confined to the Hellenized Jews of the Delta, now began to make rapid progress among the native Egyptians. . . .

Christianity travelled rapidly up the Nile, leaving temple-worship, already moribund, stricken to death. At Thebes, where the cult of Imhotep and Amenhotep as healing deities had lingered on . . . , the old priests were chased away, and little Christian basilicas were set up in the courts and halls of the temples. Philae, the sacred island much patronized by Ptolemaic kings and Roman emperors, was the last stronghold of the ancient religion to fall.

Paul Johnson, *The Civilization of Ancient Egypt*, 1978.

scholars to their capital. With royal cooperation these scholars established the ancient world's largest collection of books written on papyrus, ultimately comprising something close to half a million volumes. . . .

The Mouseion was an original establishment that foreshadowed a modern university in many ways. Royal subsidies enabled scholars from all over the Greek world to live, study, and lecture in its congenial environment. . . .

But Alexandria was never a city where the Egyptians felt at home. Their unofficial capital was a new city, opposite Memphis, built where the canal leading to the Gulf of Suez diverged from the Nile. Its name, Babylon-in-Egypt, has been given two explanations. According to one, Chaldean workmen brought to Memphis from Babylon revolted against their Persian masters and established themselves on a mound on the east bank. Having been granted an amnesty, they were allowed to settle the area and name it after their home city on the Euphrates. Another explanation sees in Babylon a corruption of Bab-li-On, the Gateway to On, the ancient name for Heliopolis. Whatever its origin, Babylon-in-Egypt was the first important settlement on the site of the future Cairo. Unlike Alexandria, it was crowded, huddled, and secret. It symbolized the chasm between triumphant Hellenism and an Egyptian culture reduced to being a poor relation in its own homeland.

Not that the Ptolemies showed outward contempt for the culture of their subjects. On the contrary, they probably prided themselves on the tolerance they showed their dark-skinned subjects, and at least to begin with, on an administration that was more just and less onerous than most. But the later Ptolemies, lacking the qualities of the first three, extracted taxes for foreign wars that exhausted the countryside or for civil wars that devastated it. Like all tax merchants, they were hated. Their scrupulous imitation of Egyptian customs seemed part of the trickery for which Greeks had been renowned since the time of Odysseus.

If the Ptolemies had persecuted the old religion, or remained contemptuously aloof from it, the Egyptians might have found in Horus and Isis standards around which to rally. But when the Egyptians entered their temples, they found the Ptolemies there, and their inscriptions. If the temples crumbled, the Ptolemies repaired them—so frequently and so well that this Macedonian dynasty ranks among the greatest builders in Egyptian history. Their shrine of Horus at Edfu and of Hathor at Dendera are two of the best-preserved temples awaiting the present-day tourist. Most of what remains of the island temple of Isis at Philae, just south of Aswan, was the result of reconstruction started by Ptolemy II (surnamed Philadelphus, or "lover of his sister") and completed by Ptolemy III (surnamed Euergetes, "doer of good works"). . . .

The End of the Dynasty

The Ptolemies ruled, with diminishing effectiveness, for three hundred years—or half a century longer than the great dynasty of Hashepsowe and Tuthmosis III. The dynasty expired with Cleopatra VII in 30 B.C. Cleopatra is as much history's first Levantine as Egypt's last Horus-sovereign. "Levantine" is an unflattering adjective coined in recent centuries for someone who lives in the Middle East without belonging to it, who speaks many languages without possessing one of his own, who has decadent tastes, whose armory springs from his wits rather than his muscle, who looks to outside forces for his succor and succubus. Cleopatra was in many respects a prototype. Her name was Greek, being found in Homer; she dressed as a Greek, except when arraying herself as Isis. Her father, Ptolemy XII, surnamed the Flute-Player, had been illegitimate, and her claim to twilight Egypt, which had by now lost Cyprus, its last shred of empire, was through marriage, first to her half brother Ptolemy XIV, then after his death in battle to one still younger, Ptolemy XV.

Cleopatra spent her life watching the struggle of outside forces: first Pompey against Caesar; then the assassins of Caesar against his avenger, Antony; then Antony against Caesar's great-nephew, the future Augustus. When Caesar invaded Egypt, she had herself smuggled to his palace wrapped in a carpet. She accompanied him to Rome and had by him a son, whose pet name was Cesarion. Through Cesarion, or Ptolemy XVI, she continued to reign, having meanwhile poisoned her fraternal spouse, Ptolemy XV.

Cleopatra's mind was in firm control of her libido, which she used effectively to beguile first Caesar, then Antony. Her sensual imagination seems to have been untiring. Her will was insatiable and opportunistic, and although her opportunities were constricted by fate, she used them to the full. As a ruler, she was a failure, and as a military ally to Antony, a disaster. The flight of sixty Egyptian ships under Cleopatra's command from the decisive battle of Actium not only reduced Antony's fleet but, in their precipitate desire to get back to Egypt, broke his battle line.

Yet behind her ruthless, European temperament—which only the Romans of the day could have equated, as they did, with the dangerous East—was a streak of identification with her people. Although by blood she was as alien to them as such later rulers as Farouk, the Egyptians accepted Cleopatra as completely as their ancestors had accepted Hashepsowe, a full-blooded Egyptian. She, for her part, had that ability to identify with a foreign people which recurs in such later figures as Lady Hester Stanhope in Lebanon or Lafcadio Hearn in Japan.

Besides Greek and Latin, Cleopatra spoke the language of her subjects—and accepted their mythology. After she had been loved as a girl by Caesar and as a mature woman by his successor, after she had sailed in gilded barges to paltry destinations, after she had accepted as a plaything a pirate kingdom in southern Anatolia, after the game was lost and she faced a choice of defeats, she chose to die royally. Her death excited the admiration of Plutarch, and through him, Shakespeare. Plutarch, eager for examples of Hellenic heroism to set against heavy Roman virtue, tells how she chose to slay herself, not with a bare bodkin, but with the very symbol of Egyptian kingship, the cobra, or uraeus. It had reared on every pharaoh's head since Narmer's, and it now reared on hers as she held the market-woman's cobra to her naked breast.

Chapter 5

The Heritage of Ancient Egyptian Civilization

Turning | Points

IN WORLD HISTORY

Egypt's Enduring Legacy

Douglas J. Brewer and Emily Teeter

Douglas J. Brewer is a professor of anthropology at the University of Illinois at Urbana-Champaign and the director of the Spurlock Museum, a museum of world history and culture located at the University of Illinois. Emily Teeter is the associate curator at the Oriental Institute Museum of the University of Chicago and the author of several books and articles. In the following excerpt from their book *Egypt and the Egyptians*, Brewer and Teeter discuss the enduring nature of ancient Egypt's legacy to the world. In particular, they maintain that many aspects of Egyptian culture have been passed down through the ages and still influence modern society. The authors conclude that ancient Egyptian civilization never truly died but was simply transformed.

Although it is common to refer to the "death" of the pharaonic civilization, there is no consensus as to what point in history it "died" or whether it was merely transformed. A basic problem with such a discussion is the definition of exactly what constitutes the death of a civilization. As defined by [social scientists] Robert Redfield and Milton Singer, civilization refers to the great traditions of a state; thus, "death" must refer to the loss of these great traditions.

On the one hand, the great traditions of the Egyptian culture—its elaborate polytheistic religion, sovereignty, system of writing, the creation of monumental art and architecture—had all vanished by the Late Antique Period (early Christian period) or shortly afterward. On the other hand, however, many aspects of ancient Egypt lived on. Economically, Egypt did not collapse. The annual inundation of the Nile ensured a renewable supply of rich arable land, and irrigation works were dependent upon local rather than central governmental power. Natural resources were never exhausted as they were in the case of the states of Mesopotamia. In addition, the basic infrastructure of the Egyptian state was relatively inexpensive to maintain— there was no great system of dikes or roads, and no standing army to exhaust the national treasury. Politically, there was no fragmentation of the Egyptian state that can be compared to the "fall" of a state such as Rome or the Inca empire. Pharaonic Egypt withstood periods of decentralization (the Intermediate Periods), foreign conquest, and occupation by Hyksos, Persians, Assyrians, Greeks, and Romans, yet the borders of the country remained largely unchanged even into the Christian and Islamic periods. Indeed, the borders of the modern state of Egypt are not appreciably different today from those that existed in the third millennium B.C., so one cannot properly speak of the physical fragmentation of the state.

Egypt's Influence

In terms of religion, the ancient theology continued to exert a strong influence. Greeks and Romans became adherents of the cult of Isis. Christians built their churches within pagan temples, such as Medinet Habu, and reconsecrated others, such as Philae, for their new monotheistic religion. Even today the pharaonic temples continue to play a part in folk religion of rural Egypt, with Coptic Christians and Muslims alike visiting the temples to gather sand that has been ground from the ancient pillars to use as a remedy for barrenness. One of the clearest surviving rituals is the annual festival of the Islamic saint Abu Haggag, which is celebrated by a procession of boats around the temple of Luxor in imitation of the ancient festival of Opet.

Finally, the influence of Egyptian art and architectural style is clearly visible in early Greek sculpture (the kouroi) and Roman monuments. The Romans also collected Egyptian art and disseminated it throughout their vast empire. The Neoplatonists (fifth century A.D.) and, much later, the Freemasons (eighteenth century) studied Egyptian iconography in their search for enlightenment, while Neoclassical artists and designers such as Giambattista Piranesi and Robert Adam inspired a mania for all things Egyptian that swept through Western Europe during the late 1770s and early 1800s. Centers of Christian piety and learning, such as St Peter's in Rome, were embellished with obelisks, a pagan symbol of sun worship. The plazas of great cities—London, Paris, Rome, Istanbul, New York— likewise imported and raised Egyptian obelisks in homage to the ancient Egyptians. Today, Egyptian motifs decorate myriad objects of daily life, from fabrics and furniture to beer cans and dishware.

It is clear that the concept of "death" does not take into account the many aspects of Egyptian culture that continued, even to the present day. Therefore, it is argued that it is more productive to consider that the culture was transformed. But how was it transformed and what factors were involved? Was there a single cause, such as military conquest or poor leadership? Surveying the 3,000 years of Egypt's history suggests that a single cause is too simplistic, and that the modification of Egyptian civilization resulted from the complex culmination of evolutionary processes.

Although perhaps not dramatic enough to constitute true demise, one cannot deny that there were changes in Egypt's economic and political systems. The Romans heavily taxed Egypt, to the extent that farms in Lower Egypt were depopulated as farmers fled to Upper Egypt or Nubia to escape their obligation to the state. Even more damaging to the long-term health of the Egyptian state was that the Romans increasingly exported the resources received through taxation to help support Roman imperial expansion instead of redistributing the goods to state workers within Egypt, as had been done in former times. Politically, Egypt did lose her sovereignty. With the rule of the Persians, Romans, Byzantines, Arabs, and, to a lesser degree, Ptolemaic, Macedonian Greeks who considered Egypt their own kingdom, Egypt was ruled by powers outside the Nile Valley and was drawn into the status of a client state. Yet the nature of each of these periods of foreign rule shared basic characteristics: each was autocratic, and each had a definite theocratic

Drawing Inspiration from Egypt

Michael Rice is a writer, public relations consultant, and museum planner and designer. He has been involved in the establishment of museums and departments of antiquities in several Middle Eastern nations. His books include Egypt's Making: A Study of the Origins of the Egyptian State, 5000–2000 B.C. *and* Egypt's Legacy: The Archetypes of Western Civilization, 3000–30 B.C., *from which the following passage is excerpted.*

To speak, as some will do, of the 'rediscovery' of Egypt at this time is to misunderstand the processes at work. Egypt had never been lost to the consciousness of the lands around the Mediterranean nor of that part of the world which draws its intellectual, religious and social inspiration from them. At first consciously, as in the case of Greece or, earlier still, of some of the Levantine lands, Egypt was the model which indicated 'the way that things were done'. Later, as time went by and as societies expanded and became more sophisticated themselves, the influences began to operate at a less conscious level, though they were always likely to erupt into visibility. In Roman times, with some mediation from Greece, public buildings, the soaring columns, statuary and the exiled Egyptian obelisks themselves gave an Egyptian stamp to the Imperial city. In the Middle Ages the stories in the Christian Bible kept Egypt's name alive with the figure of 'Pharaoh' looming formidably over the fortunes of the Christians' notional confessional ancestors, the Jews and their supposed 'captivity'. Without an awareness of Egyptian architecture and many of its decorative elements, the Renaissance is hardly thinkable; the decipherment of hieroglyphs became something of a passion amongst scholars who believed that all manner of mysteries and wisdom were contained in their beautiful and innocent shapes.

Michael Rice, *Egypt's Legacy: The Archetypes of Western Civilization, 3000–30 B.C.*, 1997.

basis—the divine Roman emperor, the Byzantine emperor, the caliph of Islam—so these political changes were easily comprehended by the majority of the Egyptian populace. One theocratic autocracy simply replaced another, and daily life continued much the same as before. Even today, life in Upper Egypt among the peasants has not changed appreciably from ancient times.

Perhaps the most obvious source of cultural transformation was the belief system, which influenced all aspects of the Egyptian culture and served as the medium through which new elements of society were introduced. Although the Greeks greatly respected Egyptian religious beliefs and, as indicated by the Ptolemaic temples whose walls are covered with liturgies, made valiant efforts to preserve the cult, their Roman successors had little interest in the native beliefs. With the conversion of Emperor Constantine (A.D. 306–337) to Christianity, the Egyptian civilization underwent a major change. Egypt's king had always served as the focus of the religious cult: the walls of the temples were covered with timeless images of the pharaoh making offerings to the gods, and it was he who functioned as the intermediary between humankind and the deities, and who ensured the protection of the land and her people. Without the king—the core of the religious system—ancient Egyptian culture was irrevocably altered. Finally, in A.D. 392 the Roman Emperor Theodosius ordered the pagan temples closed and a 3,000-year tradition came to an end.

The Endurance of Egyptian Culture

Although the ancient Egyptian civilization is traditionally considered to have "died" (its death placed variously at the end of the Ramesside Period, or at the Persian, Greek, or Roman conquests), many aspects of the culture were simply transformed. The political boundaries of the land are largely unchanged from 4,500 years ago, and, for much of the modern era, Egypt continued to be a theocracy as the rule of the semi-divine pharaoh was replaced by the Roman and Byzantine emperors and by the caliph of Islam. Indeed, life for the Egyptian peasant class has not changed significantly in the last few millennia, and even today popular folk traditions contain an echo of the pharaonic past.

An indication of the endurance of Egyptian culture—its transformation rather than true demise—is seen in the fascination that modern cultures have for the ancient past, and in the ways other cultures have incorporated many aspects of Egyptian civilization into their own.

Egypt's Influence on Ancient Greece

William A. Ward

In the following selection from his book *The Spirit of Ancient Egypt*, William A. Ward asserts that Egyptian civilization had a significant impact on the development of Greek culture. The ancient Greeks borrowed heavily from Egyptian artistic innovations and ideas, Ward maintains. Perhaps most importantly, the Greeks gained much of their early scientific knowledge from the Egyptians, the author contends, laying the foundation for Greece's remarkable achievements in science and mathematics. Ward, a noted Egyptologist and Near Eastern scholar, taught for many years at the American University of Beirut in Lebanon and at Brown University in Providence, Rhode Island. His books include *Pharaoh's Workers: The Villagers of Deir el-Medina* and *Egypt and the East Mediterranean World, 2000–1900 B.C.: Studies in Egyptian Foreign Relations During the First Intermediate Period*.

It is important for us to realize that "Western Culture" is not solely the product of Graeco-Roman civilization, but owes much to the ancient Near East. Historians, in recent years, have become more aware that the great civilizations of antiquity had mutual influence on each other long before the advent of the classical world. The peoples of the second millennium B.C. had already established an East Mediterranean civilization with as much coherence and cultural interaction as our own Western Civilization. Minoans and Mycenaeans, Hittites, Canaanites, Egyptians and the great Assyro-Babylonian tradition of Mesopotamia, all these made their contributions to

From William A. Ward, *The Spirit of Ancient Egypt* (Beirut, Lebanon: Khayats, 1965). Reprinted by permission of the Estate of William A. Ward.

this broader cultural concept and each gained from participation. The fundamental channels by which the various native cultures of the East Mediterranean world welded themselves into a cultural community, were trade and the fluid "middle class" of artisans, merchants and craftsmen who moved about freely throughout the whole area. . . .

The end product was an international civilization belonging to no specific country, yet belonging to all. This international civilization spread over the entire East Mediterranean coastal area as early as the middle centuries of the second millennium B.C. This internationalism never dominated the indigenous culture in any one area. It was a more subtle movement—the sum total of the contributions made by individuals. This concept of an East Mediterranean civilization involves cultural, not political penetration. Historians have accepted the fact that the classical and late Near Eastern traditions came together in that huge amalgamation of civilization we call the Hellenistic Age when the conquests of Alexander brushed aside the litter of previous empires and moved mankind into a new era. But the hellenization of the ancient world was the last stage in a process that had been going on for centuries. Alexander simply added impetus to cultural interchanges that had begun in the Bronze Age.

The Egyptian Spirit

There was, however, a break in this exchange between East and West. The Dorian migrations wiped out Bronze Age civilization in the Aegean and ushered in the Dark Age of Greece. Similar catastrophes destroyed much in the Near East during the same period (ca. 1150–800 B.C.). Egypt suffered along with the rest; while the Greeks took a step backward from Mycenaean kingdoms into obscure and isolated local states, the Egyptian Empire came to its end. When Archaic Greek civilization rose from the Dorian plague, it looked eastward to new empires emerging from the dust. Assyria and Babylonia had replaced Egypt as the greater powers, but still the Egyptian spirit, or its shadow, was there.

One of those fascinating coincidences of history saw the

last major attempt to revive native Egyptian power and culture at the time when the major thrust of Archaic Greece took place in the Orient. In the seventh century B.C. the paths of Egypt and Greece met once again, though both were vastly different political entities from what they had been. When Greece found Egypt again, it was at the time of the Saïte Renaissance, the Twenty-sixth Dynasty, when Egypt was again proclaiming her ancient glories. The Saïte revival was more than an imitation of past ages. For a while the old Egypt was alive again and it was this new-old Egypt that welcomed Greece into her circle of intimates. From this time on Egypt remained within the orbit of western interests.

Thus we could say that Egypt remained more or less in touch with the precursors of Western Civilization from the early second millennium B.C. until the collapse of the Roman Empire, roughly a period of about two thousand years. It is impossible to say that in this period Egypt produced no lasting effect on what would ultimately become our own heritage. If it is agreed that each society must build on the triumphs and failures of its predecessors, then, faced with the undeniable influence of Egypt on her contemporaries, it must be concluded that Egypt was in fact a contributor to our civilization. Without the existence of Egyptian civilization, the ancient world would not have been quite the same, and our own ancestry might have taken a somewhat different course. It is taken for granted that western culture is based on classical Greece, but classical Greece owed much to the periods that preceded it. The perfection of fifth century Athens was only the culmination of all past centuries which laid the foundation for the flowering of the Greek genius. Throughout those formative centuries, Egypt exerted a decided influence on Aegean civilization.

Tracing "influences" depends mainly on personal judgement. Scholars have noted many supposed Egyptian elements in Mycenaean civilization, brought to the Aegean during the Middle and Late Bronze Ages (roughly 2000–1100 B.C.). It has been suggested, for example, that the burial customs of Late Bronze Mycenae owed much to Egypt. Whether the chamber-tombs, the use of death-masks in the shaft-graves, the one example of embalming found there and the stelae erected over the shaft-graves are really examples of Egyptian influence remains to be seen. The death-masks are an intrusive element in Mycenaean culture and may well have been copied from similar Egyptian usage. Conversely, many find it difficult to accept the conclusion that the chamber-tombs of Mycenae were adapted from Egyptian rock-cut tombs of the late Twelfth Dynasty. Competent scholars have supported both views. Students of antiquity are often at odds in delineating foreign influence. In the final analysis, personal judgement does much to form conclusions.

Influences in Art

There are many evidences of Egyptian influence in the Mycenaean culture. An inlaid dagger found at Mycenae shows an unmistakably Egyptian scene which can be paralleled in Egyptian tomb paintings. A rock-crystal bowl also from Mycenae in the form of a duck with the head bending gracefully over backwards to form a handle likewise has excellent Egyptian prototypes. This style has been found elsewhere in the Aegean (in later contexts) and in Phoenicia.

One may well question the process of determining the presence of foreign influence in the material culture of a civilization. Basically the process is as follows. If a new element suddenly appears in a given culture, which does not fit into the normal pattern of that culture, we may justifiably suggest cultural borrowing. This may take many forms—a direct import, an artisan who has migrated to a new home, or local imitation. In the case of the Mycenaean duck-bowl, this is the earliest example of this motive in Aegean art. Duck-bowls were manufactured in Egypt from very early times and we know that Mycenaean Greece was in close contact with Egypt via the Mediterranean trade routes. Hence we can assume that Egypt was the homeland of the duck-bowl type and, through normal trade relations, this type was borrowed both by the Phoenicians and Mycenaeans. When a particular art motive, type of object, architectural element or pottery style has a long history in one culture and suddenly appears with no prior development in another, we can be reasonably sure that it was borrowed from the first by the second.

This is evident in the art motives shown on a silver plate from Idalion, Cyprus, dating to the eighth or seventh century B.C. The central motive, that of a Pharaoh holding the hair of his enemy in one hand, and a club upraised in the other, is as old as Egyptian dynastic art. The theme is as Egyptian as the pyramids and is an eloquent expression of the contact between Egypt and the archaic Mediterranean ancestors of classical civilization. . . . Egyptian art became a major influence in the formation of Archaic Greek culture.

This influence is nowhere shown as clearly as in the *kouroi*, or young athlete, statues which are typical of Aegean sculpture during the Archaic Period. This style of sculpture in the round was new in the Aegean artistic tradition at this time. It is now almost universally conceded that it was derived from the classical Egyptian style. The torso is four-sided, the head in cubic form, the left foot is generally advanced beyond the right, and the arms hang straight against the sides with clenched fists. Here, in an early Greek context, the canonical artistic tradition of ancient Egypt reappeared. A statue from Cyprus of the early sixth century B.C. not only shows a typical Egyptian pose, but also has an Egyptian kilt. While obviously of local manufacture, this statue is a patent imitation of Egyptian art. Finally a capital from Kition, Cyprus, reflects a purely Egyptian architectural motive known as early as the Twelfth Dynasty and continued into the later periods. Such examples as these are positive evidence of a strong Egyptian influence on Greek art of the Archaic Period. This influence was one result of the renewed contacts between Egypt and the Aegean during the seventh century B.C.

These few illustrations could be augmented by a much longer list of specific art objects. Mycenaean and Archaic Greek art borrowed much from Egypt and, since these were the antecedents of the classical style of Greek art, it can be suggested without hesitation that Egypt made definite contributions to the Greek classical style. It may plausibly be argued that such influences were ultimately discarded by, or absorbed into the Greek classical style. While this may be true, we must still concede that Egypt offered the Greek-speaking world part of its own rich heritage and that this influence appeared in the formative centuries of Western Civilization. The most prominent Egyptian feature of Archaic Greek art—the *kouroi* statues—eventually developed into the classic perfection we expect of later Greece. In its origin this style was an Egyptian donation to the new vibrant age dawning in the Aegean world.

A Scientific Awakening

A more subtle Egyptian influence may be found in the scientific awakening of Archaic Greece, an influence which was partially responsible for the stimulation of classical Greek thought culminating in the magnificent fifth century B.C. The Egyptian Twenty-sixth Dynasty (663–525 B.C.) gained and held its power with the aid of mercenary troops from the Ionian states of the Anatolian coast. The Pharaohs of this age rewarded their allies by allowing them to establish an important trading city, Naukratis, in the Delta. This commercial enterprise brought Greek tourists, as well as merchants to the ancient land of the Nile. Here began the myth of Egyptian "secret wisdom" which has plagued history to the present day. These Greeks, the most prominent of whom was Herodotus, were deeply impressed by the antiquity of Egyptian civilization and were receptive to the fanciful tales and traditions they heard from Egyptian priests.

The Greeks gained more than the fabled wisdom of Egypt. Greek science, it is true, was a great improvement over Egyptian science, but Greek scholars found the elementary knowledge of geometry and astronomy in Egypt. They went far beyond their Egyptian predecessors, though they began where the Egyptians left off. It was the Greeks who added theory to the practical science of Egypt. Probably the true measure of Greece's dependence on Egyptian science will never be known. The Greeks acknowledged their debt and we may assume that the Egyptians made a definite contribution to Greek science, hence to our own. We may well wonder if the founders of Greek scientific thinking would have made the advances they did without the stimulation of the much older nation they found along the banks of the Nile.

The Greeks might have developed precisely as they did without Egyptian help. Using the same methods of trial and error, the Greeks as any other people, could have discovered all the fundamental principles upon which they founded their great advances in science, but they did not have to. When Thales and the other fathers of Greek scientific thought broke away from the ancient prison of mythology, they took advantage of the practical thinking which had been going on for centuries in Egypt. Classical Greek thought developed and waned in a relatively short time. A scant two hundred years after Thales, the Golden Age of Greece had already come and gone, Athens had suffered ignominious defeat in the Peloponnesian War and Greece was on the decline. Greek civilization might never have flowered as brilliantly as it did in the fifth century B.C. if Greece had found it necessary to start at the beginning. But Greece did not have to. She built upon the earlier Egyptian foundations, now no longer Egyptian since they were infused with the unique Greek genius for logic and its insatiable search for truth.

Meroe: The African Heir of Ancient Egypt

P.L. Shinnie

A specialist in West African archeology, P.L. Shinnie is a professor emeritus at the University of Calgary in Alberta, Canada; he has also taught at the University of Ghana and the University of Khartoum in the Sudan. Among his numerous books are *The Capital of Kush, Ancient Nubia, Medieval Nubia, The African Iron Age,* and *Meroe: Civilization of the Sudan.* In the following article, Shinnie explores the Egyptian contributions to the cultures of sub-Saharan Africa. In the author's opinion, the ancient African civilization of Meroe adopted many Egyptian ideas, including hieroglyphic writing. Meroe maintained Egypt's legacy long after the fall of the Egyptian Empire, he writes, and a few traces can still be found among the African people living in the region today.

Any attempt to describe the legacy of Egypt to Africa is faced with a difficulty of terminology. What is meant in this context by Africa? If used in its proper geographical sense of the continent of Africa it includes Egypt itself, and it is not our purpose here to describe the influences of ancient on modern Egypt.

Egypt and Africa

Egypt certainly lies in Africa and is in that sense African, but it is at a vital world cross-roads close to Western Asia and open to many influences that scarcely penetrated further west or south, and therefore developed a distinctive civilization in many ways different from that of the rest of Africa.

Reprinted from P.L. Shinnie, "The Legacy to Africa," in *The Legacy of Egypt,* edited by J.R. Harris (2nd edition, 1971), by permission of Oxford University Press. Copyright © Oxford University Press 1971.

The northern littoral of the continent has always been in close contact with southern Europe and has formed part of a Mediterranean culture area, so it, too, is excluded, and the many and interesting traces of Egyptian influence in Carthage and Libya will not be treated here as they more properly form part of a study of the Egyptian legacy to the Mediterranean and the Near East.

The Africa considered here is that major part of the continent known clumsily as sub-Saharan Africa, or sometimes to French scholars as *Afrique noire* [black Africa]. Both these terms are themselves inadequate since there is no barrier along the southern edge of the Sahara, nor are all the peoples lying south of it black. But some definition is necessary, and rather than use some more complicated and inevitably inaccurate term, Africa and African will be used here to refer to that part of the continent that lies outside the frontiers of modern Egypt and south of the Sahara, an area that is largely, but not exclusively, inhabited by negroid peoples.

It is by no means a homogeneous area, either geographically, linguistically, or culturally, and as much variation can be found here as in any other of the great land masses of the world. But there is also some unity, and there are common features which, though hard to analyse or define, make it possible in general terms to speak of African culture, and to use the word African to describe the social and artistic elements found in ancient Egypt which are neither peculiar to Egypt itself, nor introduced from Asia or the Mediterranean—and to use it also to describe that geographical and cultural area whose debt to ancient Egypt we shall consider.

To define this legacy of Egypt to Africa is a matter of some difficulty and much uncertainty. The paucity of sources in a largely illiterate continent and the still early stage of research into its history make such gaps in knowledge that much of what is said must be speculative, and detailed study of the history of Africa and the influences on it must remain full of queries and guesses for many years to come.

It is desirable that an attempt should be made to analyse this legacy, since in recent years much attention has been devoted to the question, and a great deal of questionable material has been published, often with little attention to the claims of scholarship or accuracy. Attempts have been made to show that some modern African peoples are either directly descended from the Egyptians or were closely influenced by them. These range from suggestions that the brass and bronze sculptures of Nigeria were directly inspired from Egypt, to attempts to bring the Yoruba or the Wolof from Egypt by claiming direct descent—or, in the case of the Yoruba, suggesting a mass migration from the Nile to western Nigeria. Tendentious works have been written to prove linguistic and cultural connections, many of them having no more truth in them than the eighteenth-century histories that sought to bring the British from Troy. . . .

These works do little to help in the appreciation of Egypt's legacy to Africa, and it is not in this way that her contribution to the development of the African continent can be discerned. But, leaving such exaggerated claims aside, there are possibilities that the civilization of Egypt had some influence on other parts of Africa, and there are here and there faint hints of a common culture or of influence of the one on the other. Through the haze of centuries of separation there is the suggestion that there were exchanges, some in the realm of ideas and institutions, some in the realm of material objects. It must be made clear, though, that in many cases there is no certainty that in these common elements we may not be seeing Africa's legacy to Egypt as much as Egypt's legacy to Africa. The resemblances which can be found in cultural, social, and religious spheres between Egypt and other parts of Africa cannot of themselves tell us which way these influences may have travelled. Only the finding of material objects can tell us this, and here there is a complete absence of factual evidence, for although some objects in use even in modern Africa are reminiscent of pharaonic Egypt, no properly attested ancient-Egyptian objects have ever been found south of the northern Sudan. . . .

The Civilization of Meroe

The only absolutely certain Egyptian influence in Africa is in the area immediately to its south. Here, in the territory of the present Republic of the Sudan, Meroitic civilization flourished from the sixth century B.C. to the end of the third century A.D. Meroe is of the utmost importance for Africa, for it seems possible that it was from here that important techniques such as iron-working, the *cire perdue* method of bronze-casting, perhaps the cultivation of cotton, and the use of the horse for transport, spread into Africa.

Meroe was heavily influenced by Egypt in all its cultural, and possibly its political, development. It was the first purely African state to use writing, and it developed forms of state organization which may have had influence further south. In considering Egyptian influences in Africa, Meroe is an obvious centre of the possible diffusion of Egyptian ideas, and it is with a study of its history and place in the continent that we should begin.

Meroe developed from the Egyptianized kingdom of Napata, whose early kings figure in Egyptian history as the Twenty-fifth Dynasty, at some time in the sixth century B.C. For reasons which are still not clear, but were presumably both political and economic, the kings moved their capital from Napata to Meroe, perhaps in the reign of Aspelta, *c.* 590 B.C. The culture of the rulers of Napata had been completely Egyptian, whatever the race and language of the kings and people may have been, and they had derived it from the Egyptians who had conquered and ruled along the Nile from the first to the fourth cataracts from the beginning of New Kingdom times. Kush, as it was known to the Egyptians, became an Egyptian colony under the rule of an Egyptian governor and clear signs of Egypt are to be seen in the ruins of towns and temples throughout Nubia.

With the withdrawal up the Nile to Meroe, this Egyptian influence, while remaining strong throughout the whole history of the Meroitic state, becomes tinged with new elements deriving from Africa. The art changes and, though showing marked Egyptian and Hellenistic elements, it has a sufficient character of its own to enable us to speak of a distinctively Meroitic art as shown in its statuary and temple reliefs. The pottery, though much of it, in later times at least, is akin to Roman pottery of the first three centuries A.D., has also characteristics of its own, and in the burnished black ware known from Faras to Sennar provides a purely African pot fabric of a type previously unknown. This pottery is similar to a wide range of African ceramic styles, many of which are still in use today. The designs are normally incised before firing, and the surface is burnished. . . .

Of the political history of the Meroitic state we know very little. . . . In the whole period from the reign of Kashta to that of the last king of Meroe, a span of nearly 1,000 years, we have approximately fixed dates only for the first kings, the Twenty-fifth Dynasty of Egypt; and, after Tanwetamani, only for Aspelta (c. 593–568 B.C.), Ergamenes (c. 268–220 B.C.), and Teqerideamani (c. A.D. 246–66), and even for these kings the dates are open to question. The remainder have to be fitted in by using average lengths of reign and by weighting the averages by such indications as size of pyramid or richness of tomb content. By this method a reasonable chronological framework has been drawn up, though the dates for each king are only a statistical expression of probability, and should not be understood as having any validity beyond that. . . .

The picture that we have of Meroe, from at least the fourth century B.C. to the end of the third century A.D., is of a stable, well organized African state, ruling from its capital, on the banks of the Nile, a great stretch of country from Maharraqa to at least as far south as Sennar.

It was a power in the ancient world during the last three centuries B.C. and the first A.D., and possibly earlier, and was known and described by classical writers as well as being mentioned in the Bible. The Biblical reference (Acts 8:27) is interesting additional information that the title Candace, though misunderstood as a name, was well known in foreign countries.

Even in the third century A.D., well on towards the end of the Meroitic kingdom, ambassadors were passing to and from the Mediterranean, and a graffito of one of them from the

Dodekaschoinos, in the reign of King Teqerideamani, gives us one of the very few fixed dates in Meroitic history by referring to the Roman Emperor Trebonianus Gallus. It is a remarkable phenomenon that in this part of Africa at this early date such a state should develop, and, although there may well have been other influences, particularly from further east, at work, the main influence and legacy came from Egypt. . . .

The buildings of Meroe, though now much ruined, were a considerable achievement. The standard of workmanship may on occasion have been crude, and walls may often have been only two outer skins of dressed stone filled with rubble, but many other countries of the ancient world also built in this way. There is no doubt that the temples of Netekamani and other rulers of Naqa, the great complex of Musawarat dating in part from the fourth century B.C., as well as the buildings of Meroe itself, with its temple to Amun, its palace, and remarkable bath-house, were major achievements, and that the main inspiration came from Egypt.

It was a literate culture, and here again it owed much to Egypt for its two forms of writing. Meroitic hieroglyphic writing, used only occasionally and only for royal inscriptions, contains a small selection of Egyptian hieroglyphs used in a slightly different manner, the signs being alphabetic and without the ideographic element of Egyptian. The other, more common, writing, misleadingly described as cursive, may be derived from the hieroglyphs or perhaps from Egyptian demotic, but it is an interesting and distinctive type of writing in its own right. Although the phonetic values of its signs are known, it can still not be translated and there is no knowledge of the nature of the Meroitic language or of its relationship to other languages, though it is a reasonable assumption that, when more is known of it, it will be found to be related to one of the existing families of African languages. . . .

The written language died with the end of Meroe at the very beginning of the fourth century A.D., or perhaps a little earlier, and no legacy of writing from Egypt continued in the rest of Africa after this date.

From a technological point of view Meroe had one outstanding contribution to make, and that was in iron-working.

The Nile valley had always been backward in metallurgy and when the Assyrians invaded Egypt in 668/7 B.C., the Egyptians and their Kushite rulers could put into the field forces armed only with bronze weapons as against the formidable iron ones of the Assyrians. But the bitter experience of defeat was not wasted, and it was not long before, in their southern homeland, the people of Meroe were working iron to an unprecedented extent. Starting in a modest way in the reign of Harsiotef (c. 416–398 B.C.), in whose tomb for the first time models of iron tools were found, the use of iron became increasingly common and the existence of the great iron slagheaps at Meroe is now well known to all historians of Africa. . . .

Traces of Egyptian Culture

Meroe came to an end probably somewhere about the end of the third century A.D. The conventional view has been that it was the invasion by Aezanes of Axum in about A.D. 350 that dealt the final blow, but there are suggestions that the Black Noba were the real destroyers of Meroe, and that Aezanes came into a land already conquered and ruled by these new people. It has been suggested that, after the fall of Meroe, the Meroitic royal house moved westwards to Darfur, thus setting in train the dispersal of the knowledge of iron-working as well as of a number of other culture traits which can be traced back to Egypt.

The evidence adduced for this westward march is not very convincing, being largely derived from the existence of modern tribal names which, it is suggested, contain the element 'Kush' and must therefore have come from the ancient Kush. Traditions amongst one of these tribes, the Kagiddi of northern Darfur, of having come from the east are also quoted as evidence. Oral traditions are notoriously unreliable and difficult to control and need extremely careful and critical handling, and it would be dangerous to accept these accounts at their face value. All the evidence we now have from many different parts of Africa suggests that reasonably reliable oral traditions go back only a few centuries and it is in the highest degree improbable that a tradition of this type would have been maintained for some 1,600 years. . . .

But, having said all this, it can be seen that, here and there, there are strong resemblances to Egyptian objects and to Egyptian culture scattered throughout Africa. In the realm of material culture a small number of objects have been found which might reasonably be supposed to have originated from Egypt. Amongst these are musical instruments such as the small harp used by the Azande and other peoples of the southern Sudan and Uganda, wooden headrests in various parts of the continent, certain types of sandals, and many other similar objects. In West Africa attention has been drawn to the use of ostrich-feather fans, very similar to pharaonic ones, in Wadai and Bagirmi and other places in the neighbourhood of Lake Chad. Such fans were certainly in use in Nubia in the Second Intermediate Period and a number were found at Kerma, but none has been depicted in any Meroitic reliefs.

In other parts of West Africa, particularly Nigeria, there are resemblances in the regalia of chiefs to the pharaonic regalia— whips, crooks, and flails have all been reported and some have seen them as direct borrowings from Egypt.

The god Shango, of the Yoruba, whose sacred animal is the ram, has been derived by some from the god Amun, and G.A. Wainwright has cited a ram-headed breastplate from Lagos which certainly very strongly suggests an Egyptian origin. . . .

Limited Influence

The attempt to prove an Egyptian origin for any resemblance of objects or ideas to known Egyptian ones has been made many times, and was the main argument of the now long-discredited 'Diffusionist School', who saw in Egypt the origins not only of African culture but also of that of peoples in many other parts of the world, even America. The idea that, wherever cultural or technological developments can be seen in Africa, they must have been brought in from elsewhere, dies very hard, and arises in part from a deep-rooted feeling amongst non-African scholars that it is somehow *impossible* for Africans to have made these advances on their own. There is now plenty of evidence to show that many parts of Africa had highly developed societies, well adapted to their environments, from early times, and that, although in Africa, as throughout the world, no society is isolated and there is a two-way traffic in ideas and techniques, it is not necessary to assume that everything in Africa came from Egypt.

Yet still most are agreed that some elements in technology, particularly in the development of metal-working, were probably spread to Africa from the Nile valley through Meroe. If the legacy is to be seen anywhere in Africa it is at Meroe, and Meroe was ancient Egypt's African heir.

Egypt's Moral Legacy: The Impact on Early Judaism

James Henry Breasted

James Henry Breasted was one of the earliest American experts in Egyptology. He held the first professorship in Egyptology in the United States, at the University of Chicago. During his tenure, he helped establish the university's Oriental Institute and served as its first director. Breasted also wrote extensively on Egypt and other regions of the ancient world, including *A History of the Ancient Egyptians*, *The Conquest of Civilization*, and *Development of Religion and Thought in Ancient Egypt*.

In the following selection from his book *The Dawn of Conscience*, Breasted examines the influence of Egyptian religion and philosophy on the early Hebrews. Comparisons between the Old Testament and ancient Egyptian literature, the author argues, reveal that the Hebrews incorporated Egyptian ideas and beliefs into their religion as it developed. Therefore, he concludes, much of the moral legacy of the modern Judeo-Christian world ultimately derives from ancient Egypt.

The Hebrews appear in the arena of history for the first time in the Tell el-Amarna Letters, the earliest of which are to be dated not long after 1400 B.C., that is, from a time far older than any surviving Hebrew literature. These cuneiform letters disclose to us bodies of the Hebrew nomads drifting into Palestine, then under Egyptian sovereignty, and entering mercenary military service there. . . .

The Hebrew people were still very largely the product of their long centuries of pastoral life as nomadic herdsmen on the desert fringes before they entered Palestine. They still carried with them the rude and barbarous habits of the desert tribesmen and even the half-savage practices of a primitive stage of life, like the slaying of first-born children as a sacrifice to the tribal god. . . .

The Egyptian Background of Moses

It is evident that some of the Hebrew nomads, after having taken refuge in Egypt in time of famine, were subjected to slavery, from which a Hebrew of statesmanlike gifts and notable powers of leadership, who placed himself at their head, delivered them and thus became the first great Hebrew leader whose name has come down to us. It is important to notice that his name, Moses, was Egyptian. It is simply the Egyptian word "mose" meaning "child," and is an abridgement of a fuller form of such names as "Amen-mose" meaning "Amon-a-child" or "Ptah-mose," meaning "Ptah-a-child," these forms themselves being likewise abbreviations for the complete form "Amon-(has-given)-a-child" or "Ptah-(has-given)-a-child." The abbreviation "child" early became a convenient rapid form for the cumbrous full name, and the name Mose, "child," is not uncommon on the Egyptian monuments. The father of Moses without doubt prefixed to his son's name that of an Egyptian god like Amon or Ptah, and this divine name was gradually lost in current usage, till the boy was called "Mose." [The final *s* is an addition drawn from the Greek translation of the Old Testament. It is not in the Hebrew which has "mosheh."] The leadership of Moses, the courage and skill with which he delivered his people from foreign bondage, the deliverance itself, accompanied by some natural catastrophe which destroyed a body of pursuing Egyptian troops—all these found an imperishable place in Hebrew tradition and gave the Hebrews an initial heritage of glory which was the earliest influence welding them together as a nation.

At some stage in these early incidents Moses had tarried in the wilderness south of Palestine among a desert tribe known as Midianites, and especially with one of their sacred ministrants named Jethro, from whom he learned of their local god, "Yahveh," or "Jahveh.". . .

Through the influence of Moses the Hebrews cast out their ancient [gods] and adopted Yahveh as their sole god. For this extraordinary deed there must have been some stronger motive than the influence of their great leader. It is evident that the deliverance from Egyptian task-masters was accompanied by some terrible manifestation of Yahveh's power. There is much basis for the view that as the Israelites pressed on in flight an eruption of Sinai, a volcanic mountain, began, and we might conjecture that it was the accompanying earthquake and a resulting tidal wave which caused the engulfment of a body of pursuing Egyptian troops. . . .

The Egyptian background out of which Moses had developed into a great national leader must in itself have contributed to his vision of Yahveh's place in the life of his people. Born in Egypt and bearing an Egyptian name, Moses enjoined his countrymen to adopt an enormously ancient Egyptian custom, the rite of circumcision, which in his day had been practiced among the Nile-dwellers for at least three thousand years and more. Hebrew tradition always attributed the origin of this rite to Moses, and the fact that he adopted as a universal distinguishing mark of the Israelite a sacred Egyptian practice, with which he had obviously been acquainted in Egypt from childhood days, is unequivocal contemporaneous evidence that he was consciously drawing upon his knowledge of Egyptian religion. He was no slavish imitator of Egyptian practices, however, as is shown by the fact that having received his god Yahveh from the Midianites, a desert people too primitive and unskilled in the arts to make images of their god, he left Yahveh unpictured and imageless, just as the Midianites had done. He retained, however, some reminiscences of Egyptian religious images. He himself carried a magically potent staff, doubtless a serpent staff, in which dwelt the power of Yahveh, and for the healing of the people he set up a shining brazen image of a serpent, obviously one of the many serpent divinities of Egypt. . . .

Down into the Christian Era the Hebrews preserved a tradition that Moses was learned in "all the wisdom of the Egyptians" (Acts 7:22), and we can hardly question the correctness of this tradition. It is only in recent years that we have been able to understand the surviving sources of Egyptian life sufficiently well to realise that the "wisdom of the Egyptians" was primarily social contemplation. Moses must therefore have been familiar with the writings of the Egyptian social prophets, the oldest of which had been in circulation for fifteen hundred years when Moses began the teaching of his people. It is obvious that a man brought up with such literature around him would feel the need of a religion of ethical content for his people. How much moral and ethical teaching Moses may have left with them, it is now very difficult to determine. The reader may decide for himself whether a leader who had set up a brazen serpent for worship by his people, an image which was preserved and worshipped for centuries in the national sanctuary, could also have laid upon each Hebrew householder the command, "Thou shalt not make unto thee a graven image, nor (the likeness of) any form that is in heaven above, or that is in the earth beneath, or that is in the water under the earth." Each commandment in the Decalogue is addressed to a householder, in the second person singular, "thou." It is obvious that when the Decalogue was written the Hebrews had already made the transition from a pastoral life on the desert grasslands to a settled agricultural life in towns, where social influences were shaping religious belief and enriching its content. Landownership, a thing unknown to the nomads, and to some extent also commercial life in towns were creating a small class of rich townsmen, while the majority were left still poor. Class rivalries, with their inevitable antipathies and resulting instructive social experience, began to arise. . . .

In a situation of sharply contrasted social classes, there developed a social arena such as arose on the Nile almost two thousand years earlier. It was conditions like these which had awakened a new sense of enduring values in Egypt. In the same way men of humane spirit and social vision among the Hebrews began to feel the voice of conscience as a social force, and the Age of Character, in response to such impulses, was beginning in Israel, as it had done so long before in Egypt. The old rites and the religious usages of ritual and sacrifice began to decline in value as contrasted with worthy character. We recall the remarkable words of the unknown Heracleopolitan king to his son Merikere, a thousand years before the day of Moses, "More acceptable is the virtue of the upright man than the ox of him that doeth iniquity." The trenchant discrimination of the old Pharaoh's moral insight had evidently not been confined to Egypt; the roll that contained his instruction to his son must have found its way to Palestine, for identically the same idea, in very similar words, appeared early in the ethical development of the Hebrews: "Behold, to obey is better than sacrifice, and to hearken than the fat of rams" (I Sam. 15:22). This emphasis on "hearkening" sounds like an echo from the Maxims of Ptahhotep, who instructed his son, over fifteen hundred years before Samuel's time, on the value of "hearkening." The superiority of character over ritual observances was set forth by the Hebrew wise men in the Book of Proverbs in words which are again an echo of the Heracleopolitan sage: "To do righteousness and justice is more acceptable to Yahveh than sacrifice" (Prov. 21:3). That the Hebrew wise man was following Egyptian thought at this point is interestingly disclosed by the immediately preceding verse (Prov. 21:2), "But Yahveh weigheth the hearts." In the ancient East there was only one faith in which we find the god *weighing* the human heart, and that was Egyptian religion with its Osirian judgment. . . .

A God of Righteousness

In an age of such moral vision the old Midianite nature god of the desert, who had led the Israelites into Palestine and had found savage pleasure in the slaughter of the Canaanites, was gradually transformed in the Hebrew conception of him, till he became a God of righteousness, who likewise demanded righteousness in the character of his worshippers. While this transformation, growing out of their own social experience, was in no small degree due to the Hebrews themselves, nevertheless the religious thinking of these dwellers in Palestine was in this instance, as in so many other similar experiences, drawing substantially from the heritage of the past as they found it in the Canaanitish communities with which they had gradually coalesced. That heritage was filled with Egyptian ideas of the character of the Sun-god as a righteous ruler of men. We find a Hebrew prophet assuring his people, "Unto you that fear my name shall the sun of righteousness arise with healing in its wings." We recall that personified "Righteousness," the goddess Maat, was believed by the Egyptians to be a daughter of the Sun-god. Identified by the possession of wings, "the sun of righteousness" of the Hebrews can be nothing else than a reference to the winged Egyptian Sun-god, for none of the old Hebrew conceptions of Yahveh had ever pictured him with wings. Excavations at Samaria have revealed the fact that these Egyptian conceptions of the righteous Sun-god were common in Palestinian life. In the ruins of the palace of the Israelitish kings at Samaria the excavators discovered some carved ivory relief plaques once forming the decorative incrustation that adorned the furniture of the Hebrew sover-

---

Egyptian Teachings

Pierre Montet points out the similarities between Egyptian maxims and the proverbs of the Hebrews in the following excerpt from his book Eternal Egypt. *Montet's other books include* Egypt and the Bible *and* Lives of the Pharaohs. *He taught Egyptology for almost thirty years at the University of Strasbourg in France.*

The maxims of Amenemope make it possible to see how much Israel owed to her long contact with Egypt. The earliest commentators were struck by the numerous analogies between the maxims and Solomon's Proverbs, particularly in the third part. The Hebrew sage leaves out the specifically Egyptian elements which abounded in his Egyptian model, but as regards essentials he follows Egyptian teaching. Both authors declare that we are in the hand of God and both believe in the dignity of the poor, and of the blind, the halt and the lame. Ill-gotten gains do not long remain in the same hands. Parents should be respected, children chastised, and hot-tempered people avoided; one should be sparing of words and always strictly honest in the matter of boundaries, weights and measures.

Pierre Montet, *Eternal Egypt*, trans. Doreen Weightman, 1964.

eigns. Among these carvings appears a piece bearing the figure of the goddess "Righteousness" (Maat) borne aloft by a solar genius of Heliopolis as he offers the figure, probably to the Sun-god. The entire design is Egyptian in content, but the workmanship shows clearly that the carving was done by Palestinian craftsmen. Hebrew workmen were therefore familiar with such Egyptian designs, and Hebrews of high station beheld these symbols of the Egyptian Sun-god's righteousness every day adorning the very chairs in which they sat.

The winged Sun-god of the Nile was not only known to the Hebrews as a God of righteousness, but also as the beneficent protector of his worshippers. Four times the Hebrew Psalmists refer to the protection found "under (or in) the shadow of thy wings." As we have before observed, Yahveh was not pictured by the Hebrews as possessing wings; on the other hand, we have impressive sculptured portraits of the Pharaohs with the Sun-god as a falcon hovering with wings outstretched in protection over the sovereign.

The Egyptian Sun-god conceived as a righteous sovereign was therefore among the influences which contributed to transform Yahveh into a righteous ruler of men. . . .

In the realm of *conduct* also the Hebrew prophets likewise drew upon the literature of proverbs and fables, which before 1000 B.C. had already gained international currency. . . .

The Hebrew prophets were greatly impressed by the contrast between the upright man and the wicked as pictured in the writings of the Egyptian wise men. . . .

The Wisdom of Amenemope

All Old Testament scholars of any weight or standing now recognise the fact that a whole section of about a chapter and a half of the Book of Proverbs is largely drawn *verbatim* from the Wisdom of Amenemope; that is, the Hebrew version is practically a literal translation from the Egyptian. It is likewise obvious that in numerous other places in the Old Testament not only in the Book of Proverbs, but also in the Hebrew law, in Job, in Samuel and Jeremiah, Amenemope's wisdom is the source of ideas, figures, moral standards, and especially of a certain warm and humane spirit of kindness. . . .

This discovery is of such far-reaching significance, that, at the risk of wearying the reader, some examples of the evidence must be presented here. The "Words of the Wise" in the Hebrew Book of Proverbs, and in the Wisdom of Amenemope, begin as follows:

Amenemope	*Proverbs*
Incline thine ears to hear my sayings,	Incline thine ear, and hear the Words of the Wise,
And apply thine heart to their comprehension.	And apply thine heart unto my knowledge.
For it is a profitable thing to put them in thy heart,	For it is a pleasant thing if thou keep them within thee,
But woe to him who transgresses them.	If they be established together upon thy lips.
(Amenemope III, 9–12)	(Prov. 22: 17–18)

The purpose of such instruction is then defined by the Proverbs, and is also indicated by Amenemope, as essentially practical efficiency in official business:

Amenemope	*Proverbs*
In order to return a report to the one that sent him.	That thou mayest carry back words of truth to them that
(Amenemope I, 6)	send thee. (Prov. 22: 21)

The phrase "words of truth" is corrupt in the Hebrew; what is intended is of course an equivalent to the Egyptian "report." Both in Proverbs and Amenemope, however, the moral purpose of the instruction is evident throughout. . . .

Amenemope is much concerned to warn youth against hotheadedness, or association with men of this type. The Hebrew editor likewise warns:

Amenemope	*Proverbs*
Fraternise not with the hot-tempered man,	Make no friendship with a man of heat,
And press not upon him for conversation.	And with a wrathful man thou shalt not go.
(Amenemope XI, 13–14)	(Prov. 22: 24)

The common word for the reckless man of hot temper in Amenemope's wisdom is simply the "hot one," and it is interesting to observe that the original Hebrew of this passage literally rendered means the "man of heat," a phrase which is not found elsewhere in the Old Testament, and is evidently an effort to carry over the Egyptian term. . . .

Much more suited to Egyptian life than to that of the Hebrews are Amenemope's admonitions regarding behaviour in the presence of lordly superiors, for in Egypt appropriate deportment on the part of a young official was absolutely indispensable to a successful career. Just as elegant court manners in Paris under the later Louis' spread to less cultivated capitals of Europe, so refined deportment and palace formalities of official intercourse freshly introduced among a people of rude desert background under the youthful Hebrew monarchy were strongly influenced by the long-established courtesies of the Pharaoh's court, whose officials had ruled Palestine for centuries. The Hebrew editor of Proverbs, therefore, did not hesitate to commend Egyptian official courtesy to the Israelites of his day:

Amenemope	*Proverbs*
Eat not bread in the presence of a great man,	When thou sittest to eat with a ruler
Nor offer thy mouth in his presence.	Consider diligently what is before thee;
If thou sate thyself with unpermissible food,	For thou wilt put a knife to thy throat
It is but pleasure of thy spittle.	If thou be a man given to appetite.
Look (only) upon the dish that is before thee,	Be not desirous of his dainties;
And let it furnish thy need.	Seeing they are deceitful food.
(Amenemope XXIII, 13–18)	(Prov. 23:1–3)

The translators of the Revised Version [of the Bible] were uncertain whether to render: "what is before thee" or "him who is before thee." Amenemope's "dish that is before thee" settles the question. The Hebrew editor has altered the order of ideas, and has shifted his "deceitful food," which corresponds to the Egyptian "unpermissible food" (literally "wrong food") to the last line. This admonition of Amenemope is very old, for it was drawn from the wisdom of Ptahhotep and was therefore some two thousand years old in Amenemope's time. In Ptahhotep's words the advice is much more intelligible: "If thou art a man of those who sit (at meat) by the seat of a man greater than thou, take when he gives to thee what he puts before thee; look not at what is before him; look (only) at what is before thee, and bombard him not (literally, "shoot him not") with many glances (do not stare at him). . . . Turn thy face downward until he addresses thee, and speak only when he has addressed thee." Here then is a Hebrew sage laying upon youthful Israelites admonitions of courtesy which had guided young Egyptian officials at the court of the Pharaohs in the days when the pyramids were rising two thousand years earlier. This passage is therefore probably the oldest material in the Old Testament. We have here a striking example of how Hebrew life in Palestine developed under the influence of millennia of social experience which had already become ancient history when the Israelitish nation arose. . . .

The Thirty Chapters

We might continue indefinitely with such parallels, but doubtless the examples cited are sufficient to demonstrate the fact that the Hebrew Book of Proverbs has embedded in it a substantial section of an earlier Egyptian book of wisdom. This borrowing was done, as was quite natural in such an age, without acknowledgment. It is not a little interesting, however, to find in the Book of Proverbs an unmistakable reference to Amenemope's book, although the reference is naturally not by title, nor in an age so remote, by mention of the Egyptian wise man's name. In the introduction to the Words of the Wise, we find the following curious inquiry, the translation of which has much puzzled the editors of the Revised Version:

> Have I not written unto thee excellent things,
> Of counsels and knowledge? (Prov. 22:20)

The Revision Committee has inserted a marginal remark regarding "excellent things," calling attention to the fact that "The word is doubtful." The early Hebrew editors themselves had some doubts about it also, for they inserted another spelling of the word in the margin of the Hebrew manuscript, and as thus spelled by the ancient Hebrew editors, the word means "*thirty*." If we accept this word, the query would then read:

> Have I not written unto thee thirty,
> Of counsels and knowledge?

At first sight this old reading seems to furnish only nonsense; but when we observe that Amenemope divided his book into thirty chapters and numbered them, all becomes clear. In Palestine the Egyptian roll must have been called something like the "Thirty Chapters of Wisdom," from which it would seem that an abbreviated form, of merely "Thirty," eventually arose. Without any change in the actual Hebrew text the proper rendering, as suggested by Hubert Grimme, furnishes us the following parallel:

Amenemope	*Proverbs*
Consider for thyself these thirty chapters,	Have I not written to thee "Thirty,"
That they are satisfaction and instruction.	Wherein are counsels and knowledge?
(Amenemope XXVII, 7–8)	(Prov. 22:20)

This extraordinary mention of the current title of a foreign work from which an Old Testament writer was liberally borrowing makes it certain that he had in his hands a Hebrew translation of Amenemope's book, which was complete, that is, contained all thirty chapters of the Egyptian original, otherwise the title "Thirty" would have had no meaning. To retain its meaning the Hebrew compiler of the Proverbs, though he did not retain all of the available thirty chapters, nevertheless employed exactly thirty proverbs in his abridged edition (Prov. 22:17–24:22). . . .

A Moral and Religious Inheritance

Just as the literatures of modern Europe have grown up saturated with our ancient inheritance from Greece and Rome, so it was in Palestine inevitable that the Hebrews should be profoundly influenced in their thinking and their writing by the literature of the great nation which had held Palestine as its cultural and political province longer than Rome held Gaul. In receiving a great and inspiring moral and religious heritage from the Hebrews, therefore, we may regard it as a demonstrated fact that we have inherited a two-fold legacy, which is made up in the *first* place of some thousands of years of human experience in the Ancient Near East, chiefly Egypt, *before the Hebrew nation arose*, and was then in the *second* place marvellously deepened and enriched out of their own social experience by the prophets and sages of Israel themselves. . . .

In law and mythology the Hebrews drew much from Babylonian civilisation; but in morals, in religion, and in social thinking in general, the Hebrews built up their life on Egyptian foundations. After they settled in Palestine the Israelites were dwelling in a land which was Egyptian territory and had been so for centuries. It remained Egyptian for centuries after the Hebrew occupation began, and even so late as the reign of Solomon, the Egyptian Pharaoh presented to the Hebrew king the city of Gezer, a strong city of Palestine which was almost under the eaves of Jerusalem.

The fundamental conclusions that form the basis of moral convictions, and continue to do so in civilised life at the present day, had already been reached in Egyptian life long before the Hebrews began their social experience in Palestine, and those Egyptian moral convictions had been available in written form in Palestine for centuries when the Hebrews settled there. The enrichment which these teachings received, as the outgrowth of Hebrew life and thought, are of priceless value to humanity; but in recognising this fact we should not fail to realise that the moral sentiments of civilised society originated in a period far earlier than the long accepted "age of revelation," and have descended to us of the present day from an epoch when the writings of the Hebrews did not yet exist. The sources of our inheritance of moral tradition are therefore far from having been confined to Palestine, but must be regarded as including also Egyptian civilisation. The channel by which this inheritance has reached the Western world has chiefly been the surviving

Hebrew literature preserved in the Old Testament. The disappearance of the ancient oriental civilisations, on the basis of which that of the Hebrews was built up, the resulting loss by the Western world of all understanding of the writing and languages of these vanished civilisations so that they lapsed into silence two thousand years ago, left Hebrew literature shining like a lonely beacon light surrounded by the deepest darkness. The recent scientific recovery of some knowledge of the lost oriental civilisations is therefore illuminating the darkness, and surrounding Israel with a light that is some thousands of years older. Had the Western world never lost all knowledge of the origins and development of civilisation, it would never have occurred to any one to place Hebrew history anywhere else than as the culmination of a long preceding development of morals and religion. Certainly no theological doctrine of one people exclusively enjoying a divine revelation could ever have arisen—a doctrine which has blinded us for centuries to our noble inheritance of universal human aspiration, not limited to the history or the experience of any one people.

Appendix of Documents

Editor's Note: The documents that follow are listed in approximate chronological order. It should be noted, however, that scholars often differ widely on the probable dates of composition of Egyptian documents. These disagreements reflect the inherent difficulty of working with ancient texts. For example, an Egyptian story that is preserved only in a manuscript from the New Kingdom may use vocabulary that indicates it was composed much earlier—perhaps sometime in the Middle Kingdom—while the subject matter may deal with events that occurred during the Old Kingdom. Determining an exact date of composition is therefore frequently impossible. Likewise, translators often use devices such as parentheses, half brackets, and question marks to indicate restorations of missing text or Egyptian words that are imperfectly understood. In a few cases in the following documents, such devices have been removed to facilitate ease of reading.

Document 1: The Cannibal Hymn

This hymn comes from the Pyramid Texts, a collection of incantations carved on the walls of the royal burial suites inside the pyramids of the pharaohs of the Fifth and Sixth Dynasties. They are the oldest surviving examples of Egyptian religious and funerary literature. The following hymn is from the tomb of Wenis, the last pharaoh of the Fifth Dynasty. He is depicted as hunting and eating the gods in order to gain their magical powers.

> The sky is overcast,
> The stars are darkened,
> The celestial expanses quiver,
> The bones of the earth-gods tremble,
> The planets are stilled,
> For they have seen the King appearing in power
> As a god who lives on his fathers
> And feeds on his mothers;
> The King is a master of wisdom
> Whose mother knows not his name.
> The glory of the King is in the sky,
> His power is in the horizon
> Like his father Atum who begot him.

He begot the King,
And the King is mightier than he. . . .
The King is the Bull of the sky,
Who conquers at will,
Who lives on the being of every god,
Who eats their entrails,
Even of those who come with their bodies full of magic
From the Island of Fire. . . .
It is the King who eats their magic
And gulps down their spirits;
Their big ones are for his morning meal,
Their middle-sized ones are for his evening meal,
Their little ones are for his night meal,
Their old men and their old women are for his incense-
  burning. . . .
For the King is a great Power
Who has power over the Powers. . . .
The King's place is at the head
Of all the august ones who are in the horizon,
For the King is a god,
Older than the oldest.
Thousands serve him,
Hundreds offer to him,
There is given to him a warrant as Great Power
By Orion, father of the gods.
The King has appeared again in the sky,
He is crowned as Lord of the horizon;
He has broken the back-bones
And has taken the hearts of the gods. . . .
The King feeds on the lungs of the Wise Ones,
And is satisfied with living on hearts and their magic. . . .
He enjoys himself when their magic is in his belly;
The King's dignities shall not be taken away from him,
For he has swallowed the intelligence of every god.
The King's lifetime is eternity,
His limit is everlastingness. . . .
Lo, their souls are in the King's belly,
Their spirits are in the King's possession. . . .
While the King is this one who ever appears and endures.

R.O. Faulkner, trans., *The Ancient Egyptian Pyramid Texts*. London: Oxford University Press, 1969.

Document 2: A Dancing Dwarf for a Boy-King

If a noble of ancient Egypt received a letter of commendation from his pharaoh, he would arrange to have the letter inscribed on the wall of his tomb so that future readers would know he had been held in high regard. The following letter comes from the facade of the tomb of Harkhuf, Lord of Elephantine and a conductor of caravans to foreign lands. During one of his expeditions, he sent word to the pharaoh, Pepy II, that he had obtained a dancing dwarf to amuse the royal court. Pepy II was at the time still a small boy, about eight or nine years old, and his reply to Harkhuf reveals his excited delight at the news. This is the only royal letter to survive completely intact from the time of the Old Kingdom.

Royal seal, year 2, third month of Yakhet, day 15.

Royal decree: O privy counsellor, lector-priest, and caravan-leader, Harkhuf. I have noted the matter of this thy letter, which thou hast sent to the King, to the palace, in order that it might be known that thou hast come down in safety from Yam with the army which was with thee. Thou hast said in this thy letter that thou hast brought all great and beautiful gifts which Hathor, Lady of Yamu, has given to the King of Upper and Lower Egypt, Neter-ka-Rê [Pepy II], who lives for ever and ever. Thou hast said in this thy letter that thou hast brought a dwarf of divine dances from the land of spirits, like the dwarf whom the Treasurer of the God, Ba-ur-dad, brought from Punt in the time of King Ysesy. Thou hast said to my Majesty, Never before has one like him been brought by any other who has visited Yam. Each year shows thee doing what thy lord desires and praises; thou spendest day and night with the caravan doing what thy lord desires, praises, and commands. His Majesty will make thy many excellent honours to be an ornament for the son of thy son for ever, so that all people will say when they hear what my Majesty does for thee: "Is there anything like this which was done for the privy counsellor Harkhuf, when he came down from Yam, because of the alertness he showed to do what his lord desired, praised, and commanded." Come northward at once to the Court. And thou must bring with thee this dwarf, alive, sound and well, from the land of spirits, for the dance of the god, and to rejoice and gladden the heart of the King of Upper and Lower Egypt, Neter-ka-Rê, living for ever. When he comes down with thee into the vessel, appoint trustworthy people who shall be beside him on each side of the vessel; take care lest he should fall into the water. When he sleeps at night, appoint trustworthy people who shall sleep beside him in his tent; inspect ten times a night. For my Majesty desires to see this dwarf more than the products of Sinai and Punt. If thou arrivest at the Court and the dwarf is with thee, alive, sound, and well, my Majesty will do for thee a greater thing than was done for the Treasurer of the god, Ba-ur-dad, in the time of King Ysesy, according to the heart's desire of my Majesty to see this dwarf. Commands have been sent to the Governor of the New Towns to command that provisions are to be taken by him in every store-city and every temple without stint.

Margaret A. Murray, *The Splendor That Was Egypt: A General Survey of Egyptian Culture and Civilization.* New York: Praeger, 1964.

Document 3: The Song of the Harper

The ancient Egyptians took great pains to ensure themselves of a comfortable life in the next world, and much of their literature focuses on the certainty of life after death. Yet a few texts, such as the following song, express a more skeptical view. This song is believed to date from the Eleventh Dynasty and may well reflect the cynicism and hedonism that prevailed during the turbulent First Intermediate Period.

The generations pass away,
While others remain,
Since the time of the ancestors,
The gods who were aforetime,
Who rest in their pyramids,
Nobles and the glorious departed likewise,
Entombed in their pyramids. . . .

None cometh from thence
That he may tell us how they fare;
That he may tell us of their fortunes,
That he may content our heart,
Until we too depart
To the place whither they have gone.

Encourage thy heart to forget it,
Making it pleasant for thee to follow thy desire,
While thou livest.
Put myrrh upon thy head,
And garments on thee of fine linen,
Imbued with marvellous luxuries,
The genuine things of the gods.

Increase yet more thy delights,
And let not thy heart languish.

Follow thy desire and thy good,
Fashion thine affairs on earth
After the mandates of thine own heart.
Till that day of lamentation, cometh to thee,
When the silent-hearted hears not their lamentation
Nor he that is in the tomb attends the mourning.

Celebrate the glad day,
Be not weary therein.
Lo, no man taketh his goods with him.
Yea, none returneth again that is gone thither.

James Henry Breasted, *The Dawn of Conscience*. New York: Scribner, 1933.

Document 4: The Dispute of a Man with His Soul

In this unique text, probably written during the First Intermediate Period, a distraught man expresses his longing for death. His ba *is opposed to suicide and threatens to leave him, which would prevent the man from being resurrected. In the following excerpt, the man tries to persuade his* ba *that suicide is a rational course. Earthly life is full of suffering, he says, but one who journeys "yonder" into the afterworld will become as a god himself.*

To whom shall I speak today?
  One's fellows are evil;
  the friends of today do not love.

To whom shall I speak today?
  Men are rapacious;
  every one seizes his neighbor's goods.

To whom shall I speak today?
  Gentleness has perished;
  insolence has access to all men.

To whom shall I speak today?
  The evil have a contented countenance;
  good is rejected in every place. . . .

To whom shall I speak today?
  No one remembers yesterday;
  no one now requites good to him who has done it.

To whom shall I speak today?
  Brothers are evil;
  a man is treated as an enemy for his uprightness. . . .

To whom shall I speak today?
I am laden with misery,
and lack a trusted friend.

To whom shall I speak today?
The evil which treads the earth,
it has no end.

Death is in my sight today
as when a sick man becomes whole,
as when one goes out after an illness.

Death is in my sight today
as the odor of myrrh,
as when sitting under sail on a breezy day.

Death is in my sight today
as the odor of lotus flowers,
as when sitting on the riverbank getting drunk.

Death is in my sight today
as a well-trodden path,
as when a man returns home to his house from war.

Death is in my sight today
as a clearing of the sky,
as a man discerning what he knew not.

Death is in my sight today
as when a man longs to see his home again
after he has spent many years in captivity.

Nay, but he who is Yonder
will be as a living god,
inflicting punishment for evil upon him who does it.

Nay, but he who is Yonder
will stand in the bark of the Sun-god
and will assign the choicest things therein to the temples.

Nay, but he who is Yonder
will be a man of knowledge,
not hindered from petitioning Ra when he speaks.

Joseph Kaster, trans. and ed., *Wings of the Falcon: Life and Thought in Ancient Egypt.* New York: Holt, Rinehart, and Winston, 1968.

Document 5: The Admonitions of Ipuwer

The invasions and revolutions that characterized the First Intermediate Period shattered the placid, orderly worldview of the ancient Egyptians. Their dismay is vividly expressed in the words of the sage Ipuwer as he admonishes the pharaoh for failing to protect his people.

We do not know what has happened in the land. The poor now have riches; he who before could not afford sandals is now a rich man.

Everyone thinks only of violence. Pestilence ravages the land. Blood flows everywhere. Masses of corpses are thrown into the river. The river has become the usual burial place.

The nobles sorrow, but the poor people rejoice.

In all cities, they say, "Let us persecute the great men among us." Look, people walk about like filthy birds of prey. Vermin overrun the country, no one wears white clothes nowadays.

The land whirls about like a potter's wheel.

Behold, the river is full of blood. When you seek to drink from it, you recoil, for after all it is water that you thirst for. The crocodiles in the river are sated with the dead they have to eat. Willingly people cast themselves to them. Evil times have fallen upon the land.

Behold, the desert is encroaching on the land. The provinces are being ravaged. Foreign hordes are descending on Egypt's land. There is no longer room for the Egyptians themselves.

Now gold and lapis lazuli, silver and malachite, carnelian and precious jewels hang about the necks of slave girls. But distinguished ladies go dressed in rags. Mothers of households sigh: "If we only had something to eat!"

Behold, the children of princes are crushed against the wall. There is no food, the princes starve in misery. But the servants are well supplied. One eats only vegetables and washes them down with water. One takes food from the mouths of swine.

No one rejoices any longer. Sorrow stalks the land, followed by lamentation and wails of woe.

High and low alike say: "If only I might die!"

Small children cry: "Would that I had never been born!"

All warehouses are plundered and the guards are slaughtered. They have broken into the state offices and carried off the tax rolls. The bondsmen make themselves lords and have slaves themselves. The records of those who keep account of the corn are destroyed. Egypt's grain becomes the property of every man.

The legal texts from the courts of justice are cast into the front hall. Men trample them in the streets. The populace rips them to shreds in the alleys.

Behold, the flame leaps high! Now happens that which has never happened before. The king is dragged away by the populace, he who was buried as a god. That which the pyramid concealed is gone. A handful of lawless men have dared to deprive the land of its king. Behold, they have dared to challenge the king's divine power. In the work of one moment, the regime has been felled. The inhabitants of the palace are gripped with fear.

Behold, so it has come to pass: the poor in the land have become rich, and the rich have been wiped out. Officials are driven from place to place. The country's leaders flee the land. The corps of officials is like a frightened herd of sheep without a shepherd.

The land weeps.

Everything lies in ruins!

Torgny Säve-Söderbergh, *Pharaohs and Mortals*, trans. Richard E. Oldenburg. Indianapolis: Bobbs-Merrill, 1958.

Document 6: Running the Household from Afar

The following letter was written in the early Middle Kingdom by a mortuary priest and farmer named Hekanakht. His priestly duties took him away from his home in the village of Nebeseyet for long stretches of time, so he periodically sent letters filled with instructions regarding the farm's operation and attempting to settle quarrels among the members of his large household. (Scholars conjecture that Merisu was Hekanakht's eldest son who was left in charge during his father's absence, while Anup and Snefru seem to have been favored younger sons.)

It is a son who speaks to his mother, namely, the mortuary priest Hekanakht his mother Ipi and to Hetepe: How are you both? Are you alive, prospering, and healthy? In the favor of Montu, lord of the Theban nome!

And to the entire household: How are you? Are you alive, prospering, and healthy? Don't worry about me, for I'm healthy and alive. Now you are the case of the one who ate until he was sated having gotten so hungry that his eyes had become glassy white. Whereas the whole land has died off, you haven't hungered; for when I came south to this place, I had fixed your food allowance in good measure. Isn't the Nile inundation very low? Since our food allowance has been fixed for us according to the nature of the Nile inundation, bear patiently, each of you, for I have succeeded so far among you in keeping you alive. . . .

Lest you be angry about this, look here, the entire household is just like my children, and I'm responsible for everything so that it should be said, "To be half alive is better than dying outright." Now it is only real hunger that should be termed hunger since they have started eating people here, and none are given such rations anywhere else. Until I come back home to you, you should comport yourselves with stout hearts, for I shall be spending the third season here.

Communication by the mortuary priest Hekanakht to Merisu and to Hety's son Nakht, who is subordinate: Only as long as my people keep on working shall you give them these rations. Take great care! Hoe every field of mine, . . . and hack with your noses in the work! Now if they are assiduous, you shall be thanked so that I will not have to make it miserable for you. . . .

Be very assiduous since you are consuming my food.

Now as for any chattel belonging to Anup which is in your possession, give it back to him! As for what is lost, reimburse him for it. Don't make me write you about this again since I've already written you about this twice.

Now if, as you say, Snefru wants to be in charge of the bulls, you should put him in charge of them. He neither wants to be with you plowing, going up and down, nor does he want to come here to be with me. Whatever else he may want, it is with what he wants that you should make him happy.

Now as for whoever of the women or men may reject these rations, he should come to me here to be with me just to live as I live. . . .

Take great care! Be very assiduous and be vigilant, since you are on good irrigated land of the region of Khepesheyet.

Edmund S. Meltzer, ed., *Letters from Ancient Egypt*, trans. Edward F. Wente. Atlanta: Scholars Press, 1990.

Document 7: Sinuhe's Return to Egypt

Judging from the number of extant copies, the story of Sinuhe was one of the most popular tales of the ancient Egyptians. Sinuhe may well have been an actual person and his adventures true. The story begins with a real historical event: the sudden death of the first pharaoh of the Twelfth Dynasty and the succession of his son, Sesostris I. Seized by inexplicable terror at the news of the pharaoh's death, Sinuhe flees into Syria and Palestine, where he lives among Asiatic tribes for many years. In his old age, however, his desire to be buried as a proper Egyptian spurs him to petition Sesostris for permission to come home.

When it dawned, very early, they came to summon me. Ten men came and ten men went to usher me into the palace. My forehead touched the ground between the sphinxes, and the royal children stood in the gateway to meet me. The courtiers who usher through the forecourt set me on the way to the audience-hall. I found his majesty on the great throne in a kiosk of gold. Stretched out on my belly, I did not know myself before him, while this god greeted me pleasantly. I was like a man seized by darkness. My *ba* was gone, my limbs trembled; my heart was not in my body, I did not know life from death.

His majesty said to one of the courtiers: "Lift him up, let him speak to me." Then his majesty said: "Now you have come, after having roamed foreign lands. Flight has taken its toll of you. You have aged, have reached old age. It is no small matter that your corpse will be interred without being escorted by Bowmen [Asiatic tribesmen]. But don't act thus, don't act thus, speechless though your name was called!" Fearful of punishment I answered with the answer of a frightened man: "What has my lord said to me, that I might answer it? It is not disrespect to the god! It is the terror which is in my body, like that which caused the fateful flight! Here I am before you. Life is yours. May your Majesty do as he wishes!"

Then the royal daughters were brought in, and his majesty said to the queen: "Here is Sinuhe, come as an Asiatic, a product of no-mads!" She uttered a very great cry, and the royal daughters shrieked all together. They said to his majesty: "Is it really he, O king, our lord?" Said his majesty: "It is really he!" Now having brought with them their necklaces, rattles, and sistra, they held them out to his majesty [and sang]:

... Slacken your bow, lay down your arrow,
Give breath to him who gasps for breath!
Give us our good gift on this good day,
Grant us the son of northwind, Bowman born in Egypt!

He made the flight in fear of you,
He left the land in dread of you!
A face that sees you shall not pale,
Eyes that see you shall not fear!

His majesty said: "He shall not fear, he shall not dread! He shall be a Companion among the nobles. He shall be among the courtiers. Proceed to the robing-room to wait on him!"

I left the audience-hall, the royal daughters giving me their hands. We went through the great portals, and I was put in the house of a prince. In it were luxuries: a bathroom and mirrors. In it were riches from the treasury: clothes of royal linen, myrrh, and the choice perfume of the king and of his favorite courtiers were in every room. Every servant was at his task. Years were removed from my body. I was shaved; my hair was combed. Thus was my squalor returned to the foreign land, my dress to the Sand-farers. I was clothed in fine linen; I was anointed with fine oil. I slept on a bed. I had returned the sand to those who dwell in it, the tree-oil to those who grease themselves with it.

I was given a house and garden that had belonged to a courtier. Many craftsmen rebuilt it, and all its woodwork was made anew. Meals were brought to me from the palace three times, four times a day, apart from what the royal children gave without a moment's pause.

A stone pyramid was built for me in the midst of the pyramids. The masons who build tombs constructed it. A master draughtsman designed in it. A master sculptor carved in it. The overseers of construction in the necropolis busied themselves with it. All the equipment that is placed in a tomb-shaft was supplied. Mortuary priests were given me. A funerary domain was made for me. It had fields and a garden in the right place, as is done for a Companion of the first rank. My statue was overlaid with gold, its skirt with electrum. It was his majesty who ordered it made. There is no commoner for whom the like has been done. I was in the favor of the king.

Miriam Lichtheim, *Ancient Egyptian Literature: A Book of Readings*, vol. I. Berkeley: University of California Press, 1973.

Document 8: Fight on Her Behalf!

According to Egyptian theology, the spirits of the dead could still interact with the living. When misfortune or illness struck, the ancient Egyptians tended to blame a malicious spirit. However, the dead could also fight on the behalf of their living relatives by confronting the troublemaking spirits in the afterworld. In the following letter from the early Twelfth Dynasty, a man writes his deceased relative asking for aid for a member of his household. The letter was inscribed on a bowl; typically such bowls were filled with food or some other sort of offering and left at the tomb of the deceased.

What Dedi sends to the priest Iniotef, born to Iunakht:

What about the maidservant Imiu, who is ill? Aren't you fighting on her behalf night and day with whoever, male or female, is acting aginst her? Why do you want your domicile desolated? Fight on her behalf anew this day that her household may be maintained and water be poured out for you. If there is nought [i.e., no help] from you, your house shall be destroyed. Can it be that you are unaware that it is this maidservant who keeps your house going among people?

Fight on her behalf: Watch over her! Rescue her from whoever, male or female, is acting against her. Then shall your house and your children be maintained. It is good if you take notice.

Edmund S. Meltzer, ed., *Letters from Ancient Egypt*, trans. Edward F. Wente. Atlanta: Scholars Press, 1990.

Document 9: Destruction and Deliverance

Ra, the sun god, becomes infuriated with humans in this Middle Kingdom tale. In order to teach the blaspheming humans a lesson, Ra unleashes the goddess Hathor among them—but he soon regrets his action when Hathor refuses to stop killing. Thinking quickly, he devises a clever ruse to save humanity from total destruction. This tale is especially fascinating in its parallels to the biblical story of Noah's flood.

The god Re, who created himself, was king over men and gods together. And mankind uttered evil words against him. They said, "Behold now, his Majesty has become old! His bones are like silver, his limbs are like gold, and his hair is like real lapis-lazuli."

Now his Majesty heard these evil words, and he [called] to his [fellow gods]. . . .

And Re spoke unto them, "O Nu, thou firstborn god, from whom I came into being, and ye, ye ancestor gods, behold mankind, who were created by mine Eye, and are uttering words against me. Tell me what ye would do concerning this. I will not slay them until I have heard what ye may say."

And the Majesty of Nu said, "Thou god who art mightier than he who created thee, and older than they that fashioned thee, sit thee down on thy throne; the fear of thee is great if thou but turn thine Eye upon those that have blasphemed thee."

And Re said, "Behold how men have taken flight into the mountains. Their hearts are afraid because of the evil words they spoke!"

Then the gods said, "Send forth thine Eye, and let it destroy those that blaspheme thee. There is not an eye upon all this earth that can resist thine when it descendeth in the form of Hathor."

And Re sent for Hathor, and the goddess went forth and slew the people upon the mountain.

Whereupon Re said, "Come, come in peace, Hathor, thy work is accomplished. I myself will gain the mastery over mankind and make them few in number."

And the goddess said, "By thy life, I have prevailed over men and that is pleasant to my heart!" And it came to pass that Hathor in the form of Sekhmet, goddess of war, waded about in the night in the blood of mankind.

Then the Majesty of Re spoke, "Cry out, and fetch me swift and speedy messengers who can run like the wind."

Straightway the messengers were brought.

And Re said, "Go to the island of Elephantine and bring me mandrake plants in great number."

Straightway the plants were brought.

Now the maidservants crushed barley to make beer, and the mandrake plants were added to this mash, and it was red as human blood. They made seven thousand vases of this beer. Re came with the gods to look at the beer, and he said, "It is doubly good."

And the day broke on which the goddess had planned to slaughter mankind as she sailed up the river.

"I must protect mankind against her," said Re. "Let them take the vases of beer to the place where men and women are to be slaughtered." Then Re commanded them to pour out this sleep-giving beer. And the fields were covered with the liquid to the height of four spans even according to the Will of the Majesty of this god.

Now when Hathor came and found the regions flooded, her face beamed with joy, and she drank of the beer, and she became drunk, and troubled mankind no further.

And Re spoke unto this goddess, "Come, come in peace, O fair and gracious goddess. There shall be prepared for thee vases of beer which shall make thee wish to sleep at every festival of the New Year. And the number thereof shall be in proportion to the number of my handmaidens."

And from that day to this at the festival of Hathor men have made vases of beer which will make them sleep, in number according to the handmaidens of Re.

Adapted from E.A. Wallis Budge, *From Fetish to God in Ancient Egypt*. London: Oxford University Press, 1934. In Josephine Mayer and Tom Prideaux, eds., *Never to Die: The Egyptians in Their Own Words*. New York: Viking, 1938.

Document 10: Magical Protection

This charm of protection is found in a papyrus dating from the late Middle Kingdom or early Second Intermediate Period. Designed to safeguard

*a sleeping child from ghosts or other evil spirits who walked the night, it
also suggests the strong love of Egyptian parents for their children.*

May she flow away—she who comes in the darkness,
Who enters in furtively
With her nose behind her, her face turned backward—
Failing in that for which she came!

Hast thou come to kiss this child?
I will not let thee kiss him!

Hast thou come to injure him?
I will not let thee injure him!

Hast thou come to take him away?
I will not let thee take him away from me!

Barbara Mertz, *Red Land, Black Land: Daily Life in Ancient Egypt.* New York: Dodd, Mead, 1978.

Document 11: Satire of the Trades

*Since only a small section of the population of ancient Egypt ever learned
to read or write, the career path of a scribe could lead to positions of great
power and rank. The following piece was often assigned as a penmanship
exercise to the schoolboys of the New Kingdom, but it probably was composed during the Second Intermediate Period. It purports to be the advice
of a father to his son who is preparing to enter school. The father exag-
gerates the drawbacks of other professions in order to emphasize to the
young boy the importance of doing well in his studies.*

I have seen many beatings—
Set your heart on books!
I watched those seized for labor—
There's nothing better than books! . . .

I'll make you love scribedom more than your mother,
I'll make its beauties stand before you;
It's the greatest of all callings,
There's none like it in the land.
Barely grown, still a child,
He is greeted, sent on errands,
Hardly returned he wears a gown.
I never saw a sculptor as envoy,
Nor is a goldsmith ever sent;
But I have seen the smith at work
At the opening of his furnace;
With fingers like claws of a crocodile

He stinks more than fish roe.

The carpenter who wields an adze,
He is wearier than a field-laborer;
His field is the timber, his hoe the adze.
There is no end to his labor,
He does more than his arms can do,
Yet at night he kindles light.
The jewel-maker bores with his chisel
In hard stone of all kinds;
When he has finished the inlay of the eye,
His arms are spent, he's weary;
Sitting down when the sun goes down,
His knees and back are cramped. . . .

The potter is under the soil,
Though as yet among the living;
He grubs in the mud more than a pig,
In order to fire his pots.
His clothes are stiff with clay,
His girdle is in shreds;
If air enters his nose,
It comes straight from the fire.
He makes a pounding with his feet,
And is himself crushed;
He grubs the yard of every house
And roams the public places. . . .

The gardener carries a yoke,
His shoulders are bent as with age;
There's a swelling on his neck
And it festers.
In the morning he waters vegetables,
The evening he spends with the herbs,
While at noon he has toiled in the orchard.
He works himself to death
More than all other professions. . . .

The weaver in the workshop,
He is worse off than a woman;
With knees against his chest,
He cannot breathe air.
If he skips a day of weaving,
He is beaten fifty strokes;

224 Ancient Egyptian Civilization

He gives food to the doorkeeper,
To let him see the light of day. . . .

The courier goes into the desert,
Leaving his goods to his children;
Fearful of lions and Asiatics,
He knows himself only when he's in Egypt.
When he reaches home at night,
The march has worn him out;
Be his home of cloth or brick,
His return is joyless. . . .

I'll speak of the fisherman also,
His is the worst of all the jobs;
He labors on the river,
Mingling with crocodiles. . . .

See, there's no profession without a boss,
Except for the scribe; he is the boss.
Hence if you know writing,
It will do better for you
Than those professions I've set before you,
Each more wretched than the other.

Miriam Lichtheim, *Ancient Egyptian Literature: A Book of Readings*, vol. I. Berkeley: University of California Press, 1973.

Document 12: The Negative Confession

Perhaps the best-known literary work of ancient Egypt, the Book of the Dead *actually consists of various papyruses written between the beginning of the New Kingdom and the Twenty-Sixth Dynasty, when they were arranged in their final form. The formulas and spells contained in the* Book of the Dead *were intended to help the deceased pass through the judgment of the gods and win eternal life. Taken from an Eighteenth Dynasty papyrus, the text that follows is often referred to as the negative confession because the deceased lists those sins he did not commit rather than confessing those he did.*

Homage to thee, O Great God, . . . I have brought myself hither that I may behold thy beauties. I know thee, and I know thy name, and I know the names of the two and forty gods who exist with thee, . . . who live as warders of sinners and who feed upon their blood on the day when the lives of men are taken into account. . . . In truth I have come to thee, and I have brought Maāt [*i.e.*, right and truth] to thee, and I have destroyed wickedness for thee. I have not done evil to mankind. I have not oppressed the members of my family, I have not wrought evil in the place of right and truth. I have had no knowledge of worthless men. I have not wrought evil. I have not made to be the first consideration of each day that excessive labor should be performed for me. I have not brought forward my name for exaltation to honors. I have not ill-treated servants. I have not thought scorn of God. I have not defrauded the oppressed one of his property. I have not done that which is an abomination unto the gods. I have not caused harm to be done to the servant by his chief. I have not caused pain. I have made no man to suffer hunger. I have made no one to weep. I have done no murder. I have not given the order for murder to be done for me. I have not inflicted pain upon mankind. I have not defrauded the temples of their oblations. I have not purloined the cakes of the gods. . . . I have not carried away the milk from the mouths of children. I have not driven away the cattle which were upon their pastures. I have not snared the feathered fowl of the preserves of the gods. . . . I have not driven off the cattle from the property of the gods. I have not repulsed God in his manifestations. I am pure. I am pure. I am pure. I am pure.

E.A. Wallis Budge, trans., "The Book of the Dead," in *Egyptian Literature*. New York: Colonial Press, 1901.

Document 13: The Divine Conception of Hatshepsut

The divinity of the pharaoh was well established by the time Hatshepsut ascended the throne. However, Hatshepsut was a woman, the first queen of the royal family to assume the title of pharaoh. In order to solidify her right to the throne, Hatshepsut created the story that the god Amon himself was her father. The excerpt below picks up after Amon, seeing the beauty of Hatshepsut's mother, decides to seduce her in the guise of her husband.

And then he came, this august god Amen, Lord of the Two Lands, and he assumed the form of the Majesty of her husband, King Thothmes. They [the god and the form of the king] found her as she was reclining in the beauty of her palace.

She awakened at the fragrant odor of the god, and laughed in joy before His Majesty. And then he came to her straightway. He was passionate for her. He gave his heart unto her. He let her see him in his divine form after he came to her. She rejoiced when she beheld his beauty; his love went through her limbs. The Palace was flooded with the divine fragrance, and all his odors were those of Punt. The dearest and loveliest one—the Majesty of this god did everything that he desired with her. She let him rejoice over her. She kissed him.

Then spoke the Wife and Mother of the God, Queen Aahmes, to the Majesty of this god, Amen, Lord of the Thrones of the Two Lands:

My Lord, how great is thy splendor! Magnificent it is to see thy presence! Thou hast filled my Majesty with thy glory! Thy sweet savor pervades all my members!

Thus she spoke after the Majesty of this god did everything that he desired with her.

Then spoke Amen, Lord of the Thrones of the Two Lands, unto her:

Hat-Shepsut ["foremost in nobility"] shall be the name of this daughter whom I have implanted in thy body. She shall exercise beneficent kingship in this entire land. My spirit shall be hers. My power shall be hers. My exaltation shall be hers. My crown shall be hers. She shall rule the Two Lands in kingship, and shall lead all the living over all that the heavens embrace and all over which I shine. I have joined unto her the Two Lands in all her names, and upon the throne of Horus of the Living. She shall be under my divine protection every day, together with the god thereof. She is my beloved daughter, out of my own seed.

Joseph Kaster, trans. and ed., *Wings of the Falcon: Life and Thought in Ancient Egypt*. New York: Holt, Rinehart, and Winston, 1968.

Document 14: The Victory Hymn of Thutmose III

Thutmose III was the first true empire-builder of the Egyptian pharaohs; through several decades of war, he greatly expanded Egypt's frontiers. To celebrate his victories, the priests of Amon-Ra in the Temple of Amon at Karnak composed the following hymn in which the god welcomes the returning hero.

It is Amon-Re who speaks, Karnak's lord:
You have come to me rejoicing when you behold my beauty,
You, my avenging son, Tuthmosis, who lives for eternity.
Out of love for you, I show myself in my bright rays.
My heart is filled with joy over your coming to my temple,
    and my hands grant your limbs protection and life.

A wonder have I wrought for you:
I give you victorious strength against all foreign highlands.
I let your power and fear of you spread through all lowlands,
    Terror of you extends to the four pillars of the sky.
I make your reputation great among all men.
I let Your Majesty's battle cry sound among the barbarians.

The princes of all foreign lands you hold in your hand.
It is I who stretch out my hands and capture them for you.
Nubians in the south I bind together like sheaves by the
    thousands and the ten thousands,
And the people of the north are taken captive by the hundred
    thousands.
I let your opponents fall beneath your foot soles.
Troublemakers you trample under your feet.
For the earth in all its length and breadth I have delivered
    over to you,
East and West are under your supervision.
Joyously you forge ahead through nations.
    In your time no one dares to attack.
For I am the one who leads you, so that you meet them.
The waters of the land of two floods you have crossed
    with strength and force which I have given you.
They hear your battle cry and flee into their dens,
Of the breath of life have I deprived them,
With terror of you have I filled their hearts.

Torgny Säve-Söderbergh, *Pharaohs and Mortals*, trans. Richard E. Oldenburg. Indianapolis: Bobbs-Merrill, 1958.

Document 15: Instructions for the Vizier

The vizier of Egypt was the most important civil officer of the state. He was directly responsible to the pharaoh and oversaw many other major officials. The following description of the vizier's moral responsibilities comes from the tomb of Rekhmire, who was the vizier of Upper Egypt during the latter half of the reign of Thutmose III. Most likely each new vizier received these or similar instructions from the pharaoh.

Look after the office of vizier and watch over everything that is done in it, for it is the constitution of the entire land. As to the office of vizier, indeed, it is not pleasant; no, it is as bitter as gall. . . . He is one who must give no special consideration to princes or councilors nor win to himself anyone as a follower. . . . Now if a petitioner comes from Upper or Lower Egypt, . . . then you must on your part see to it that everything is done according to law and that everything is conducted in the proper manner, while every man is accorded his rights.

Now as for an official who hears in public, the water and the wind announce everything that he does, so that no one is ignorant of his actions. . . . Now the best safeguard for a prince is to act according to regulation. . . . For one whose case has been decided must not say: "I have not been accorded my rights." . . . Look upon him whom you know as on him whom you do not know, the one who is close to you as the one who is distant from you. For an official who so conducts himself will succeed here in this position. Pass over no petitioner without hearing his case. . . . Show anger to no man wrongfully and be angry only at that which deserves anger. Instil fear of yourself that you may be held in fear, for a true official is an official who is feared. The distinction of an official is that he does justice. But if a man instils fear in an excessive manner, there being in him a modicum of insincerity in the estimation of men, then they do not say of him: "That is a just man." . . . What one expects of the conduct of the vizier is the performance of justice; for it is the vizier who has been its proper keeper since the rule of the god. . . . The vizier is the one who before all other men shall practice justice.

Now a man shall continue in his office, while he officiates in accordance with the instructions which have been given to him. Unassailable is the man who acts according to what has been said to him. Perform not your own desire in affairs about which the law is known. And touching on arrogance—the king prefers the timid to the arrogant. Conduct yourself, therefore, according to the instructions which have been given to you.

George Steindorff and Keith C. Seele, *When Egypt Ruled the East*. Chicago: University of Chicago Press, 1957.

Document 16: A Princess of Egypt

Amenhotep III maintained an active correspondence with the kings of Babylonia, most of which centered on fostering trade and maintaining friendly ties between the two countries. In order to cement these ties more closely, Amenhotep asked for the hand of a Babylonian princess in marriage. King Kadashman-Bel agreed, but he asked to wed a princess of Egypt in return. Amenhotep refused flat out: Never before had any ruler been so rash as to ask for one of the divine princesses of Egypt, who were expected to intermarry into the Egyptian royal family. Kadashman-Bel sent the following letter in response—and soon received his princess.

To Amenhotep, King of Egypt, My Brother—from Kadashman-Bel, King of Babylonia, Your Brother.

May it be well with you, with your house, your wives, your land, your chariots, your horses, your chief men, may it be very well.

Now, my brother, when I wrote to you to marry your daughter you said you would not give her, in these words: "From of old a daughter of the king of Egypt has not been given to anyone."

Why is that? A king are you, and you can do according to your heart's wish. If you give her, who shall say anything against it?

When they told me your answer I wrote: "There are grown-up daughters and beautiful women. If there is any beautiful woman there, send her. Who shall say: 'She is not a king's daughter'? If, however, you do not send anyone at all, then you will have no regard for brotherhood and friendship."

That we might be nearer related to one another you wrote me of marriage; and I, for this very reason, for brotherhood and friendship, have written to you of marriage. Why did not my brother send me a wife? If you do not send one, then I, like you, will withhold from you a wife.

Adapted from Hugo Winckler, *The Tell-el-Amarna Letters*. New York: Lemcke and Buechner, 1896. In Josephine Mayer and Tom Prideaux, eds., *Never to Die: The Egyptians in Their Own Words*. New York: Viking, 1938.

Document 17: The Great Hymn to the Aten

Around the middle of the fourteenth century B.C., Akhenaton took the remarkable step of instituting a monotheistic religion, with the sun-disk Aten established as the sole god. Possibly composed by Akhenaton himself, this hymn presents the fullest expression of the short-lived faith.

Beautiful is your shining forth on the horizon
    O living Aten, beginning of life!
When you arise on the eastern horizon,
    you fill every land with your beauty.
You are bright and great and gleaming,
    and are high above every land.
Your rays envelop the lands,
    as far as all you have created.
You are Ra, and you reach unto their end,
    and subdue them all for your beloved son.
You are afar, yet are your rays upon earth;
    you are before their face, yet one knows not their going! . . .

All beasts are content upon their pasture,
    and the trees and herbs are verdant.
The birds fly out of their nests,
    and their wings praise your Divine Essence.
All wild beasts prance upon their feet,
    and all that fly and alight.
        They live when you shine forth for them! . . .

You who bring children into being in women,

and make fluid into mankind,
Who nourishes the son in the womb of his mother,
   who soothes him so that he weeps not,
      O nurse in the womb!
Who gives breath in order to keep alive
   all that he has made;
When he comes forth from the womb on the day of his birth,
   you open his mouth in speech, and give all that he needs. . . .

How manifold are the things which you have made,
   and they are hidden from before man!
      O unique god, who has no second to him!
You have created the earth according to your desire,
   while you were alone,
With men, cattle, and wild beasts,
   all that is upon earth and goes upon feet,
      and all that soars above and flies with its wings.

The lands of Syria and Kush,
   and the land of Egypt,
You put every man in his place,
   and supply their needs.
Each one has provision
   and his lifetime is reckoned.
Their tongues are diverse in speech,
   and their form likewise;
Their skins are distinguished,
   for you distinguish the peoples of foreign lands. . . .

Your rays suckle every field,
   and when you shine forth
      they live and flourish for you.
You make the seasons
   to cause to continue all you have created:
The winter to cool them,
   and the warmth that they may taste of you.
You have made the sky afar off to shine therein,
   in order to behold all you have made.
You are alone, shining in your forms as living Aten,
   appearing, shining, withdrawing, returning,
      you make millions of forms of yourself alone!
Cities, townships, fields, road, and river,
   all eyes behold you against them,
      O Aten of the day above the earth!

You are in my heart,
> and there is no one who knows you save your son,

Nefer-Khepru-Ra Wa-en-Ra [Akhenaton],
> whom you made understanding of your designs and your
> > might.

The earth came into being by your hand,
> even as you have created them.

When you arise they live,
> and when you set they die.

But you have eternity in your members,
> and all creatures live in you.

The eyes look on your beauty until you set;
> all work is laid aside when you set in the west.

When you rise you make all to flourish for the King,
> you who made the foundations of the earth.

You raise them up for your son,
> he who came forth from your body.

Joseph Kaster, trans. and ed., *Wings of the Falcon: Life and Thought in Ancient Egypt*. New York: Holt, Rinehart, and Winston, 1968.

Document 18: An Appeal for Aid

While Akhenaton occupied himself with establishing his new religion and defending his actions against the outraged priests of Amon, Egypt's borders and client states came under attack. The following letter to Akhenaton from the king of Jerusalem is just one example of many desperate pleas for help he received from the rulers of various sections of the Egyptian Empire—all of which he appears to have ignored.

To the king, My Lord, say I, Abdi-Cheba, your servant. At the feet of my royal master I bow down seven times seven times.

So long as my royal master lives and so long as messengers travel, I shall say again and again: "The king's lands are being laid waste."

But you do not listen to me.

All the princes fall away—not a single prince will remain to my king. May the king turn his countenance toward the army, so that the soldiers may move into the field.

None of the king's lands will remain. The Chabiru plunder all his lands.

If the Egyptian troops come here this year, my royal master's lands will be retained. But if they do not come, my royal master's lands will be lost.

To my royal master's clerks says Abdi-Cheba, your servant: "Put these words clearly before my royal master: All my royal master's lands are being laid waste!"

Torgny Säve-Söderbergh, *Pharaohs and Mortals*, trans. Richard E. Oldenburg. Indianapolis: Bobbs-Merrill, 1958.

Document 19: Restoring the Gods and Goddesses

During his brief reign, Tutankhamen disavowed the monotheistic faith of the Aten and recommitted the royal family to the ancient Egyptian religion. On a stela at the Temple of Amon at Karnak, the young pharaoh recounted the measures he took to refurbish the temples and restore the worship of the gods and goddesses.

Now when his majesty appeared as king, the temples of the gods and goddesses from Elephantine to the Delta marshes . . . had fallen into neglect; their shrines had gone to ruin, having become tracts overgrown with thorns, their chapels were as if they had never been, and their temples had become trodden roads. The land was topsy-turvy, and as for the gods, they had turned their backs to this land. If troops were sent to Djahi to extend the boundaries of Egypt, their efforts came to naught. If one besought a god with a request for anything, he did not come at all; if one petitioned any goddess likewise, she would not come either—for their hearts were angry in their bodies, because they [the heretics of the Aton movement?] had destroyed what had been made.

But now when some days had passed after these things, his majesty appeared on the throne of his father and ruled the regions of Horus; Egypt and the foreign desert lands were under his control and every land bowed to his might.

Now when his majesty was in his palace which is in the estate of Okheperkare, then his majesty administered the affairs of this land and the daily needs of the Two Regions. . . . His majesty took counsel with his heart, searching out every proper means and seeking what would be beneficial to his father Amun for fashioning his august image of genuine *djam*-gold. . . . His majesty made monuments for all the gods, fashioning their statues of genuine *djam*-gold, restoring their sanctuaries as monuments enduring forever, providing them with perpetual endowments, investing them with divine offerings for the daily service, and supplying their provisions on earth.

George Steindorff and Keith C. Seele, *When Egypt Ruled the East*. Chicago: University of Chicago Press, 1957.

Document 20: I Gave Them a Taste of My Hand

In the fifth year of his reign, Ramses II led a military campaign into northern Syria to regain lost territory from the Khatti and their allies. At the fortified town of Kadesh, the two armies met in battle. An epic poem was later written to commemorate the occasion. The following excerpt, undoubtedly exaggerated, describes how Ramses II took on the entire Khatti army singlehandedly.

No officer was with me, no charioteer,
No soldier of the army, no shield-bearer;
My infantry, my chariotry yielded before them,
Not one of them stood firm to fight with them.
His majesty spoke: "What is this, father Amun?
Is it right for a father to ignore his son?
Are my deeds a matter for you to ignore?
Do I not walk and stand at your word?
I have not neglected an order you gave.
Too great is he, the great lord of Egypt,
To allow aliens to step on his path!
What are these Asiatics to you, O Amun,
The wretches ignorant of god?
Have I not made for you many great monuments,
Filled your temple with my booty,
Built for you my mansion of Millions-of-Years,
Given you all my wealth as endowment? . . .
I call to you, my father Amun,
I am among a host of strangers;
All countries are arrayed against me,
I am alone, there's none with me!
My numerous troops have deserted me,
Not one of my chariotry looks for me;
I keep on shouting for them,
But none of them heeds my call.
I know Amun helps me more than a million troops,
More than a hundred thousand charioteers,
More than ten thousand brothers and sons
Who are united as one heart.
The labors of many people are nothing,
Amun is more helpful than they;
I came here by the command of your mouth,
O Amun, I have not transgressed your command!"

Now though I prayed in the distant land,

My voice resounded in Southern On [Thebes].
I found Amun came when I called to him,
He gave me his hand and I rejoiced.
He called from behind as if near by:
"Forward, I am with you,
I, your father, my hand is with you,
I prevail over a hundred thousand men,
I am lord of victory, lover of valor!"
I found my heart stout, my breast in joy,
All I did succeeded, I was like Mont.
I shot on my right, grasped with my left,
I was before them like Seth in his moment.
I found the mass of chariots in whose midst I was
Scattering before my horses;
Not one of them found his hand to fight,
Their hearts failed in their bodies through fear of me.
Their arms all slackened, they could not shoot,
They had no heart to grasp their spears;
I made them plunge into the water as crocodiles plunge,
They fell on their faces one on the other.
I slaughtered among them at my will,
Not one looked behind him,
Not one turned around,
Whoever fell down did not rise.

And the wretched Chief of Khatti stood among his troops and
    chariots, . . .
Stood turning, shrinking, afraid.
Then he caused many chiefs to come,
Each of them with his chariotry,
Equipped with their weapons of warfare:
The chief of Arzawa and he of Masa,
The chief of Irun and he of Luka,
He of Dardany, the chief of Carchemish,
The chief of Karkisha, he of Khaleb,
The brothers of him of Khatti all together,
Their total of a thousand chariots came straight into the fire.
I charged toward them, being like Mont,
In a moment I gave them a taste of my hand,
I slaughtered among them, they were slain on the spot,
One called out to the other saying:
"No man is he who is among us,

It is Seth great-of-strength, Baal in person;
Not deeds of man are these his doings,
They are of one who is unique,
Who fights a hundred thousand without soldiers and chariots,
Come quick, flee before him,
To seek life and breathe air;
For he who attempts to get close to him,
His hands, all his limbs grow limp.
One cannot hold either bow or spears,
When one sees him come racing along!"
My majesty hunted them like a griffin,
I slaughtered among them unceasingly.

Miriam Lichtheim, *Ancient Egyptian Literature: A Book of Readings*, vol. II. Berkeley: University of California Press, 1976.

Document 21: The Israel Stela

This hymn of victory is inscribed on a stela in the mortuary temple of Merneptah. It describes how he drove Libyan invaders out of Egypt during the fifth year of his reign. Especially significant is the hymn's inclusion of Israel among the conquered peoples and places, for it is the only time the name of Israel is ever mentioned in an Egyptian text.

The sun, uncovering the cloud which had been over Egypt
    And letting Egypt see the rays of the sun disc;
Removing the mountain of metal from the neck of the people,
    So that he might give breath to the folk who had been shut in;
Appeasing the heart of Memphis over their enemies,
    And making Ta-tenen rejoice over those rebellious to him;
Opening the doors of Memphis which had been barred
    And letting its temples receive their food again . . .

Great joy has arisen in Egypt;
    Jubilation has gone forth in the towns of Egypt.
They talk about the victories
    Which Mer-ne-Ptah Hotep-hir-Maat made in Tehenu:
"How amiable is he, the victorious ruler!
    How exalted is the king among the gods!
How fortunate is he, the lord of command!
    Ah, how pleasant it is to sit when there is gossip!"

One walks with unhindered stride on the way, for there is no fear at all in the heart of the people. The forts are left to themselves, the wells lie open, accessible to the messengers. The battlements of the wall are calm in the sun until their watchers may awake. . . . There is no cry of people as when there is mourning. Towns are settled anew again. He who plows his harvest will eat it. Re has turned himself around again to Egypt. He was born as the one destined to be her protector, the King of Upper and Lower Egypt: Ba-en-Re Meri-Amon; the Son of Re: Mer-ne-Ptah Hotep-hir-Maat.

The princes are prostrate, saying: "Mercy!"
　　Not one raises his head among the Nine Bows.
Desolation is for Tehenu; Hatti is pacified;
　　Plundered is the Canaan with every evil;
Carried off is Ashkelon; seized upon is Gezer;
　　Yanoam is made as that which does not exist;
Israel is laid waste, his seed is not;
　　Hurru is become a widow for Egypt!
All lands together, they are pacified;
Everyone who was restless, he has been bound.

James B. Pritchard, ed., *Ancient Near Eastern Texts Relating to the Old Testament*, trans. John A. Wilson. Princeton, NJ: Princeton University Press, 1950.

Document 22: Sick with Love

Quite a few love songs survive from the New Kingdom, the golden age of lyric poetry in ancient Egypt. The lovers refer to each other as "brother" or "sister," these being the customary terms of affection among the ancient Egyptians.

Seven days have I not seen my sister.
A sickness has crept into me,
　　my limbs have become heavy, and my body does not know
　　　itself.
Even should the master physicians come to me,
　　my heart would not be soothed by their remedies.
As for the magician-priests, there is no resource in them;
　　my illness cannot be diagnosed.
But to say to me, "Here she is!"—
　　that will make me live again!
Her name is what will revive me;
　　the coming and going of her messengers is what will give
　　　life to my heart. . . .
When I see her, then I am well;
　　when she opens her eyes, my limbs are young again;
　　when she speaks, then I am strong;

when I embrace her, she banishes evil from me.
But she is gone from me for seven days!

Joseph Kaster, trans. and ed., *Wings of the Falcon: Life and Thought in Ancient Egypt*. New York: Holt, Rinehart, and Winston, 1968.

Document 23: The Report of Wenamun

As with the earlier story of Sinuhe, the report of Wenamun may relate actual historical events, or it may be a fictionalized account that reflects the tenor of the times. At the end of the Twentieth Dynasty, the empire had been lost, Egyptian prestige had decayed abroad, and Ramses XI was only in nominal control of Egypt. The southern part of Egypt was ruled by Herihor, the high priest of Amon at Thebes. In this story, Herihor sends his envoy Wenamun to Lebanon to obtain timber to repair the bark of Amon, which floated on the Nile during sacred festivals. Wenamun is robbed along the way and so appears in Byblos with no payment for the wood. The prince of Byblos repeatedly orders Wenamum to leave before finally granting him an audience. The following excerpt begins at this point in Wenamun's report.

He spoke to me, saying: "On what business have you come?" I said to him: "I have come in quest of timber for the great noble bark of Amen-Re, King of Gods. What your father did, what the father of your father did, you too will do it." So I said to him. He said to me: "True, they did it. If you pay me for doing it, I will do it. My relations carried out this business after Pharaoh had sent six ships laden with the goods of Egypt, and they had been unloaded into their storehouses. You, what have you brought for me?"

He had the daybook of his forefathers brought and had it read before me. They found entered in his book a thousand *deben* of silver and all sorts of things. He said to me: "If the ruler of Egypt were the lord of what is mine and I were his servant, he would not have sent silver and gold to say: 'Carry out the business of Amun.' It was not a royal gift that they gave to my father! I too, I am not your servant, nor am I the servant of him who sent you! If I shout aloud to the Lebanon, the sky opens and the logs lie here on the shore of the sea! . . . Indeed, Amun has founded all the lands. He founded them after having first founded the land of Egypt from which you have come. Thus craftsmanship came from it in order to reach the place where I am! Thus learning came from it in order to reach the place where I am! What are these foolish travels they made you do?"

I said to him: "Wrong! These are not foolish travels that I am doing. There is no ship on the river that does not belong to Amun. His is the sea and his the Lebanon of which you say, 'It is mine.' It is a growing ground for Amen-user-he, the lord of every ship. Truly, it was Amen-Re, King of Gods, who said to Herihor, my master: 'Send me!' And he made me come with this great god. But look, you have let this great god spend these twenty-nine days moored in your harbor. Did you not know that he was here? Is he not he who he was? You are prepared to haggle over the Lebanon with Amun, its lord? As to your saying, the former kings sent silver and gold: If they had owned life and health, they would not have sent these things. It was in place of life and health that they sent these things to your fathers! But Amen-Re, King of Gods, he is the lord of life and health, and he was the lord of your fathers! They passed their lifetimes offering to Amun. You too, you are the servant of Amun! . . ."

[Wenamun arranges for gold, silver, and other goods to be brought from Egypt for the prince.]

The prince rejoiced. He assigned three hundred men and three hundred oxen, and he set supervisors over them to have them fell the timbers. They were felled and they lay there during the winter. In the third month of summer they dragged them to the shore of the sea. The prince came out and stood by them, and he sent to me, saying: "Come!" . . .

As I stood before him, he addressed me, saying: "Look, the business my fathers did in the past, I have done it, although you did not do for me what your fathers did for mine. Look, the last of your timber has arrived and is ready. Do as I wish, and come to load it. For has it not been given to you? Do not come to look at the terror of the sea. For if you look at the terror of the sea, you will see my own!"

Miriam Lichtheim, *Ancient Egyptian Literature: A Book of Readings*, vol. II. Berkeley: University of California Press, 1976.

Glossary

akb Along with the *ba* and the *ka*, one of the three immortal and unchangeable elements of the human soul or identity.

ba An immortal element of the human soul that was able to leave the mummy and travel to places outside the tomb.

canopic jars Four jars, often made of stone, containing the embalmed stomach, liver, lungs, and intestines from a mummified body.

cubit An ancient Egyptian measurement based on the length of the forearm from the elbow to the tip of the thumb; equivalent to 52.5 centimeters.

cuneiform The wedge-shaped characters used for writing in ancient Mesopotamia.

deben A weight of approximately ninety-one grams.

demotic A very cursive script that evolved from the **hieratic** script beginning at approximately 700 B.C. and that was primarily used for everyday business, legal, and administrative documents.

hieratic A simplified and cursive form of **hieroglyphs**, adapted to the medium of ink and brush on papyrus. It first occurs at the same time as hieroglyphs and was used for both religious and secular documents before being replaced by the **demotic** script.

hieroglyphs A pictorial script designed for carving or large-scale painting. This script first appeared fully developed around 3100 B.C. and was used primarily for religious and literary texts.

Hyksos An Asiatic people of unknown origin who infiltrated the delta during the Middle Kingdom and became rulers of Lower Egypt during the Second Intermediate Period.

ka An essential and immortal element of the human soul; created at birth as a person's double, it was released from the body at death and resided within a statue in the tomb chapel, where it received food and drink offerings.

kouroi Plural form of *kouros*; an ancient statue of a nude male youth standing with the left leg forward and both arms at the sides.

maat This word encompasses the concepts of divine order, morality, justice, truth, correct attitudes, and balance.

mastaba Low mud-brick or stone tombs, built on a rectangular ground plan with slightly inclining walls.

menyet Heavy beads that were strung onto a necklace; often used as a rattle to accompany songs.

necropolis Greek for "city of the dead"; refers to Egyptian cemeteries dating from all periods.

nome A province or administrative district, controlled by a governor or nomarch. Egypt was divided into forty-two nomes, twenty-two in Upper Egypt and twenty in Lower Egypt.

ostraca Fragments of pottery or limestone used as a cheap alternative to papyrus for letters, notes, or sketches.

sarcophagus The protective rectangular or oval stone container in which the coffins and mummified body were placed.

scarab The Egyptian dung beetle, which was associated with spontaneous creation; also refers to stone or faience representations of the beetle used as talismans, ornaments, and symbols of resurrection.

Sea Peoples The collective name given to the sea-faring northerners who unsuccessfully tried to invade Egypt during the reigns of Merneptah and Ramses III.

sistrum A sacred rattle; it consisted of a forked metal stick with discs threaded onto a bar across the prongs.

stela or **stele** (pl. **stelae**) A rectangular slab of stone or wood, usually with straight sides and a rounded top, decorated with inscriptions that memorialized a dead person, commemorated a victory or other notable event, or set forth a formal decree. Sometimes refers to a similar inscription carved on the face of a wall or a cliff.

uraeus The royal cobra motif worn as part of the crown as a symbol of sovereignty.

wadi A desert riverbed that is dry except during the rainy season.

ziggurat A Mesopotamian temple in the shape of a step pyramid.

Discussion Questions

Chapter 1: The Rise of Egyptian Civilization

1. According to John A. Wilson, how did the periodic flooding of the Nile and the constant sunshine of Egypt affect the world-view of the early Egyptians? In particular, what religious significance did the Egyptians find in these natural phenomena?

2. What examples does Barbara Mertz cite to bolster her thesis that the development of early Egyptian civilization was greatly influenced by Mesopotamia? How does she account for the dissimilar aspects between these two cultures? In your opinion, does she provide sufficient proof to support her argument? Why or why not?

3. Jill Kamil maintains that the unification of Upper and Lower Egypt took several generations. What evidence does she give? In Kamil's opinion, how did the establishment of the divinity of the pharaoh solidify the unification of the Two Lands?

Chapter 2: Royalty and Religion in Ancient Egypt

1. According to Jon Manchip White, what was the reason for intermarriage within the royal family? Explain the three different types of wives that a pharaoh might have. What purpose did the "political wives" serve?

2. In Cyril Aldred's view, which deities did the queen embody? Did a queen necessarily need to be of royal blood, according to Aldred? Why or why not?

3. Lionel Casson discusses religious concepts and the development of the pantheon at different times in Egyptian history. In Casson's opinion, how did the early Egyptian gods evolve? How do these early gods differ from deities that were introduced at a later date? What differences does Casson note between local and national deities?

4. What types of provisions were supplied for the dead in their tombs, as described by Rosalie David? What purpose did the wall drawings serve? List the beliefs held by the Egyptians concerning the afterlife that led them to treat their dead in such a fashion.

5. According to A.J. Spencer, why did the animal cults persist throughout Egyptian history? What political considerations may have influenced the rise in animal worship during the waning years of the Egyptian Empire?

Chapter 3: The Accomplishments of Ancient Egyptian Civilization

1. Barbara Sewell describes the three different types of writing that the Egyptians developed. Explain the differences and similarities of these writing styles. What different functions were the three types eventually used for? How did this separation of functions affect the evolution of each style?

2. Eugen Strouhal depicts Egyptian medicine as a mixture of medical expertise and superstitious ritual. Based on your reading, how much of Egyptian medicine was useful? Did the Egyptians enjoy a high or low standard of medical care for their time? Explain, citing the text to support your answer.

3. According to M. Abdel-Kader Hatem, the annual flooding of the Nile inspired the ancient Egyptians to create a calendar. What aspects of the flooding most influenced the development of this calendar? How did the Egyptians resolve the differences between the Nile year and the astronomical year?

4. John Romer characterizes the pyramids of the Fourth Dynasty as the greatest in Egypt. What evidence does he give to support this contention? Do you agree or disagree? Explain your answer.

5. How did the concept of *maat* affect the development of Egyptian art, in the opinion of Paul Johnson? In what way was art related to the hieroglyphic system of writing? Explain the effects that this relationship had on the ancient Egyptian art style.

6. Of the various achievements of ancient Egypt that were discussed in this chapter, which one do you feel was most important or impressive? Defend your answer, using examples from the articles.

Chapter 4: The Decline of the Egyptian Empire

1. Elizabeth Riefstahl writes that Akhenaton's monotheistic religion was in some ways similar to the old polytheistic religion of Egypt. Discuss these similarities, and explain in what ways the faith of the Aten differed from the old religion. In Riefstahl's

opinion, why did the new religion fail to appeal to the masses?

2. Why does Torgny Säve-Söderbergh consider Ramses III to be the last great pharaoh of ancient Egypt? In what ways was Ramses's rule less outstanding than he proclaimed, according to the author?

3. According to Lionel Casson, how many different peoples conquered Egypt between 950 B.C. and 525 B.C.? How many of these peoples had themselves previously been ruled over or influenced by the Egyptians? What factors enabled these foreign groups to invade Egypt?

4. What Greek ideas did the Ptolemies import to Egypt, according to Desmond Stewart? Which Egyptian concepts and beliefs did the Ptolemies adopt? How well did the Egyptians accept Greek rule, in the author's view?

Chapter 5: The Heritage of Ancient Egyptian Civilization

1. Douglas J. Brewer and Emily Teeter argue that Egyptian culture never really died. According to the authors, what elements of ancient Egyptian civilization continue to affect modern society? Do you find the examples they give convincing proof of their argument concerning Egypt's long-lasting influence? Why or why not?

2. William A. Ward maintains that the Egyptians significantly boosted the achievement of classical Greece during its golden age. According to the author, could the Greeks have advanced as far without Egyptian help? Why or why not? Cite evidence from the text to support your answer.

3. What aspects of the African civilization of Meroe does P.L. Shinnie attribute to Egyptian influences? According to Shinnie, what technological advancement did the Egyptians learn from Meroe?

4. The Egyptian influence on the development of Judaism was significant, in the view of James Henry Breasted. The author provides examples of similar quotes from the Bible and Egyptian literature to bolster his argument. Compare and contrast his examples. Do you agree with Breasted that the similarities between the quotes prove that the Hebrews borrowed from Egyptian literature? Why or why not?

Chronology

ca. 5500–3200 B.C.
Predynastic Period. Agriculture develops in the Nile valley. Regional rulers govern increasingly larger areas, including city-states.

ca. 3200–2700 B.C.
Archaic or Early Dynastic Period. First and Second Dynasties. Menes unites Upper and Lower Egypt. Memphis becomes the capital of Egypt. Hieroglyphic writing is introduced.

ca. 2700–2200 B.C.
Old Kingdom. Third to Sixth Dynasties. The pyramids are built. An Egyptian colony is established at Byblos.

ca. 2200–2050 B.C.
First Intermediate Period. During the Seventh to Tenth Dynasties, the Old Kingdom collapses and the country is racked by invasions, civil war, and famines. During the first half of the Eleventh Dynasty, strong pharaohs reunite Egypt and establish a capital at Thebes.

ca. 2050–1650 B.C.
Middle Kingdom. The pharaohs of the second half of the Eleventh Dynasty solidify their rule over all of Egypt and restore order to the land. The pharaohs of the Twelfth Dynasty expand into Nubia and western Asia. Literature and art flourish.

ca. 1650–1550 B.C.
Second Intermediate Period. Thirteenth to Seventeenth Dynasties. The Middle Kingdom collapses as the Hyksos invade and conquer Egypt. The horse and chariot is introduced into the Nile valley. The last pharaohs of the Seventeenth Dynasty begin driving the Hyksos from Egypt.

ca. 1550–1070 B.C.
New Kingdom. The first pharaoh of the Eighteenth Dynasty completes the repulsion of the Hyksos from Egypt and reunifies the land. Many strong pharaohs follow who build an empire. Construction of tombs begins in the Valley of the Kings. Hatshepsut, the first female pharaoh, rules ca. 1472–1457. Akhenaton introduces the religion of the Aten ca. 1350. The pharaohs of the Nine-

teenth Dynasty and the early Twentieth Dynasty reconquer the areas of the empire lost by Akhenaton and protect Egypt from invasion by the Sea Peoples. The later pharaohs of the Twentieth Dynasty lose control of the government to local rulers.

ca. 1070–663 B.C.

Third Intermediate Period. The country splits into Upper and Lower Egypt; rival dynasties often overlap during this period. During the Twenty-First Dynasty, Nubia sets up an independent state under its own kings. Egypt is under Libyan rule throughout the Twenty-Second to Twenty-Fourth Dynasties. Nubian princes conquer Egypt in the late 700s and establish the Twenty-Fifth Dynasty. In 670, the Assyrians conquer Egypt and drive out the Nubians.

663–525 B.C.

Saïte Period. The Egyptians expel the Assyrians and retake control of their country. The Saïte pharaohs of the Twenty-Sixth Dynasty usher in a period of renaissance that imitates the art and literature of the golden age. They also make an unsuccessful attempt to rebuild the former empire.

525–332 B.C.

Persian Period. The Persians conquer Egypt and incorporate it into their empire. Persian kings rule the country as the Twenty-Seventh Dynasty. In the 400s, the Egyptians revolt against the Persian Empire. The Egyptian pharaohs of the Twenty-Eighth to Thirtieth Dynasties rule from 404 until 343, when the Persians put down the rebellion and establish the Thirty-First Dynasty.

332–30 B.C.

Ptolemaic Period. Alexander the Great conquers Egypt. The Macedonian Greek family of the Ptolemies rules Egypt until the death of Cleopatra VII in 30 B.C.

30 B.C.–A.D. 395

Egypt becomes a province of the Roman Empire in 30 B.C. It remains under Roman rule until the division of the empire in A.D. 395.

For Further Research

Collections of Primary Sources

Adolf Erman, *The Ancient Egyptians: A Sourcebook of Their Writings*, trans. Aylward M. Blackman. New York: Harper & Row, 1966.

R.O. Faulkner, trans., *The Ancient Egyptian Pyramid Texts*. London: Oxford University Press, 1969.

Joseph Kaster, trans. and ed., *Wings of the Falcon: Life and Thought in Ancient Egypt*. New York: Holt, Rinehart, and Winston, 1968.

Miriam Lichtheim, *Ancient Egyptian Literature: A Book of Readings*, 2 vols. Berkeley: University of California Press, 1973–76.

Josephine Mayer and Tom Prideaux, eds., *Never to Die: The Egyptians in Their Own Words*. New York: Viking, 1938.

Edmund S. Meltzer, ed., *Letters from Ancient Egypt*, trans. Edward F. Wente. Atlanta: Scholars Press, 1990.

Ezra Pound and Noel Stock, trans., *Love Poems of Ancient Egypt*. Norfolk, CT: New Directions, 1962.

James B. Pritchard, ed., *Ancient Near Eastern Texts Relating to the Old Testament*. Princeton, NJ: Princeton University Press, 1950.

William Kelly Simpson, ed., *The Literature of Ancient Egypt: An Anthology of Stories, Instructions, and Poetry*. New Haven, CT: Yale University Press, 1972.

General Histories of Ancient Egypt

Cyril Aldred, *Egypt to the End of the Old Kingdom*. New York: McGraw-Hill, 1965.

James Henry Breasted, *A History of Egypt*. New York: Scribner, 1919.

Peter A. Clayton, *Chronicles of the Pharaohs*. London: Thames and Hudson, 1995.

Walter B. Emery, *Archaic Egypt*. Baltimore, MD: Penguin Books, 1961.

Alan Gardiner, *Egypt of the Pharaohs: An Introduction*. Oxford, UK: Oxford University Press, 1961.

Nicolas Grimal, *A History of Ancient Egypt*, trans. Ian Shaw. Cambridge, MA: Blackwell, 1992.

Jacquetta Hawkes, *Pharaohs of Egypt*. New York: American Heritage, 1965.

K.A. Kitchen, *The Third Intermediate Period in Egypt (1100–650 B.C.)*, Warminster, UK: Aris and Phillips, 1973.

P.H. Newby, *Warrior Pharaohs: The Rise and Fall of the Egyptian Empire*. London: Faber and Faber, 1980.

George Steindorff and Keith C. Seele, *When Egypt Ruled the East*. Chicago: University of Chicago Press, 1957.

Barbara Watterson, *The Egyptians*. Cambridge, MA: Blackwell, 1997.

Ancient Egyptian Civilization and Society

Cyril Aldred, *Egyptian Art in the Days of the Pharaohs, 3100–320 B.C.* New York: Oxford University Press, 1980.

E.A. Wallis Budge. *The Mummy: A Handbook of Egyptian Funerary Archaeology*. London: KPI Limited, 1987.

Aidan Dodson, *Monarchs of the Nile*. London: The Rubicon Press, 1995.

Humphrey Evans, *The Mystery of the Pyramids*. New York: Thomas Y. Crowell, 1979.

Ahmed Fakhry, *The Pyramids*. Chicago: The University of Chicago Press, 1961.

Paul Ghalioungui, *Magic and Medical Science in Ancient Egypt*. New York: Barnes and Noble, 1965.

James Hamilton-Paterson and Carol Andrews, *Mummies: Death and Life in Ancient Egypt*. London: Collins, 1978.

Christine Hobson, *Exploring the World of the Pharaohs*. London: Thames and Hudson, 1987.

T.G.H. James, *Pharaoh's People: Scenes from Life in Imperial Egypt*. Chicago: University of Chicago Press, 1984.

Rosalind M. and Jac. J. Janssen, *Getting Old in Ancient Egypt*. London: Rubicon Press, 1996.

Lise Manniche, *Music and Musicians in Ancient Egypt*. London: British Museum Press, 1991.

Siegfried Morenz, *Egyptian Religion*, trans. Ann E. Keep. Ithaca, NY: Cornell University Press, 1992.

William J. Murnane, *The Penguin Guide to Ancient Egypt*. London: Penguin Books, 1983.

Margaret A. Murray, *The Splendor That Was Egypt: A General Survey of Egyptian Culture and Civilization*. New York: Praeger, 1964.

Timothy R. Roberts, *Gift of the Nile: Chronicles of Ancient Egypt*. New York: MetroBooks, 1999.

John Romer, *Ancient Lives: Daily Life in the Egypt of the Pharaohs*. New York: Holt, Rinehart, and Winston, 1984.

W. Stevenson Smith, *The Art and Architecture of Ancient Egypt*. New Haven, CT: Yale University Press, 1999.

Studies of Important Egyptians

Cyril Aldred, *Akhenaten, King of Egypt*. London: Thames and Hudson, 1988.

F. Gladstone Bratton, *The Heretic Pharaoh*. London: Hale, 1962.

Bob Brier, *The Murder of Tutankhamen: A True Story*. New York: Putnam, 1998.

Michael Carter, *Tutankhamen the Golden Monarch*. New York: McKay, 1972.

Joy Collier, *The Heretic Pharaoh*. New York: John Day, 1970.

Leonard Cottrell, *Lady of the Two Lands: Five Queens of Ancient Egypt*. Indianapolis: Bobbs-Merrill, 1967.

K.A. Kitchen, *Pharaoh Triumphant: The Life and Times of Ramesses II, King of Egypt*. Warminster, UK: Aris and Phillips, 1982.

Bernadette Menu, *Ramses II: Greatest of the Pharaohs*. New York: Harry N. Abrams, 1999.

Joyce Tyldesley, *Hatchepsut: The Female Pharaoh*. London: Penguin Books, 1998.

Evelyn Wells, *Nefertiti*. London: Hale, 1964.

Index